Great
COMPOSERS

Great COMPOSERS

LULU BRITZ GMOSER

SMITHMARK
PUBLISHERS

A FRIEDMAN GROUP BOOK

This edition published in 1997 by SMITHMARK Publishers, a division of U.S. Media Holdings, Inc., 115 West 18th Street, New York, NY 10011

SMITHMARK books are available for bulk purchase for sales promotion and premium use. For details write or call the manager of special sales, SMITHMARK Publishers, 115 West 18th Street New York, NY 10011; (212) 519-1300.

ISBN 0-7651-9327-2

Great Composers
was prepared and produced by
Michael Friedman Publishing Group, Inc.
15 West 26th Street
New York, New York 10010

Editor: Celeste Sollod
Art Director: Jeff Batzli
Designer: Joan Peckolick
Photography Editor: Karen Barr

Color separations by HK Scanner Arts Int'l Ltd.
Printed in the United Kingdom by Butler & Tanner

HALF-TITLE PAGE: GIACOMO PUCCINI'S (SEE CHAPTER 4, PAGE 109) SMALL BOOK *LA MESSA* FEATURES ONE OF THE GREATEST WORKS THE COMPOSER WROTE.

FRONTISPIECE: THE COVENT GARDEN OPERA HOUSE, IN LONDON, ENGLAND, HAS BEEN HOME TO THE WORKS OF HUNDREDS OF COMPOSERS, INCLUDING GEORGE FRIDERIC HANDEL (SEE CHAPTER 2, PAGE 27), CLAUDE DEBUSSY (SEE CHAPTER 6, PAGE 124), AND BENJAMIN BRITTEN (SEE CHAPTER 7, PAGE 167).

PAGE 5: THIS MUSICAL EXCERPT FROM BOLERO WAS SIGNED BY MAURICE RAVEL (SEE CHAPTER 6, PAGE 128) IN 1930.

PAGES 6-7: COMPOSER LEONARD BERNSTEIN (SEE CHAPTER 7, PAGE 168) DRAMATICALLY CONDUCTS THE BOSTON SYMPHONY ORCHESTRA IN JULY, 1970. THE SELL-OUT CROWD GAVE THE COMPOSER A ONE-MINUTE OVATION.

DEDICATION

For Carl

CONTENTS

INTRODUCTION

BEGINNINGS

" *The language of music is common to all generations and nations; it is understood by everybody, since it is understood with heart.* "

GIOACCHINO ROSSINI, COMPOSER, 1792-1868

That's all you need to appreciate music—heart! Neither your age nor your ethnic background matters. A musical education—any education—is entirely unnecessary. Music can be understood and enjoyed by anyone. All you need are your senses and your feelings—your heart.

Music has forever been part of society, going back thousands of years. There are references in the Bible to musical instruments, and the biblical psalms are actually songs. Psalm 150 encourages listeners to praise the Lord with trumpet sound, lute and harp, timbrel and dance, strings and pipe, and loud clashing cymbals.

Before biblical times, the Egyptian civilization, born around 4,000 B.C., had ceremonial choirs, martial bands, and royal musicians. Artifacts and paintings on the walls of temples and tombs portray bands and musicians and the instruments they used. People in ancient China created music based on a five-note scale. People in India made music with wind, string, and percussion instruments. In Greece, there was an alphabet that represented musical tones. The first pipe organ, operated by water pressure, was unearthed in a Rome sports arena, forerunner of electric organs in today's ballparks.

The creators of music in all these cultures were the composers. However, we know very little about many composers before medieval times. Since early medieval music was largely tied to religion, it is logical that one of the first known composers was a woman of the cloth, Abbess Hildegard of Bingen. The Abbess wrote plainsong or chant; as simple as the word implies, plainsong was a single line of vocal music. Another composer was St. Ambrose, who expanded plainsong into hymn singing. A big change in music came when composers started using multiple melodies blended in harmony in their works, a style called polyphony. Guido d'Arezzo, a Benedictine monk and music teacher, was probably the creator of the musical staff—the four (later expanded to five) horizontal lines on music manuscript paper—and the namer of the first six notes of the scale: ut (found difficult to sing, it was later changed to do), re, mi, fa, sol, la. A composite of sol and mi, si, subsequently changed to ti, was added later.

A new field opened up for composers as troubadours spread out across Europe and secular music was added to the religious as medieval times turned into the Renaissance, around the middle of the fifteenth century, which is where our story of composers begins. Since western secular music was developed, music has been composed for all purposes and all occasions: weddings, funerals, anniversaries, storytelling, and pure entertainment. *Great Composers* introduces you to some of the most well-known, prolific, and influential masters of the art of creating music.

CHAPTER 1

GIOVANNI PALESTRINA

The Renaissance

The Renaissance was a transitional time from the medieval to modern eras, and music was a part of the general rebirth and flowering of the arts of the period. The Renaissance was a time of growth and development for the visual arts, literature, exploration, religion, philosophy, and science. Botticelli painted the *Birth of Venus*. Michelangelo painted the ceiling of the Sistine Chapel and sculpted *David*. Cervantes wrote *Don Quixote*, Dante wrote *The Divine Comedy*, and Shakespeare wrote *King Lear*, *Romeo and Juliet*, *Macbeth*, and *Hamlet*, among other masterpieces. Vasco da Gama and Magellan explored the world by sea, seeking new ways to bring the spices of the Far East back to Europe. Martin Luther protested the excesses he saw in the Catholic Church, thus establishing Protestantism. Copernicus and Galileo explored the heavens, changing Europe's view of their place in the world. Leonardo da Vinci, the exemplary Renaissance man, painted *Mona Lisa* and *The Last Supper*, dissected the human body and described its organs, and developed new engineering concepts.

The atmosphere of innovation that fostered this period of creativity also influenced the development of new forms of music. While it remained primarily religious in its purpose, music was beginning to go from churches into palaces and humble homes. Its concentration in the monasteries of rural France now extended to the cities of urban Italy and beyond. Dukes, princes, and nobles who had the means became patrons of the arts, supporting artists and their work. Patrons sought out those who showed promise as composers, educated them, and made them members of their households. Many extended noble households included musicians-in-residence.

The time frame for the Renaissance period varies considerably depending on what historians choose to include, but generally, the Renaissance in music took place from 1450 to 1600.

The development of printing, credited to Johannes Gutenberg (1395–1468), contributed a great deal to the spread of music. Gutenberg perfected the technique of movable type and a printing press on which to use it. One of the earliest existing examples of his craftsmanship is the Gutenberg Bible, the first book ever printed. The printing press allowed printers to make hundreds of copies of sheet music far more efficiently than scribes writing by hand could. Starting in 1465, this was a big factor in making music available to the middle class as well as to the royals.

Secular music was spreading, abetted by itinerant musicians, in the form of the madrigal, the secular equivalent of the religious motet, both being unaccompanied songs written and sung in parts. Secular motets, however, are found pre-Renaissance as early as the mid-1200s. Basically, a major factor in Renaissance music is that standards and methods of composition were becoming established.

The Renaissance was widespread throughout Europe, and this was no less true for music than for any other field. From England there were, among others, Thomas Tallis, William Byrd, and Thomas Morley; from France, Guillaume Dufay, Jachet da Mantova, Guillaume Costeley, and Clement Janequin; from Italy, Bartolommeo Spontone, Orfeo Vecchia, and Girolamo Frescobaldi; from Spain, Antonio de Cabezon, Tomas Luis de Victoria, and Fernando Las Infantas. One of the best representatives of the Renaissance composers is Giovanni Palestrina of Italy.

GIOVANNI PALESTRINA HOLDS THE MOST EXALTED POSITION AMONG composers of sacred music.

Palestrina was born in 1525 or 1526 in the Sabine Hills, about 20 miles (32km) from Rome, in a town called Palestrina—hence his name, Giovanni Pierluigi da Palestrina. He started his musical career as a choirboy at the Rome church of St. Maria Maggiore around 1537 and progressed to become a teacher and organist at the Cathedral of St. Agapito in Palestrina in 1544. When Julius III, who had been Bishop of Palestrina and was therefore very aware of the young man's talents, became Pope in 1550, he brought Palestrina into the musical limelight of religious Rome. In 1551 Palestrina was appointed to the Cappella Giulia of St. Peter's as Master of the Chapel and subsequently to the Cappella Sistina (the Sistine Chapel), the pope's own chapel, in 1555. Unfortunately, Palestrina was dismissed from the papal choir that same year when Pope Julius III died and Pope Paul IV, Julius's successor, prohibited married men from being in the choir.

Palestrina had wed Lucrezia Gori in 1547, and they had three sons. Tragically, Lucrezia, the two older boys, and one, or possibly two, of Palestrina's brothers died of the plague between 1572 and 1581. Distraught, Palestrina prepared to enter the priesthood, but then married Virginia Dormoli, widow of a wealthy fur merchant.

Effectively managing not only the fur business but also real estate investments, Palestrina divided his time between business and composing. His business acumen carried over to his music, for there are a number of known occasions when he turned down desirable composing jobs because his fee was not met.

Palestrina's *First Book of Masses* was published in 1554 under the patronage of Pope Julius III, to whom the composer

GIOVANNI (c.1525–1594)
PALESTRINA

dedicated his first published work. He often dedicated his compositions to popes, patrons, and rulers, apparently trying to curry their favor, but he was never in such good standing with subsequent popes as he was with Pope Julius III, though he worked with them, too.

In 1562 Pope Pius IV gathered his cardinals for the Council of Trent to deal with complaints of the Church's excesses, including the accusation that the music was becoming too secular. Some cardinals wanted to remove all music except Gregorian chants from the Church. Several composers were designated to write masses that would be acceptable. Palestrina composed *Missa Papae Marcelli* ("The Mass of Pope Marcellus"), which won over the council and reinforced the use of music in the Catholic church.

From 1566 to 1571 Cardinal Ippolito II d'Este engaged Palestrina to supervise the music at his summer estate outside Rome and to serve him in general year-round. Palestrina also taught music at the Seminario Romano to provide education for his sons. Palestrina was a mentor to many students and his expertise was sought at all levels. Duke Guglielmo Gonzaga had written some music and solicited Palestrina's evaluation. Discussions of the Duke's music are the basis of the only twelve surviving letters written by Palestrina.

The Renaissance

In 1571 Palestrina returned to the Cappella Giulia as choirmaster, a post he held until he died in 1594.

It is said that Palestrina did more composing than any of his contemporaries, including William Byrd (1543–1623), a highly regarded composer and a pioneer in printing music, and Orlandus di Lasso (1532–1594), an eminent Dutch composer and conductor. Palestrina wrote 104 masses, more than 375 motets and 65 hymns, 68 offertories, 35 magnificats, and an assortment of lamentations, litanies, and psalms. Even with his more than 140 madrigals, most of what he composed was sacred music rather than secular. Nearly three hundred years after Palestrina died in 1594, the master Italian opera composer Giuseppe Verdi observed, "[Palestrina] is the real king of sacred music, and the Eternal Father of Italian music." ♪

PALESTRINA HANDS THE POPE HIS NEW MASS, *MISSA PAPAE MARCELLI*, WHICH BECAME A MODEL OF CHURCH MUSIC, COMBINING AN EVOCATIVE MOOD WITH A CLEAR INTERPRETATION OF THE TEXT.

CHAPTER 2

The Baroque Period

The Baroque Period

"There exists a common fallacy that all music of the first half of the eighteenth century not written by Bach was written by Handel," states Percy M. Young in his biography of Handel. Johann Sebastian Bach and George Frideric Handel were the leaders of the Baroque period in music, but numerous other composers must not be underestimated.

Baroque music spans the years 1600 to 1750. Amazing things were happening in and around the world during this period. Britain's Oliver Cromwell (1599–1658) became a respected but controversial leader. Jonathan Swift (1667–1745) wrote *Gulliver's Travels*. The plays of William Shakespeare (1564–1616) appeared at the Globe Theatre in London. Sir Isaac Newton (1642–1727) conducted scientific experiments that resulted in the discovery of the law of gravity. Voltaire (1694–1778) in France and Benjamin Franklin (1706–1790) were writing philosophy on opposite sides of the Atlantic Ocean. The Dutch settled New Amsterdam, which eventually became New York, in 1624. Painters flourishing at the time include the Spanish El Greco (1541–1614), the Flemish Peter Paul Rubens (1577–1640), and the Dutch Rembrandt van Rijn (1606–1669).

The word "baroque" derives from the Portugese word "barroco," meaning a pearl of irregular shape. At first, the word "baroque" was used pejoratively to describe art and music that did not fit Renaissance standards. During the Renaissance, monody—music for a solo singer rather than for ensembles—flourished. In the Baroque period, monody was crucial to the creation of opera; it also allowed the Renaissance oratorio and cantata musical forms to develop. At the same time, new styles of instrumental music, such as fugues, concertos, and sonatas, developed.

Music was continuing to become more available to the populace. Public concerts were offered at private academies; probably the first school to invite the public in was the Academia Filarmonica in Verona. Some of these music academies were also orphanages, and some of the most influential Italian Baroque composers were the teachers and the students. In England concerts were sponsored in schools, homes, and taverns; the first documented public performance in England was at London's Mitre Inn during 1664. Handel's successful concerts at Oxford were likely responsible for creating a hall just for concerts, the Holywell Music Room. By the 1700s, most sizable towns had music societies that fostered public concerts. Performances in palaces continued for the royalty and private programs in the homes of the well-to-do. And of course, music for the church was still a major avenue for composers, especially in Germany.

It needs to be kept in mind that much of what was written by musicians and authors in the 1600s and earlier has deteriorated, been destroyed, or been lost through the subsequent centuries. In the seventeenth century, many compositions were lost during the Thirty Years' War. However, detective work has pieced together the creative output of composers like Jacopo Peri, Claudio Monteverdi, Heinrich Schütz, and their contemporaries.

JACOPO PERI
(1561–1633)

JACOPO PERI, WHO WAS BORN IN ROME AND DIED IN FLORENCE, IS regarded as one of the fathers of opera. In 1600 he finished *Euridice*, an entire play-with-music for the nuptial celebrations of King Henri IV of France (1553–1610) and Maria de' Medici (1573–1642). *Daphne,* sometimes referred to as a short pastoral, with music by Peri, certain arias by Giulio Caccini, and the libretto by Ottavio Rinuccini, was an operatic forerunner dating to 1597. But *Euridice*, on which Rinuccini also collaborated, is the earliest opera for which both the music and the score still exist.

Early precursors of opera included incidental music, music written to accompany dramatic works. In 1583, for instance, Peri wrote incidental music for *Le Due Persilie*, a comedy by Giovanni Fedini, and in 1589 he participated in the wedding festivities for Ferdinando and Christine of Lorraine by writing music for *La Pellegrina*, by Girolamo Bargagli. As a staff musician at the Mantua Court, one of Peri's tasks was setting poems written by members of the court to music.

Opera and incidental music for drama were not Peri's only musical formats. In 1609 he published a collection of songs, *Le Varie Musiche*, including sonnets, madrigals, and arias. It was not unusual for Peri also to be one of the singers in a presentation. In *La Pellegrina*, for instance, he sang an aria he had composed and drew a most favorable critique: "He captivated the audience, accompanying himself with amazing skill on the chitarrone [a double guitar]." It is also likely that Peri sang the role of Orpheus in *Euridice*.

Peri was slender and of medium height; his distinguishing feature was his flowing blond hair, which prompted the nickname Il Zazzerino ("the long-haired"). Though enthusiastic, Peri was a slow writer, which possibly accounts for his having left many compositions incomplete. While manuscripts of some of Peri's music have never been found, evidence of their existence has been traced in preserved letters and other documents of the period.

Peri also continued to write for weddings. In 1628, when Duke Odoardo Farnese of Parma married Margherita de' Medici, Peri collaborated on an opera, *La Flora* ("The Flower"), that was presented at the festivities. The text dealt with the characters Zeffiro and Clori and the origin of flowers—blossoms were created from the tears of happiness shed by Zeffiro upon winning the love of his adored Clori. In creating operas like *La Flora*, Peri founded a monumental form of musical expression that has survived ever since.

CLAUDIO (1567–1643) MONTEVERDI

PIONEERS ARE NOT ONLY THOSE HARDY SOULS WHO FORGE OVER AND through unchartered terrain, but also the talented who visualize beyond those things that exist in an artistic or technological field and create another dimension of their chosen field. Claudio Monteverdi was such a pioneer.

It was Monteverdi who brought opera, first introduced by Jacopo Peri in 1600, out of the palaces and into the public theaters. Recitative—a monotonous form of singing set to limited accompaniment—was the prevailing opera style when Monteverdi started composing. He added his creativity to the form, giving it considerably more expressiveness and emotion.

Monteverdi was born in Cremona, Italy. His father, a surgeon, engaged Marc Antonio Ingegneri, Master of the Chapel (director of music) of the cathedral in Cremona, where the

Monteverdis resided, to instruct Claudio and his brother in music. By the time Monteverdi was in his midteens, his madrigals, which would eventually number 250, and motets were being published.

When Monteverdi was in his early twenties, he had jobs playing stringed instruments at the Court of the Gonzaga family in Mantua, which led to full employment as maestro

to Duke Vincenzo I. Monteverdi also accompanied the Duke on his travels to Austria and Hungary. Soon after his marriage in 1599 to Claudia de Cattaneis, one of the court singers, Monteverdi was called to join the Duke on a trip to Flanders. Claudia died in 1607, leaving her husband with two sons (a daughter had died in infancy).

CLAUDIO MONTEVERDI MASTERED COMPOSITION AT A VERY EARLY AGE—A COLLECTION OF HIS THREE-PART MOTETS WAS PUBLISHED IN VENICE WHEN HE WAS ONLY FIFTEEN.

The Baroque Period

There is some debate as to whether Monteverdi's first opera was *Orfeo* or *Arianne*, since they appeared around the same time, 1608, and records are unavailable. The only extant part of *Arianne* is the "Lament," one of the most popular vocals in its time. For *Orfeo*, Monteverdi introduced an orchestra of thirty-six instruments, an exceptionally high number by the standards of the day. He also experimented with progressions of harmonies. Monteverdi was a man so ahead of his time that the composer, teacher, lecturer, and historian William Rockstro (a.k.a. Rackstraw, 1823–1895) compared the preludes in *Orfeo* to the writings of Wagner.

When Duke Vincenzo died in 1612, his successor dismissed Monteverdi. Soon after, the composer was appointed music director at St. Mark's in Venice. Credited with revitalizing the choir, Monteverdi also gained a reputation for being a good administrator. While he composed for St. Mark's, he simultaneously developed a staff of composers, which allowed him time to freelance. Around then he composed ballet music for *Tirsi E Clori,* which was produced in Mantua in 1616. But his loyalty to St. Mark's kept Monteverdi from completing other music that had been commissioned.

Around 1629 Monteverdi apparently became less active as a composer, perhaps partly due to wars that interferred with ducal commissions and a major plague that hit Venice between 1630 and 1631. But plague was also a source of ideas—the Black Plague inspired Monteverdi to compose a Mass of Thanksgiving for deliverance from the scourge.

The first opera house, the Teatro di St. Cassiano, opened in Venice in 1637. By that year, Monteverdi had long been an established composer, so now his operas were sought after for the public opera house; this helped to make Venice the era's opera center of Italy.

In the 1630s—some historians say 1632, others 1636—Monteverdi took holy orders. A decade later, when the composer was seventy-five years old, he composed one of his best-known operas, *L'Incoronazione di Poppea* ("The Coronation of Poppaea"). The following year, en route to the city where he was born, Monteverdi became ill and was helped back to Venice, where he died shortly thereafter. The highly regarded Monteverdi was given a funeral fit for a king. ₰

ABOVE: FOR THIS OPERA, *ORFEO*, MONTEVERDI BROKE WITH TRADITION IN USING AN EXCEPTIONALLY LARGE ORCHESTRA FOR HIS TIME. OPPOSITE: HEINRICH SCHUTZ OWES HIS PLACE IN MUSIC HISTORY TO HIS ASTUTE ADAPTATION OF THE STYLES OF CONTEMPORARY ITALIAN INNOVATORS, INCLUDING CLAUDIO MONTEVERDI AND GIOVANNI GABRIELI.

Schütz is regarded as the greatest German composer of the seventeenth century and generally considered to be the first composer of international reputation. He was born in the German town of Kostritz in 1585, but the family moved to Weissenfels around 1590. Schütz's parents were innkeepers. One day, a guest, the Landgrave Moritz of Hessen-Kassel, happened to hear young Heinrich sing and was impressed to the point of inviting the boy to join his *kapelle*, a musical ensemble customarily part of seventeenth-century privileged households. At first Heinrich's parents did not want their son to go, but eventually they gave their permission. Heinrich was fourteen when he became a choirboy in the Landgrave Moritz's kapelle; as such, he received a varied education, in which he excelled at languages. In 1608 Schütz went to the University of Marburg to study law, but was drawn back to music the following year when Landgrave Moritz offered him the opportunity to journey to Venice to study with Giovanni Gabrieli (1553–1612), a highly regarded composer and teacher and an organist at St. Mark's Cathedral. Schütz greatly appreciated his mentors; he always credited Gabrieli as his teacher and he dedicated his graduation thesis, the *Book of Five-Voice Madrigals,* to Moritz, who financed most of his study in Italy.

HEINRICH SCHÜTZ
(1585–1672)

Soon after Schütz's return to the Moritz household, negotiations for his services began between the Landgrave and Johann Georg I of Saxony, who had learned of the accomplished young musician. In January 1617 Moritz acquiesced and Schütz went to Dresden to work for Johann Georg as an organist and music director, eventually earning the title of kapellmeister (director of the court choir). Among Schütz's early assignments from Georg was composing a ballet to honor the visit of Emperor Matthias and music for the centenary of the Reformation.

Schütz composed the first German opera as part of the entertainment for the wedding festivities of Princess Sophia Eleanore of Saxony to Landgrave Georg II of Hessen-Darmstadt. Drawing on the libretto *Dafne* used by composer Jacopo Peri thirty years earlier for what is acknowledged to be the first opera ever (also written for a royal wedding), Schütz prepared a tragicomedy to entertain the wedding guests. Subsequently, he also wrote other stage works, including an opera-ballet based on *Orpheus* for the wedding of Prince Johann Georg and Princess Magdalena Sybilla of Brandenburg.

The composer's own wedding was in 1619, and Schütz "never knew or heard a more lovely sound or song than when he heard the voice and word of his precious wife," said Hoe von Hoenegg in his funeral oration for Schütz's wife, Magdalena, who died just six years after she and the composer were married. After her death, their two daughters were cared for by Magdalena's mother.

Schütz's study in Italy enabled him to introduce new techniques of composition to Germany, and it is possible he benefited from the influence of Claudio Monteverdi as well as Gabrieli. He also brought several Italian musicans into Georg's Kapelle. Between 1642 and 1644, Schütz extended his expertise to Denmark, where he was court conductor in Copenhagen.

A further Schütz innovation was the use of musical copyright. In 1637 Schütz had King Ferdinand III write a disclaimer governing unauthorized reprinting of Schütz's work.

The disclaimer covered a period of five years, after which Schütz requested a renewal of the copyright.

In 1645 Schütz, feeling—both physically and creatively—that it was time to retire, petitioned Johann Georg, but was granted only semiretirement. As he aged, Schütz frequently repeated his request, but it was overlooked time and again. He even took his case to a legal court, where it was also ignored. Schütz's desire to leave the Kapelle was intensified by the miserable financial conditions largely brought on by the Thirty Years' War, which left the royal households in disarray. Schütz was concerned not only for himself but for the instrumentalists and singers who were not being paid; Schütz always showed a personal warmth in his responsibility toward his musicians.

Schütz's wish for retirement was granted after Johann Georg died in 1656. He had served Johann Georg for more than forty years and, in spite of the antagonistic relationship related to Schütz's retirement, Schütz composed his employer's funeral music, twin settings of the German *Nunc Dimittis* segment of Catholic liturgy. Schütz received a pension, composed for major events, and received the emeritus title of chief (or senior) Kapellmeister after he retired.

Schütz lived to be eighty-seven years old, outliving both his daughters. In 1660 he composed the earliest known German musical setting of the Christmas story in recitative form. The last evidence of music composed by him is dated 1668. Upon his death in 1672, his body was interred at the Frauenkirche in Dresden, but the grave was destroyed when the church was rebuilt in 1721. ⁊

JEAN-BAPTISTE LULLY (1632–1678)

STROLLING THROUGH THE STREETS ONE DAY IN HIS HOMETOWN OF Florence, Jean-Baptiste Lully tagged along after a group of wandering players who were performing for the crowds gathered for carnival. Soon the fourteen-year-old joined in the entertainment, and before long he attracted the attention of Roger de Lorraine, Chevalier de Guise. The chevalier hired the boy as a kitchen scullion for the Parisian court of Mademoiselle de Montpensier, a cousin of the boy king of France, Louis XIV. De Montpensier soon discovered that Lully had musical ability and assigned him to lead a small group of violin players; Lully remained in her service for six years.

In one of the many political upheavals of the period, de Montpensier was exiled; Lully, however, was allowed to remain. He entered the service of King Louis XIV as a ballet dancer, composer, and member of the ensemble referred to as the "24 Violons du Roi" ("The King's 24 Violins"). Already showing traits of entrepreneurial know-how, Lully persuaded Louis to allow him to form his own ensemble, which was made up of seventeen to twenty-one musicians and became known as "Les Petits-Violons du Roi" ("The King's Small Violins").

Talent coupled with energy and perhaps a bit of wiliness enabled Lully to rise through the ranks at court, culminating in the position of Music Master to the Royal Family in 1662. Eventually, Lully sought naturalization in France, and when filing his papers, he claimed that his father, a miller, was a Florentine gentleman. This subterfuge was accepted and Lully was regarded as a gentleman of the French court. Lully was held in such high esteem by the royal family that when he wed Madeleine Lambert, daughter of a court musician, he was given the rare compliment of having the marriage contract signed by the king, the queen, and the queen-mother.

The playwright Molière (Jean Baptiste Poquelin,1622–1673) and Lully were collaborators for approximately ten years on what might be called vocal-comedy-ballet performances, a stepping stone to French opera. The first of several such entertainments was *Le Mariage Force* in 1664, and the last was *Le Bourgeoise Gentilhomme* in 1670.

Early attempts at producing opera in Paris were a dismal failure financially. Lully, being in favor with the king, obtained permission to take over the royal opera. His company was known as the Académie Royale de Musique, the forerunner of the Paris Opéra. Not only did Lully compose, direct, conduct, and coach, but he also managed his company with great skill; he was disciplined and he instilled discipline in his musicians, singers, and associates. The inaugural offering was *Les Fetes de L'Amour et de Bacchus* ("The Festivities of Cupid and Bacchus") in 1672. Lully held something of a monopoly on musical theater due to a decree issued in 1673 forbidding other theaters to employ more than two singers and six instrumentalists, and Lully's operas were actively performed for nearly a century. To his credit, Lully developed French opera into a truly popular art, available to the commoner as well as to the nobility. He introduced ballet into his operas and used overtures and choruses more often to augment the solo singing. Lully based many of his operas on Greek legend and history, including *Alceste* (1674), *Thesée* (1675), *Psyche* (1678), and *Acis et Galatée* (1686).

At the height of his career, with fame and power his, Lully was brought down by a strange death at age fifty-four. While conducting, he inadvertently jabbed his foot with a long staff with which he was beating time. This precipitated a fatal infection. Ironically, the composition Lully was conducting was a Te Deum celebrating Louis XIV's recovery from a serious illness. ♪

OPPOSITE: THE ITALIAN-BORN JEAN-BAPTISTE LULLY WORKED FOR ABOUT A DECADE WITH THE RENOWNED PLAYWRIGHT MOLIÈRE, CREATING WORKS THAT COMBINED MUSIC, VOCALS, COMEDY, AND BALLET—THE PRECURSORS OF FRENCH OPERA.

DIETRICH BUXTEHUDE (1637–1707)

WHILE WE DON'T KNOW WHETHER DIETRICH BUXTEHUDE WAS BORN in Germany or Denmark, or exactly when, we do know that he was one of the outstanding composers and organists of the seventeenth century. A tribute to his reputation is the oft-told story that Johann Sebastian Bach, the musical master of the first half of the eighteenth century, walked two hundred miles (320km) to hear Buxtehude perform on the organ. Buxtehude is acknowledged to have had a definite effect on Bach as both organist and composer; for example, Bach interpolated Buxtehude's D Minor Passacaglia theme into his C Minor Passacaglia for Organ.

Dietrich's family came from the town of Buxtehude, southwest of Hamburg, Germany, hence the family surname. Dietrich's father was an organist and schoolmaster in Oldesloe in the Duchy of Holstein until 1638, after which he went to Helsingborg, Sweden, becoming organist at a major church there. Around 1641 the older Buxtehude proceeded to Helsingor, Denmark, to become an organist at the Olaikirche; he apparently remained there for the rest of his life. So if Dietrich's birth date of 1637 is accurate, we may assume that he was born in Oldesloe and grew up in Helsingor. He probably attended the Lateinschule there but received his musical education from his father.

By 1657 he was playing the organ at his father's former church in Helsingborg and then, in 1660, he returned to Helsingor, as his father had done, to pursue his musical career.

In 1668 the younger Buxtehude was chosen over several qualified musicians to succeed Franz Tunder as organist at the Marienkirche in Lubeck. The Marienkirche was one of the most important churches in northern Germany, and the post of organist there was prestigious. Buxtehude remained there until he died thirty-nine years later, also serving as Werkmeister, or general manager, of the church. He was a major force in establishing Marienkirche as northern Europe's most important music center of the time.

The same year Buxtehude became organist, he married Anna Margarethe Tunder, his predecessor's younger daughter. There is speculation that marrying Fraulein Tunder was,

The Baroque Period

according to custom, one of the conditions imposed on Buxtehude upon his acceptance of the organist position. Tunder's older daughter, Augusta Sophie, was already married to the Kantor, the musical leader of the church, Samuel Franck.

Beyond his routine duties at the Marienkirche, Buxtehude reinstated Abendmusik, a series of five annual Sunday afternoon concerts in the church. These are the concerts that enticed Bach to walk from Arnstadt in 1705 to hear Buxtehude play the organ. The Abendmusik series, started in 1673, was popular with the public, and the programs continued into the 1800s. Of the five annual concerts, two took place during Trinity and three during Advent. Buxtehude composed a variety of choral settings for the concerts. Most of his instrumental music was writ-

ten for the organ, but he did compose chamber music and suites for the harpsichord and clavichord.

Very little of Buxtehude's music was published during his lifetime and much of it has therefore been lost. Those few pieces that have been saved or reconstructed are treasures of the Baroque period. ≷

ABOVE: DIETRICH BUXTEHUDE, ORGANIST AND GENERAL MANAGER OF THE MARIENKIRCHE IN LUBECK, GERMANY, HELPED TO MAKE THIS CHURCH THE ERA'S MOST IMPORTANT MUSIC CENTER IN NORTHERN EUROPE. OPPOSITE: BURIED IN WESTMINSTER ABBEY, HENRY PURCELL IS MEMORIALIZED BY THE INSCRIPTION, "HERE LYES HENRY PURCELL, ESQ.; WHO LEFT THIS LIFE, AND IS GONE TO THAT BLESSED PLACE WHERE ONLY HIS HARMONY CAN BE EXCEEDED."

HENRY PURCELL (1659–1695)

ALTHOUGH HE LIVED FOR ONLY THIRTY-SIX YEARS, HENRY PURCELL WAS highly regarded as a composer during his short lifetime. The younger Henry Purcell (Henry was also the first name of his father, a musician) was born in England (probably London) in 1659 to a musical family and became the most individualistic English composer of his time. Performances of his music lapsed for a while, but since a revival in the late 1800s, his reputation has endured.

Purcell was a chorister at the Chapel Royal until his voice changed around the age of fourteen. His knowledge of musical instruments helped him earn an appointment as an assistant caring for the King's keyboards and woodwinds in 1673; he became keeper of the royal instruments just ten years later. Soon he was the organ tuner at Westminster Abbey, and when Purcell was twenty, he succeeded composer John Blow

(1649–1708) as the abbey's organist. With this appointment came a decent salary and rent, and it was around this time that Purcell married and had several children. In his twenties, he became one of three organists at Chapel Royal, the private musical entourage of British kings and queens.

Dido and Aeneas, based on the fourth book of Virgil's Aeneid, was Purcell's masterpiece and the first substantial English opera. Particularly noteworthy are his entwining of music, text, and dance in the play. The lament of Dido, Queen of Carthage, "When I Am Laid in Earth," has entered the modern-day mezzo soprano's repertoire. Purcell collaborated with librettist Nahum Tate, an Irish playwright and poet, on this short opera, which was performed at Josias Priest's School for Young Ladies in Chelsea in 1689.

Purcell also composed in other musical forms. He wrote what are referred to as "welcome odes" for King Charles II (1660–1685), roughly the equivalent of "Hail to the Chief" for the president of the United States. Queen Mary II (1662–1694) was honored on her birthday with the Purcell ode "Come, Ye Sons of Art," and the composer also wrote her funeral music. For St. Cecilia's Day, Purcell wrote compositions that became part of the annual celebrations of that occasion: Te Deum and Jubilate in D. Purcell's talent extended to the religious with such choral anthems as "Hear My Prayer, O Lord" and "Remember Not, Lord, Our Offences." There were also verse anthems that indicated sections for solo voices. When James II (1633–1701) succeeded his brother, Charles II, as king in 1685, Purcell was one of the composers designated to write anthems for the Coronation.

Purcell's later years were primarily taken up with writing for the theater. His prodigious output of music for thirty-seven plays between 1690 and 1695 includes *Dioclesian, King Arthur, The Fairy Queen, The Indian Queen,* and *The Tempest,* with the latter two based on Shakespeare plays. In *King Arthur,* there is a passage referred to as the "cold scene" in which Purcell musically describes a person shivering with teeth clacking; this same musical play produced a popular song of the day, "Fairest Isle."

When Purcell died, his funeral was held at Westminster Abbey with the combined choirs of the Abbey and Chapel Royal participating; his body was interred under the aisle adjoining the organ. ♪

ANTONIO VIVALDI (1678–1741)

The Baroque Period

SOMEWHAT LIKE RIP VAN WINKLE, THE MUSIC OF ANTONIO VIVALDI lay dormant until fairly recently, when his music was rediscovered and woke to a generation of music lovers eager to receive it.

Vivaldi's music began to awaken in 1905 when music historian Arnold Schering cited the importance to music history of the evolution of the concerto. This inevitably pointed to Vivaldi, inasmuch as development of the concerto form was his greatest contribution to music. In the 1920s, Vivaldi's personal collection of sacred and secular scores was discovered by Alberto Gentili. In 1947 the publisher Ricordi issued a collected edition of Vivaldi's instrumental compositions, followed in 1955 by an extensively researched book on Vivaldi by Marc Pincherle, critic, musicologist, and president of the Societé Francaise de Musicologie from 1948 to 1955.

The public was awake to Vivaldi's music during his lifetime, but after a few decades it slumbered away. Antonio, born in Venice, Italy, was the eldest of six children and the only one to follow in the footsteps of their father, a professional violinist. As a boy, he studied music with his father and a local teacher, but at fifteen he trained for the priesthood. For the ten-year period of clerical preparation, he was permitted to live at home, probably due to his severe asthma. Known as the "Red Priest" because of the color of his hair, Antonio was ordained in 1703, but soon after ceased saying Mass. It is unknown whether the reason was his health or his preference for a musical career.

It was not long before Vivaldi was hired as Master of Violin at the Pio Ospedale della Pieta, a school for orphaned, abandoned, or wayward girls. Emphasis at the school was on music; the student concerts were quite impressive and were therefore attended by music lovers from near and far. Vivaldi served the school, on and off, from 1704 to 1740, acting not only as violin teacher but also as conductor, composer, and music director.

Around 1738, Vivaldi went to Amsterdam, where he wrote a concerto and directed performances for the centenary of the city's Schouwberg Theatre.

There is evidence of Vivaldi being a careless spender, and he was in a state of poverty when he died in Vienna. His remains were interred the same day at the Hospital Burial Ground.

Because he was a nonconformist, both as a person and as a musician, Vivaldi was easily the object of criticism, to which he was extremely sensitive. Being a spendthrift was not Vivaldi's only vice. His ego was quite large and he bragged about the prominent people he knew and the quantity of works he had published. Vivaldi claimed, for instance, to have written ninety-four operas, whereas fewer than fifty are known to have existed. Twenty-one opera scores survive, although not all are intact; his first and last operas, *Ottone in Villa* and *Rosmira*, are among the survivors.

Unquestionably, Vivaldi was a violin virtuoso. Much praise was given to his dexterity and to the expression with which he played. Of the approximately five hundred concertos Vivaldi composed, about 230 were for the violin. He also wrote cantatas, motets, serenatas, and about ninety sonatas. His skill as a composer so impressed Johann Sebastian Bach that the younger composer made transcriptions of Vivaldi's compositions.

In 1725 Vivaldi published *Il cimento dell'armonica e dell'inventioni* ("The Trial of Harmony and Invention"), which consisted of twelve concertos; the first four of these works are titled *Le Quattro Stagione*, "The Four Seasons." For each season, Vivaldi wrote not only music but also a poem of considerable eloquence. *The Four Seasons* has become his most popular work. ≹

Although he tried to resist music, GEORG PHILIPP TELEMANN was repeatedly drawn to it. An early sense of financial responsibility led him to pursue the study of law and he enrolled at the University of Leipzig. But his musical talent was irrepressible: he turned out an estimated three thousand compositions, but there is little evidence of his ever having practiced law. This is especially impressive when one considers that he was a mostly self-taught musician.

Telemann was born in 1681 in Magdeburg, Germany. As a child, he had learned to play numerous instruments and showed a propensity for composing—he tried his hand at writing an opera when he was twelve. As he approached adulthood, however, his widowed mother insisted that he take up a reliable profession. He heeded her advice and set off for the University of Leipzig.

Telemann encountered several musically distracting influences along his path to law, including an acquaintance with the already well-known George Frideric Handel. Handel appraised Telemann by saying that he "could write a motet for eight voices more quickly than one could write a letter."

In his student days, Telemann founded the Collegium Musicum at the University of Leipzig and later reorganized the Hamburg University's Collegium Musicum, which had been founded in 1660. He did likewise in other cities, and these groups brought concerts on a regular basis to the general public. Telemann is therefore credited with being one of the first to make music accessible, not only to professional musicians and his patrons, but also to amateurs and the middle class.

At the university in Leipzig, a psalm-set-to-music by Telemann was inadvertently discovered and brought to the attention of those in charge at one of the city's churches, where it was performed. Well received, it launched Telemann on writing on a regular basis for the church. In the early 1700s, he was known as "the father of sacred music."

GEORG PHILIPP TELEMANN (1681–1767)

Eventually, he became music director of five churches in Hamburg, where he decided to live.

Johann Sebastian Bach, a contemporary of Telemann's, is now regarded as the supreme composer of their period. But that was not necessarily so at the time, for Telemann was chosen over Bach as music director in Leipzig's St. Thomas Church. Bach accepted the position after Telemann and composer Johann Graupner (1683–1760) declined.

Domestically, Telemann had less success than he did professionally. His first wife died in childbirth. Telemann married a second time and he and his new wife had eight children, but only two survived. In time Frau Telemann left her husband for another man, and this became a topic of much gossip in Hamburg.

Telemann's tremendous musical output included not only forty operas and a vast amount of church music— including six oratorios, among them *Der Tag des Gerichts* ("The Day of Judgment")—but also numerous serenades and more than six hundred instrumental compositions, including the Concerto in D for Trumpet and Strings, Fantasies for Flute, and the Trio Sonatas. Telemann's *Tafelmusik* ("Table Music") was expressly written as background for banquets and similar events. He also served as musical director for the Leipzig Opera (around 1702) and the Hamburg Opera (from 1722 to 1738). Telemann continued writing until he died in Hamburg in 1767, at the age of eighty-six.

OPPOSITE: ANTONIO VIVALDI IS BEST KNOWN TODAY FOR *THE FOUR SEASONS*, A GROUP OF CONCERTOS FOR WHICH THE COMPOSER ALSO WROTE ACCOMPANYING POEMS. <u>ABOVE</u>: GEORG PHILIPP TELEMANN'S STYLE WAS AN EXEMPLAR OF GERMAN BAROQUE DURING ITS HEIGHT.

The Baroque Period

JOHANN SEBASTIAN BACH (1685–1750)

CURIOUSLY, CONSIDERING HIS EXALTED POSITION NOW, JOHANN Sebastian Bach was not regarded as a particularly important composer in his lifetime, probably due to lack of publication of his works and his limited travel. Bach's reputation as a composer languished until 1829, the year that Mendelssohn brought prestige to the late composer when he rediscovered Bach's *St. Matthew Passion* and conducted it in concert.

Bach was a member of an intensely musical family, from his great-grandfather, who was apparently a minstrel and fiddler, to several of Johann Sebastian's sons, who became acknowledged composers. Sebastian—as he was often called (probably because there were so many other Johanns in his family)—was born in Eisenach, Germany, but was orphaned at age ten and went to live with his eldest brother, Johann Christoph, who was an organist at Ohrdruf. It is said that the elder brother did not recognize his sibling's talents and forbade him to handle certain music manuscripts on the bookshelf. Sebastian, therefore, stealthily borrowed the manuscripts at night and clandestinely copied the music by the light of the moon. Supposedly, Sebastian severely strained his eyes in doing so, which may or may not have contributed to his blindness late in life.

The first of the "Three Great Bs"—the other two are Beethoven and Brahms—Bach could also be identified with "Three Great Cs"—court, church, and civic—for it was in all of those environs that Bach composed his music.

Bach's first major job—the first C—was an appointment in 1708 to the main court at Weimar, where Duke Wilhelm Ernst allowed him free time to develop his talents. This was Bach's greatest period of composing for the organ. He also became skilled at organ design and repair, and his expertise was often sought by his colleagues. Five years later, when Bach was offered the post of principal organist at Halle, the Duke raised his wages and expanded his responsibilities in order to retain him in his employ. In 1717 Bach wanted to leave for a position in the court at Cothen, but his approach to Wilhelm Ernst was inopportune and the duke had Bach jailed for a month and then discharged him from his court.

Bach finally got to Cothen, where he became kapellmeister (director of the court orchestra) to Prince Leopold, who was enthusiastic about music and about Bach. This was the start of Sebastian's orchestral, chamber music, and keyboard compositions. Leopold's bride, however, was less enthusiastic about music, and after the wedding in 1720 the impor-

tance of music and of Bach in Leopold's household decreased.

The second C represents Bach's tremendous involvement in church music. This started in a substantial way after his falling-out at Prince Leopold's court, although previously there had been for Bach an overlap of court and church music. In 1723 Bach went to Leipzig, becoming cantor at St. Thomas' Church, a position he would hold for the twenty-seven remaining years of his life. In this position, Bach was responsible for overseeing, as well as providing, the music in Leipzig's four principal churches. An estimated 75 percent of

Bach's 1,080 catalogued compositions were written for worship services; this is not surprising, keeping in mind that the church was an integral part of the eighteenth-century lifestyle. Bach compositions are numbered with the prefix BWV (Bach Werke Verzeichnis) or simply "S," for Schmieder, in either case referring to the catalog assembled by noted music librarian Wolfgang Schmieder.

The third C, for civic, brings in another overlap, for along with Bach's place as music director at St. Thomas' Church went supervision of the music activities in the city. Leipzig around that time was uniquely a self-governing municipality.

BACH & SONS

The Bach family was impressive not only for its sheer size, but also for the amazing quantity of musicians it produced—seven generations of them. The family's genealogy goes back at least to the year 1561. Annual reunions of the family nucleus have been documented to the mid-eighteenth century, and at that time about 120 Bachs and Bachs-in-law attended.

The musical offspring of Johann Sebastian Bach did not form a corporation or even a partnership; they shared a love of music and a vocation, but they never worked together. His best-known musical sons are Carl Philipp Emanuel (1714–1788), referred to as the "Berlin Bach" or the "Hamburg Bach"; Johann Christoph Friedrich (1732–1795), called the "Buckeburg Bach"; and Johann Christian (1735–1782), remembered as the "London Bach" (these nicknames are derived from the cities in which these musicians primarily operated). Not to be forgotten, however, is Sebastian's eldest son, Wilhelm Friedemann (1710–1784), who was a proficient organist and dabbled in composing.

One thing all the composer-sons had in common was that their first music instruction came from their father. With twenty children (not all of whom survived past infancy), the lessons may have been given at home for

financial reasons, but it may also have been simply because Sebastian was the best teacher around.

The Bach boys composed large quantities of sonatas, trios, and quartets, as well as symphonies and concertos. Although they all were busy, Carl Philipp Emanuel and Johann Christian seem to have had the most interesting careers.

Carl Philipp Emanuel (often referred to as C.P.E.) was twenty-four years old when he became harpsichord accompanist for the Prussian crown prince, who enjoyed playing flute; two years later, in 1740, when the prince became Frederick the Great, C.P.E. became court chamber musician. C.P.E. stayed in Frederick's court until 1767, when he moved on to succeed Georg Philipp Telemann as cantor, music director of five churches in Hamburg.

Opera was not a Bach forte, except for Johann Christian, who traveled to Italy and had his operas staged in Turin and Naples. To obtain church work, he converted to Catholicism, after which he became organist at the Milan Cathedral. In 1762 Johann Christian journeyed to London to hear his opera *Orione* performed. When the prodigy Wolfgang Mozart was in London, he improvised on the keyboard with Johann Christian and the two developed a sincere lifelong mutual admiration.

In 1707, immediately preceding Bach's Weimar years, he married a cousin, Maria Barbara Bach, and the couple had seven children, three of whom survived; two of these children, Wilhelm Friedemann and Carl Philipp Emanuel, grew up to become established composers in their own right. Maria Barbara died in 1720, and the following year Bach married Anna Magdalene Wulken. Daughter of a trumpeter at the Weissenfels court, Anna was musically adept and assisted her husband by writing out the parts for his cantatas. They had thirteen children, and at least one—Johann Christian (1735-1782)—became a composer, while several others also had musical careers (see sidebar, page 26).

Three years before Bach died, he was afforded a particular honor when he was invited by the Prussian king Frederick the Great to be a guest at his Potsdam palace. Bach went from room to room trying out the many pianos in the palace, followed appreciatively by Frederick and his court musicians. The king was especially pleased when a theme he had written was improvised by Bach and turned up in *The Musical Offering*, which includes Bach's Trio Sonata. Bach dedicated *The Musical Offering* to Frederick.

Of course, the Cs can be extended from the environs in which he worked to the forms his compositions took—cantata, canon, chaconne, concerto. But not all his favored forms began with "c"; he also wrote sonatas, preludes and fugues, partitas, masses and passions, and oratorios, among other forms. And every Bach fan has a favorite. In the category of cantata, it might be *Christ lag in Todesbanden* or the "Coffee Cantata." Among the concertos, the favorite could well be one of the Brandenburg Concertos, a group of six works dedicated to Christian Ludwig, the Margrave of Brandenburg, who offhandedly commissioned the work, had it filed away, and probably never heard it. The masses include the great one in B Minor, the oratorios include the *Christmas Oratorio*, and the passions include the *St. Matthew Passion* and the *St. John Passion*. The list of preludes and fugues is seemingly endless, with the Great G Minor and Little G Minor ranking high among them.

His eyesight failing, Bach had surgery twice in 1749, but he became totally blind for a brief period anyway. In July, 1750, his eyesight unexpectedly returned, but he died late that month of a brain hemorrhage. Bach's physical remains were interred in Leipzig at St. John's Church, but his musical remains will never be buried. ♩

GEORGE FRIDERIC HANDEL (1685-1759)

FOR A LONG TIME THE DARLING OF LONDON IN THE EYES OF BOTH THE nobility and the commoners, George Frideric Handel first made his mark there in the autumn of 1710. By that date, the twenty-five-year-old Handel had already garnered substantial acclaim in his native Germany and in Italy.

As an adult, Handel was greeted with musical success after musical success, but in his earlier years, apparently to appease his father, Handel studied law at the university in Halle, where he had been born. At the same time, he was being trained by Friederich Zachow, organist, cantor, and composer at the Halle Cathedral Church, in various facets of music. In his late teens, Handel ventured to Hamburg, which was then considered the opera center of Germany, and joined the opera orchestra as second violinist, all the while working on writing opera. His first work in this form, *Almira*,

GEORGE FRIDERIC HANDEL RECEIVED WIDE POPULAR ACCLAIM DURING HIS LIFETIME AND IS BEST KNOWN TODAY FOR THE *MESSIAH*, AN ORATORIO THAT IS PERFORMED ANNUALLY AT CHRISTMASTIME CONCERTS AROUND THE WORLD.

premiered in January 1705 and was an immediate success; another hit, *Nero*, followed the next month. Handel's geographic horizons widened rapidly after a Medici prince persuaded him to visit Italy, the mecca of music, late in 1706. The Italians, finding it difficult to pronounce Handel's name, referred to him as "Il Sassone" ("The Saxon"). The oratorio *La Resurezzione*, performed in Rome, and the opera *Agrippina*, staged in Venice, were among Il Sassone's early successes in Italy. It is remarkable that the work of a German was so well received at that time, the homeland of opera.

Upon his return to Germany, Handel became kapellmeister (director of the court orchestra) to the Elector of Hanover, George Ludwig (1660–1727), who later became King George I of England, but Handel soon took a leave of absence to go to London. In only two weeks, Handel composed his opera *Rinaldo*, which premiered at the Haymarket Theater to resounding acclaim. His music was enhanced by dramatic and elaborate staging that included fire-exhaling dragons and a flock of live sparrows released concurrently with the aria "Little Birds That Sing." One Handel opera followed another, among them *Il Pastor Fido* ("The Faithful Shepherd") and *Taseo*.

In 1719, Handel and impresario John Jacob Heidegger (1659–1749) founded the Royal Academy of Music, privately subsidized but called "Royal" because George I patronized it. Queen Anne had given Handel no less support, and he had written an ode for her birthday the year before she died in 1714. Upon Anne's death, George of Hanover was proclaimed king. *Radamisto* was Handel's first opera for the Royal Academy in 1720 and it proved to be the composer's finest to date.

The greatest singers of the day performed in Handel's operas, including soprano Francesca Cuzzoni and contralto castrato Francesco Senesino in 1724's *Giulio Cesare*, who were joined in 1726 by soprano Faustina Bordoni in *Alessandro*.

Handel's fortunes soon changed. With the 1728 play *The Beggar's Opera*, by John Gay (1685–1732), a turning point in opera had been reached wherein English ballads replaced the florid Italian-style singing, making opera more comprehensible to the British public. The exaggerated singing and acting of the Handel style was going out of favor. To make matters worse, the Opera of the Nobility, a company to rival the Royal Academy, was formed in London in 1729.

Fortunately for Handel, his oratorios brought him new prominence. The most famous of these is the *Messiah*. Considering the monumental scope of this work, it is amazing to learn that Handel composed it in just over three weeks, between August 22 and September 14 of 1741. Although it was an overwhelming success when it premiered in Dublin on April 13, 1742, London audiences were slow to accept it. The world premiere had benefited three Irish charities, and not until Handel used a *Messiah* performance to benefit the Foundling Hospital in London in 1754 was the oratorio genuinely a success there. Handel's other numerous oratorios, most based on Old Testament personages, include *Saul* (1739), *Samson* (1743), *Judas Maccabaeus* (1746), and his last, *Jephthah* (1752).

Among the single musical selections by which Handel is often identified is the Largo ("Ombra mai piu") from his one major comic opera, *Serse* ("Xerxes"), and instrumental favorites such as *Music for Royal Fireworks* (1748), which was written to accompany the pyrotechnics in London's St. James Park on the occasion of the signing of the peace of Aix-la-Chapelle, ending St. George's War.

Another of Handel's frequently performed concert pieces is the *Water Music,* and more than one legend of its origin has been heard. Simply stated, the composition was written in 1717 to entertain George I and his entourage during a boating party on the Thames River. When Handel and his fifty-piece orchestra, stationed on one of the boats, played the *Water Music*, the delighted king, not caring that the piece was a full hour in length, requested that it be repeated before and after they dined.

As Handel aged, he went almost totally blind in spite of three eye operations. Remarkably, he continued to compose, play organ concerts, and conduct performances of his oratorios. Eight days before his death in 1759, Handel collapsed while seated at the organ at Covent Garden for a performance of the *Messiah*. Having become a naturalized British subject in 1726, he was was given a splendid funeral and buried at Westminster Abbey. ⟨

KING GEORGE I WAS HANDEL'S LOYAL AND SUPPORTIVE PATRON. IN RETURN, HANDEL GAVE CONCERTS FOR THE KING, INCLUDING A RIVER CONCERT THAT THE MONARCH LISTENED TO FROM HIS ROYAL BARGE.

The Baroque Period

THOMAS ARNE (1710–1778)

"Rule Brittania," Great Britain's universally known nationalistic song of the sea, was not the inspiration of a naval hero but of the popular eighteenth-century theater composer Thomas Arne. He created the rousing song for the finale in his score for a successful masque entitled *Alfred*. Masques, elaborate entertainments encompassing all elements of theater arts, were popular from the late 1500s through the mid-1700s, particularly in England. Creating masques attracted such gifted men as writers John Milton (1608–1674) and Ben Jonson (1572–1637) and composers George Frideric Handel and Henry Purcell.

Arne's first theatrical effort, however, was an opera, *Rosamond*, which premiered in 1733. It was well received, but even more successful was the masque *Comus*, considered Arne's most important work. *Comus's* text by poet John Milton had been set to music a century earlier by composer Henry Lawes (1596–1662). Appearing in Arne's 1738 interpretation was an accomplished singer of the day, Cecilia Young, who was highly praised by Handel. Arne had a reputation of being a womanizer, but he focused on Cecilia and they were married the year before *Comus* was produced.

Major London theaters figured prominently in Arne's career. One of his first successful masques, *Dido and Aeneas*, played the Haymarket Theatre in 1734, and he had several productions at Covent Garden, the forerunner of today's famous opera house. In 1745 Arne was designated official composer for Vauxhall Gardens, a mecca for dancing, poetry readings, and general merriment. For approximately forty years, Arne was involved with productions at the Drury Lane Theatre. Arne composed music for more than eighty stage works and contributed to about twenty others.

Although he had little formal training, he was often addressed as "Doctor Arne," thanks in part to an honorary degree in music from Oxford University.

CHRISTOPH (1714–1787) WILLIBALD GLUCK

THE FEUD BETWEEN THE GLUCKS AND THE PICCINIS CONSISTED OF A dissent over what style of opera should prevail. While it was not, fortunately, a dispute involving physical violence, differences were vehemently aired in public for a number of years.

Christoph Willibald Gluck and his followers were striving to bring opera back to its original intent of drama-with-music in an aura of simplicity. Those who fought to maintain the florid Italian approach to opera, with focus on virtuoso singing, enlisted the esteemed composer Niccolò Piccini (1728–1800) to write an opera and override Gluck and his French-style opera.

ABOVE: AS A BOY, CHRISTOPH WILLIBALD GLUCK PROMISED AN OLDER FRIEND, A PRIEST, THAT HE WOULD DEVOTE HIMSELF TO HIS MUSICAL EDUCATION. THE PRIEST WROTE TO THE BOY'S FATHER, ENCOURAGING HIM TO LET HIS SON PURSUE A MUSICAL CAREER. RIGHT: GLUCK IS PERHAPS BEST REMEMBERED FOR HIS EFFORTS TO RE-CREATE OPERA, TO TURN IT AROUND FROM WHAT HE FELT WAS ITS BOMBASTIC ITALIAN STYLE AND RETURN IT TO ITS ORIGINAL SIMPLE BLEND OF MUSIC AND DRAMA.

Apparently, Piccini and Gluck were writing—coincidentally or not—on the same subject, and Piccini's opera, *Roland*, would precede Gluck's into production at the Opéra in Paris. Reportedly, Gluck burned his manuscript and published a vindictive letter, which brought forth a surge of oppositional pamphlets that were distributed to the public. Hence the Gluck and Piccini feud, which actually was French-style opera versus Italian-style opera.

Though his opera was known as French, Gluck was not a Frenchman—he was born in Erasbach, Bavaria, where his father was a forester and head gameskeeper for a nobleman. At the age of twelve, nurtured in peasant surroundings, Christoph was sent to the Jesuit College at Komotau, where he spent six years. He studied various musical instruments, of which the cello was his favorite. At eighteen, he ventured out into the world, settling for a while in Prague, where he used his musical education to earn a living by playing not only at concerts, but also at churches and dances. The next stop was Vienna, where Gluck was employed in the household of Prince Ferdinand Lobkowitz. Gluck's studies were furthered when a patron, Prince Melzi, took the budding composer to Italy to study harmony and counterpoint with Giovanni Battista Sammartini in Milan. Four years later, in 1741, Gluck's first opera, *Artaserse* ("Artaxerxes"), was produced, and it was sufficiently successful to earn Gluck several commissions to write opera in Italy.

After the *Roland* episode, the Opéra, in an apparent attempt to settle the feud, deliberately assigned Gluck and Piccini the same subject: *Iphigenie en Tauride* ("Iphigenia in Taurus"). This time, Gluck's preceded Piccini's into production and was so highly acclaimed that Piccini urged his opera be withdrawn; it was nevertheless performed 17 times, though overshadowed by Gluck's *Iphigenie en Tauride*.

Gluck was supposed to compose the opera to herald the opening of La Scala (Teatro alla Scala) in Milan, but commitments in Paris prevented this, so he recommended

Antonio Salieri (see Chapter 3, page 39). Certainly this was a boon for Salieri, and on August 3, 1778, La Scala opened with Salieri's *Europa Riconosciuta* ("Europe Recognized"). Salieri also finished Gluck's cantata *Das Jungste Gericht*, one of the elder composer's few nonopera compositions.

Gluck's most famous opera is undoubtedly *Orfeo et Euridice*, and for this he had Raniero de Calzabigi (1714–1795) as librettist. A worldly man, Calzabigi supplemented Gluck's talents by supplying him with subjects; later, he also wrote the text for Gluck's *Alceste* and *Paride et Elena*.

Gluck, Calzabigi, and Count Giacomo Durazzo, director of the court theaters in Vienna, joined forces to promote opera in the French vein, although their first coordinated effort was a ballet performance of *Don Juan* in 1761. Unfortunately, the operas they produced—*Orfeo et Euridice*, *Alceste*, and *Paride et Elena*—failed to please the Viennese public.

After these failures, Gluck ventured to Paris, but there he found the same resistance to his operas. At the intervention of Marie Antoinette (1755–1793), who had been a pupil of Gluck's, *Iphigenie en Aulide* was produced at the Opera in 1774—and it was a hit. Gluck met with success again the following year with *Orfeo et Euridice*. Although he had made his mark, Gluck's last opera, *Echo et Narcisse*, produced in Paris in 1779, was not well received.

Gluck is best remembered for effecting reform in opera, returning it to a blend of music and drama. Common sense instilled during his peasant upbringing was melded with a substantial education. A propitious marriage to Marianne Pergin in 1750 enabled him to travel and thus to broaden his experience. He died in 1787 in Vienna; his tombstone inscription reads "Here lies an honest German, an ardent Christian, a faithful husband."

Of his ongoing battle of reform, Gluck said, "My chief endeavor should be to attain a grand simplicity, and consequently I have avoided making a parade of difficulties at the cost of clearness." ⸮

GLUCK CONDUCTED REHEARSALS WITH GREAT PAS-SION AND VERVE. HE ONCE GREW SO ANIMATED THAT HIS WIG FLEW OFF HIS HEAD. IT WAS RETURNED TO HIM BY THE ACTRESS PLAYING THE PART OF IPHIGENIE IN *IPHIGENIE AND TAURIDE*.

CHAPTER 3

The Classical *Period*

FRANZ JOSEPH HAYDN

ANDRE GRÉTRY

ANTONIO SALIERI

WOLFGANG AMADEUS MOZART

LUDWIG VAN BEETHOVEN

CARL MARIA VON WEBER

GIACOMO MEYERBEER

GIOACCHINO ROSSINI

GAETANO DONIZETTI

FRANZ SCHUBERT

VINCENZO BELLINI

The term "classical music" encompasses the genres known as Renaissance, Baroque, Classical, Romantic, Nationalist, Impressionist, and Twentieth Century. The Classical period, or Classicism, as it is sometimes called, was a relatively short one, ranging from around 1775 to 1825. To some extent, the above periods overlap, but Classical might be regarded as a segue between the Baroque and Romantic periods. Many composers contributed to making that fifty-year bridge a solid passage.

The Classical period was a time of great transition not only in music but also in politics. In North America, there was rebellion against British rule, which crystallized in the Declaration of Independence, brought about the American Revolution, and made George Washington (1732-1799), Thomas Jefferson (1743–1826), and John Adams (1735–1826) well known throughout much of the Western world. At nearly the same time, the citizens of France rose up against the aristocracy, leading to the French Revolution and the Reign of Terror; this was the time of Robespierre (1758–1794) and Napoleon (1769–1821).

Each period of history has its classics, not only in music but also in art, literature, and philosophy. From the late 1700s to the early 1800s, Jean-Jacques Rousseau (1712–1778), Washington Irving (1783–1859), Jane Austen (1775–1817), Lord Byron (1788–1824), and E.T.A. Hoffmann (1776–1822) were among the prominent writers. J.M.W. Turner (1775–1851), Jean Ingres (1780–1867), and Francisco Goya (1746–1828) were some of the lasting painters.

The leading Classical composers—Ludwig van Beethoven, Franz Joseph Haydn, and Wolfgang Amadeus Mozart—were not directly touched by the upheavals of the eighteenth century. Through their genius, they churned out volumes of music, but their output was never enough for the insatiable public. The idea of hearing the same opera or the same symphony over and over again, for instance, had little appeal for music lovers, and the concept of a composition becoming lasting—of becoming a classic—did not necessarily occur to them. It was up to future generations to realize that true classics—timeless works of art—had indeed been composed in the Classical period.

FRANZ JOSEPH HAYDN (1732–1809)

THE ORIGIN OF FRANZ JOSEPH HAYDN'S MOST COMMONLY USED NICKname, "Papa," is rather vague. Perhaps it refers to his kindly ways or to the fact that he is generally referred to as the father of the symphony, even though "godfather" would be more apt, inasmuch as the symphony form had been conceived some time before Haydn came along. In any case, "Papa" composed more than one hundred symphonies.

While Haydn certainly showed musical promise as a child, it was not until he reached adulthood that he came to be considered an outstanding composer. Born in 1732 in Rohrau, Austria, his initial training in voice and instruments was guided by a qualified cousin. Haydn sang in the St. Stephen's Cathedral choir in Vienna from the age of eight until his voice changed, after which his brother Johann Michael (1737–1806) took his place. The younger Haydn also had a career in music as organist, teacher, and composer, primarily of church music.

With borrowed money, the teenage Franz Joseph bought a second-hand clavier, rented space in Vienna, and set himself up as a teacher. Much later in his teaching career, Haydn took on a certain Ludwig van Beethoven as his pupil. Beethoven later said of his teacher: "Though I had some instruction from Haydn, I never learned anything from him." This is an indication either of Beethoven's utter arrogance or his pure genius—it may have been that he was simply so good that no one could have taught him anything.

In Vienna, Haydn lived with his wife. The marriage, however, was not a happy one, and Haydn reportedly stayed away from his home as much as possible in order to avoid his spouse. He had married in strange circumstances: he had been in love, but the object of his affections had decided to become a nun. In 1760, on the rebound, Haydn married her sister, Maria Anna Keller, who apparently had no real fondness for the composer or for music. They remained together in little more than name only, and Haydn sought and received affection elsewhere.

Professionally, however, Haydn was doing very well. Through various contacts, he was hired by Count Morzin to conduct his private orchestra; while working for the count, he was noticed by Prince Paul Esterhazy, who in 1761 appointed Haydn as second to his kapellmeister (director of his court orchestra). The Esterhazys had a castle at Eisenstadt, 30 miles (48km) from Vienna, and an ostentatious summer palace across the border in Hungary. The prince died within the year, and his brother Nikolaus took over, which further improved Haydn's position. Nikolaus played the barytonhorn, a valved brass instrument, and was eager for Haydn to come up with specially designed music for him; this desire led to Haydn creating 150 compositions for the barytonhorn. In 1766 the kapellmeister died and Haydn took his place.

In 1768 Prince Nikolaus built a four-hundred-seat music hall to house daily performances of one form or another. With all his official duties—not to mention any composition he might want to do for his own satisfaction—Haydn was an extremely busy man. When Nikolaus added the marionette theater, it provided the necessary performing space for Haydn's operas, and in one year there were 125 performances of 17 operas, written not only by Haydn but also by other composers. In 1790, Prince Nikolaus died and was succeeded by his son Anton, for whom music was not a priority. Prince Anton pulled in the financial reins; Haydn was retained on a pension and was at liberty to freelance.

When impresario Johann Salomon invited Haydn to London in 1791 to compose and direct, the composer was free to accept. Treated as a celebrity, Haydn was presented at the royal court and given an honorary doctor of music degree by Oxford University. He stayed in London into the next year, went home to Vienna for a short time, then returned to London in 1794, again staying into the following year. During these visits, he wrote twelve symphonies—the London symphonies.

Haydn, now wealthy and internationally famous, returned to the Esterhazys and Vienna in 1795. When Anton died, Prince Nikolaus II, his successor, renewed the interest in music around the palace. Haydn stayed on staff until he was almost seventy, when failing health forced him to step down. All in all, he had musically enriched the Esterhazy household for forty years.

AS CELEBRATED IN ENGLAND AS HE WAS IN HIS NATIVE AUSTRIA, FRANZ JOSEPH HAYDN WAS THE COMPOSER OF *THE CREATION*, THE GREATEST ORATORIO IN HISTORY AFTER HANDEL'S *MESSIAH*.

Haydn's interest in choral music had been stimulated on his first visit to London, when he attended a concert commemorating George Frideric Handel (see Chapter 2, page 27) at Westminster Abbey, where Handel is buried. This inspiration led to *The Creation*, which is regarded as the finest oratorio after Handel's *Messiah*. Handel had been approached with the text for *The Creation* in the 1750s and had turned it down; approximately forty years later, in 1798, Haydn, a man of devout faith, accepted the task of writing this great religious work. (Of course, writing spiritual works was not new to him, for in 1785 he had composed *The Seven Words on the Cross* for Good Friday worship at the Cathedral of Cádiz, Spain.) *The Creation* is made up of three sections: the Creation of the earth, of living creatures, and of Adam and Eve. In the middle segment, Haydn assigned a contrabassoon, a rare instrument in his time, to emulate a hippopotamus. Haydn's other particularly noteworthy—and monumental—choral work was *The Seasons*, which was secular in content, based on a poem by the Scottish poet James Thomson (1700–1748).

In addition to oratorios, Haydn excelled at quartets and symphonies. Most of the latter are up-tempo and, according to symphony standards, on the short side; many have nicknames, most notably the "Surprise" Symphony in G Major, No. 94. Really, there are two surprises in this work. One is hearing a familiar childhood rhyme reminiscent of the old French tune "Twinkle, Twinkle, Little Star." And as the listeners drift along in nostalgia, a fortissimo chord jolts them back into reality—the second surprise! Haydn also wrote opera, but this was the least of his talents.

In 1809, as Haydn was dying, Napoleon's troops were invading Vienna. Informed of the esteemed composer's condition, the French emperor ordered a protective guard of honor at Haydn's house. Haydn, however, was probably not entirely pleased with this; he had deep patriotic feelings for Austria, and around 1797 had composed the song—his personal favorite—that was adopted as the Austrian national anthem. ♩

THE FINAL SCENE OF HAYDN'S OPERA *L'INCONTRO IMPROVISO* WAS PERFORMED UNDER THE COMPOSER'S DIRECTION AT THE ESTERHAZY FAMILY PALACE IN HUNGARY.

The Classical Period

ANDRE GRÉTRY
(1741–1813)

SOME PEOPLE FIGURATIVELY LEAVE THEIR HEART TO A BELOVED HOMEtown or city, but André Grétry did so literally. Per his instructions, Grétry's heart was placed in a protective lead receptacle, returned to his birthplace of Liège in Belgium, and sealed in the plinth of a sculpted bust of the composer. This was in 1828, fifteen years after Grétry died. Subsequently, in 1842, Grétry's heart was relocated to a bronze statue in his likeness placed in front of the opera house at Liège.

So Grétry left his heart in Liège, where he had been born in 1741, although his adult life was lived in various other European cities. As a boy, he sang and became proficient on the violin. When Grétry was in his early twenties, he studied in Rome on scholarship. He spent most of this time composing sacred music. Unfortunately, much of what he wrote during this period, including compositions for flute and for harpsichord, has been lost.

In his childhood, Grétry had been entranced by the music of Giovanni Battista Pergolesi (1710–1736), in particular the opera *La serva padrona* ("The Maid as Mistress"), and the Pergolesi style influenced the youngster. Grétry's first opera was *La Vendemmiatrice*, successfully performed in Rome in 1765. There followed *Le Huron* (1768), based on the comedy of the same name by the French author Jean-François Marmontel (1723–1799), the rights to which were secured with the help of the Swedish ambassador in Paris; *Le Tableau Parlant* ("The Talking Picture," 1769); *Zemire et Azor* (1771), an Oriental adaptation of *Beauty and the Beast* with libretto by Marmontel; and *Cephale et Procris, ou L'Amour Conjugal*

("Cephale and Procris, or Conjugal Love," 1773), also with libretto by Marmontel. In a little over two decades, he composed approximately fifty operas, gaining both royal and public approval. By the late 1700s, Grétry was the predominant composer of French opéra comique, a form of opera which features spoken dialogue and usually uses a lighter tone in music and text than standard opera.

Unfortunately, around 1784, Grétry's musical inspiration seemed to wane, perhaps precipitated by several failures following his successful *Richard Coeur de Lion* ("Richard the Lion-Hearted"), written in 1784. This period also brought much personal tragedy: three of Grétry's daughters died from tuberculosis, a disease from which he also suffered. His daughter Lucile, no doubt the namesake of one of her father's early operatic successes, wrote an opera at age thirteen, *Le Mariage d'Antonio,* which was well-received.

Grétry's diminishing musical creativity coincided with the French Revolution, and Grétry aligned himself with the cause of the common man, even though he had enjoyed the patronage of Marie Antoinette (1755–1793). When the monarchy was reinstituted, Grétry became popular with Napoleon, who bestowed the Legion of Honor on the composer in 1802 and provided him with a pension.

Grétry's writing, however, was not limited to music—he also resorted to the author's pen in expounding on his political views as well as writing his very extensive personal memoirs. *Reflexions d'un Solitaire* extended to eight volumes; written during the years immediately preceding his death in 1813, they were not published until more than a century later, in 1919.

Attesting to Grétry's place among opera composers, there is a statue of him—albeit "heartless"—under the peristyle of the Opéra-Comique in Paris. ♪

ANTONIO SALIERI
(1750–1825)

RIMSKY-KORSAKOV'S OPERA *MOZART AND SALIERI*, BASED ON A POEM by the great Russian poet Aleksandr Pushkin (1799–1837), has Antonio Salieri claiming that he poisoned Mozart. This supposed theory, held by others as well, was made more melodramatic with the Peter Shaffer play and subsequent film *Amadeus*. Research, however, has virtually disproved the murder concept, and even the idea that there was a "poisonous" relationship between the two composers is doubtful.

Salieri was the fifth son of a wealthy merchant in Verona, Italy, who died when Antonio was fifteen years old. A family friend—a Venetian nobleman by the name of Giovanni Mocenigo—stepped in. Recognizing the young man's talents, Mocenigo took Salieri to Vienna to be introduced to Florian Leopold Gassmann (1723–1774), who was considered the principal opera composer of Vienna at that time; he also wrote church music, secular cantatas, chamber works, and thirty-three symphonies. Gassman had succeeded Christoph Willibald Gluck (Chapter 2, page 30) as composer to the Viennese court. In 1766 Gassmann became Salieri's teacher; in 1772 he became court kapellmeister.

When Gassmann died in 1774, Salieri was appointed court composer and later, kapellmeister; in the end, Salieri would serve the Viennese court for fifty years (thirty-six of them as kapellmeister), retiring in 1824 with a full salary. In 1775 Salieri married Theresia Helferstorfer, and in time they had eight children. Around 1780, he succeeded his teacher as Vienna's favorite opera composer, while also composing for the opera houses of Paris, Venice, Rome, and Milan.

A crowning achievement for Salieri was having one of his operas, *Europa riconosciuta* ("Europe Recognized"), open Milan's La Scala opera house on August 3, 1778; it has been one of the world's leading opera houses ever since. Salieri composed forty operas, and none startled the public more than *Les Danaides* ("The Danaids"), with its shocking subject matter concerning the horrors of Hell. Gluck advised Salieri with this opera, and when it premiered in Paris in 1784, it was billed as a joint venture. After its success had been established, however, Gluck gave Salieri full credit. Salieri's greatest operatic success is generally considered to be *Tarare*, which was written in 1787 and pretty much established Salieri as Gluck's musical heir. Originally based on a play by Pierre Beaumarchais, this was adapted by librettist Lorenzo da Ponte, retitled *Axur, Re d'Ormus*, and performed in celebration of the wedding of Archduke Franz to the Princess of Württemberg.

As musical tastes changed, Salieri gradually turned away from opera and began concentrating on church music; he also wrote symphonies, concertos, and songs. In his later years, until 1818, he frequently conducted concerts of the famous Tonkunstler-Sozietat; and also composed works for the society's twenty-fifth and fiftieth anniversaries. This society, later known as the Haydn-Societat, was founded by Gassmann in 1771 to assist widows and orphans of musicians. Salieri brought to the society astute administration of the organization and its archives, concern for the welfare of the musicians, and encouragement to aspiring young people.

OPPOSITE: KNOWN AS THE "MOLIÈRE OF MUSIC" FOR HIS FOUNDING OF THE SCHOOL OF FRENCH OPÉRA COMIQUE, ANDRE GRÉTRY WAS INCLINED TOWARD WRITING OPERA AFTER AN ITALIAN OPERA COMPANY PERFORMED A SEASON IN HIS NATIVE LIÈGE AROUND 1754. ABOVE: ANTONIO SALIERI, CHIEF COMPOSER TO THE VIENNESE COURT DURING MOZART'S HEYDAY, WAS ONCE RUMORED TO HAVE POISONED THE YOUNGER COMPOSER, BUT THIS HAS BEEN DISPROVED.

As a teacher, Salieri trained Gassmann's two daughters to become accomplished opera singers. Salieri's ability as a teacher is further demonstrated in the success of his pupils, who included Franz Joseph Haydn, Ludwig van Beethoven, Franz Liszt (see Chapter 4, page 72), and Franz Schubert.

Returning to the question of this composer's relationship with the young Wolfgang Amadeus Mozart, let it be said that the musical accomplishments and reputation of Salieri may have intimidated Mozart, and that there are reports of rivalry between the two. Regardless of any animosity that may have existed, however, after the younger composer died, Salieri offered assistance to Mozart's son. ♪

WOLFGANG (1756-1791) AMADEUS MOZART

THE SICKER HE GOT AND THE MORE TENSE HE BECAME, THE MORE HE composed and the more magnificent were his works. Only thirty-five years old when he died, Wolfgang Amadeus Mozart wrote his most acclaimed compositions during the last few years of his life. Fraught as he was with various ailments, Mozart may have sensed that there was not much time left to him and so struggled to give to the world as much of the music that was within him as possible.

The last year of Mozart's life, 1791, was an important one for the composer: *La clemenza di Tito* ("The Clemency of Titus") had a Prague premiere on September 6 and *Die Zauberflöte* ("The Magic Flute") premiered in Vienna on September 30. In a period of only seven weeks in 1788, Mozart wrote his final symphony, No. 41, known as the "Jupiter," and symphonies No. 39 and 40; these quickly rendered works are considered among his very finest symphonic compositions.

With the Requiem on which he was working unfinished, Mozart died on December 5, 1791. One of the most oft-told stories about Mozart's life (or in this case, his death) is the

THE FLAMBOYANT WOLFGANG AMADEUS MOZART, WHO BECAME FAMOUS AS A COMPOSER AND PERFORMER BEFORE HE REACHED THE AGE OF TEN AND THEN DIED WHEN HE WAS ONLY THIRTY-FIVE, VIRTUALLY EPITOMIZED THE CONCEPT OF *WÜNDERKIND*.

bizarre circumstance of the Requiem's commission. According to the legend, a stranger came to Mozart's lodgings to commission him to compose a mass for the dead—a requiem. As part of the arrangement, the work was to be done in secret. High-strung and in bad health, Mozart misinterpreted this directive as a pronouncement of his own doom. Frantically, he worked to finish the mass, but in vain. After Mozart's death, his pupil Franz Xaver Süssmayr rounded out the Mozart Requiem, and word leaked out that the foreboding stranger was a representative of Count Franz von Walsegg, a would-be composer who apparently often worked such devious machinations in order to obtain compositions that he could claim as his own.

Although he died in misery and penury, life began much more brightly for Wolfgang Amadeus Mozart. Born in 1756 in Salzburg, Austria (then Bavaria), he was a prodigy, as was his older sister Maria Anna (1751–1829). Leopold, their father, was an accomplished and respected musician who delighted in having his brilliant children, keyboard specialists, perform in public—not in school recitals or church musicales, but in the court palaces and concert halls throughout Europe. Setting forth in 1762, when Wolfgang was six and Maria eleven, the family toured the major cities of Europe. Two weeks were spent at Versailles, where Louis XV (1710–1774) and his court were charmed by the skillful young musicians. In 1764 the family journeyed to London, where the teenage Wolfgang wrote three symphonies while his father convalesced following an illness. The famous Johann Christian Bach, son of the even more famous Johann Sebastian Bach (see Chapter 2, page 24), and the British queen's music master, immediately befriended the Mozarts. The Mozart family's last journey with Wolfgang still a child was a performance tour of Italy.

As the little boy hit his teen years, he found that the "awkward age" experienced by teenagers had added problems for him. No longer was he a novelty, nor was he readily accepted by mature musicians. But he was strong of will, and he was not deterred.

On one of his later tours, Mozart met Aloysia Weber, an accomplished soprano, in Mannheim, Germany. A romance between them soon blossomed, and just at the point Mozart needed to be on his way, he found himself contemplating marriage. He left without making a decision, and when the two next met, Aloysia was already married. Mozart's affec-

tions turned to Aloysia's sister, Constanze, who married the composer in Vienna's St. Stephen's Cathedral in 1782. In the next nine years, she gave birth to six children, only two of whom survived: Franz, who became a composer, pianist, and teacher, and Carl, who, as far as is known, did not pursue a musical career.

Throughout his career, Mozart constantly sought court employment for the sake of financial security. In Salzburg, Mozart was hired to provide music for the household of Archbishop Hieronymus von Colloredo. Treated like a servant, Mozart confronted his employer and was rudely dismissed. Mozart spent a few years as chamber musician and court composer to Emperor Joseph II, but when Joseph II died, his successor, Leopold II, showed less appreciation for the talented Mozart.

In part, the sheer volume of Mozart's work was a result of financial necessity. Some piano concertos (of which there are twenty-seven) and sonatas (of which there are forty-two) were written for his own purpose of performance. There were also concertos for other instruments and more than thirty string quartets, of which six are titled in the name of

Franz Joseph Haydn—the two composers had profound mutual regard for each other. Paris was the city where Mozart's first compositions—a series of sonatas—were published; the composer was seven years old at the time. Despite all this work, however, Mozart never made much money. Few works, other than those listed above, were published during his lifetime, and he augmented his income by teaching. In the case of the operas, after being paid for the first performance, he received no royalties.

Opera, according to indications by Mozart, was his favorite musical medium. Before he reached his teens, Mozart composed *Apollo et Hyacinthus*, *La finta semplice*

BELOW: THIS ARTISITIC RENDITION OF A PIVOTAL SCENE FROM ONE OF MOZART'S BEST-KNOWN OPERAS, *THE MAGIC FLUTE*, CAPTURES THE FANTASTIC TONE OF THE WORK. OPPOSITE: MOZART ENJOYED GREAT SUCCESS WITH HIS OPERA *IDOMENEO*, BASED ON A STORY FROM GREEK MYTHOLOGY AND COMPOSED FOR THE COURT THEATER IN MUNICH IN 1781.

("The Make-Believe Simpleton"), *Bastien und Bastienne*, and *Mitridate, Rè di Ponto* ("Mithridates, King of Pontus"). His extensive travels, with the family and on his own, gave him awareness of the different ethnicities and distinctive styles of opera and other musical forms. Lorenzo da Ponte, poet of the court theaters in Vienna, became partner (as librettist) in three of Mozart's greatest operatic successes: *Le nozze di Figaro* ("The Marriage of Figaro"), based on Pierre Beaumarchais' play knocking the aristocracy and celebrating the common man (this was a risky venture at the time and the play was banned in Austria); *Don Giovanni*; and *Così fan tutte* ("All Women Do the Same").

IDOMENEO.
DRAMMA
PER
MUSICA
DA RAPPRESENTARSI
NEL TEATRO NUOVO DI
CORTE
PER COMANDO
DI S. A. S. E.
CARLO TEODORO
Conte Palatino del Rheno, Duca dell' alta, e baſsa Baviera, e del Palatinato Superiore, etc. etc. Archidapifero, et Elettore, etc. etc.
NEL CARNOVALE
1781.

La Poeſia è del Signor Abate Gianbattista Vareſco Capellano di Corte di S. A. R. l'Arcivescovo, e Principe di Saliſburgo.
La Muſica è del Signor Maeſtro Wolfgango Amadeo Mozart Academico di Bologna, e di Verona, in in attual ſervizio di S. A. R. l'Arcivescovo, e Principe di Saliſburgo.
La Traduzione è del Signor Andrea Schachtner, pure in attual ſervizio di S. A. R. l'Arcivescovo, e Principe di Saliſburgo.

MONACO.
Appreſſo Francesco Giuseppe Thuille.

Mozart's last two operas, like much of his work, were commissioned. *La clemenza di Tito* was written for the crowning of Leopold II as King of Bohemia and *The Magic Flute* was composed for Vienna's Theater-auf-der-Wieden, commissioned by its impresario Emanuel Schikaneder, who devised the libretto. Mozart and Schikaneder were Freemasons, members of a fraternal organization that professes equality and brotherhood, and there is much Masonic symbolism written into *The Magic Flute*. Masonic brothers of the day included Johann Wolfgang von Goethe (1749–1832), Friedrich von Schiller (1759–1805), Voltaire (1694–1778), Benjamin Franklin (1706–1790), and George Washington (1732–1799).

Mozart's works are also interesting archivally. Unlike other musician's works, which are generally cataloged according to opus number, all of Mozart's compositions—whether opera or mass, symphony or concerto—are catalogued chronologically by number, preceded with the letter K. K stands for Ludwig Köchel, a nineteenth-century lawyer who compiled and catalogued Mozart's compositions.

LEOPOLD MOZART (1719-1787)

The shadow of a well-known parent sometimes prevents the light of the child from being seen; with the Mozarts, however, it was the child who outshone the parent. Leopold Mozart might have fared better in musical history and memory if it weren't for his genius son, Wolfgang Amadeus, for the senior Mozart was certainly a highly regarded musician.

Leopold had studied philosophy and law at the Benedictine University in Salzburg. In a time when many royal households of the eighteenth century had their own music ensembles, Leopold was engaged by the Count of Thurn-Valsassina und Taxis and then was a violinist in the court orchestra of the Prince-Archbishop of Salzburg. He taught violin and keyboard to the cathedral choirboys, and in 1757 advanced to the position of court composer. By 1762 Mozart was deputy kapellmeister.

An expert at playing and teaching the violin, Leopold wrote a violin instruction book that was quite popular in the late 1700s; his *Nannerl-Notenbuch* was considered an ideal children's musical primer and its use extended into the next two centuries.

Compositions by Leopold Mozart are numerous. In fact, Leopold was chosen over his son to write a piece for a special occasion by one of Salzburg's leading citizens, Sigmund Haffner. But the father passed the commission along to son, and Wolfgang wrote a six-movement serenade that he later adapted into his Symphony No. 35, which became known as the Haffner Symphony.

In 1747, he married Anna Maria Pertl; the couple had seven children, but only Anna Maria (nicknamed Nannerl) and Wolfgang Amadeus lived beyond babyhood. Talented children often have their mother taking every opportunity to push them into the performers' spotlight, hence the expression "stage mother." With the Mozart siblings, however, it was their father who fulfilled that role. While his methods are sometimes recalled as excessive, he did indeed provide great impetus for Wolfgang's career.

LUDWIG VAN BEETHOVEN (1770–1827)

BORN IN BONN IN 1770, LUDWIG WAS ONLY ELEVEN YEARS OLD WHEN he became assistant court organist and twelve when he was named harpsichordist for the court orchestra and violist for the theater orchestra. The prediction by one of his teachers that Beethoven would become the "second Mozart" turned out to have little relevance, for he became the one and only Beethoven. That teacher was court organist to the Elector of Cologne at Bonn, where Beethoven's grandfather had been kapellmeister and his father the appointed tenor.

Beethoven may have had a lesson from Mozart in Vienna, for he went to the Austrian capital in 1787 for that purpose; he may or may not have had the lesson, for his mother died and he had to return to Bonn after only two weeks. After the death of his wife, Beethoven's father became a heavy drinker and even before he died in 1792, the responsibility of his two younger sons was entrusted to his eldest, Ludwig. When Carl and Caspar were old enough to be on their own, Ludwig settled in Vienna. Nonetheless, he maintained his family ties, and when Caspar died, Ludwig went through five years of legal proceedings to adopt his nephew.

Vienna was the cultural center of Europe, and with his skill at the piano Beethoven had no difficulty getting hired for private parties and public performances. He also was able to establish his reputation beyond Vienna, making his mark in Leipzig, Prague, Dresden, Berlin, and other European cities. By the time he was thirty years old, Beethoven had become a highly successful composer and pianist and rarely had a financial problem. Like many artists of the time, Beethoven benefited from a certain amount of patronage; one of his patrons was Archduke Rudolph, younger brother of the Emperor of Austria. Beethoven had been the archduke's music teacher for three years in the early 1800s, and in 1809 the archduke provided Beethoven with an annuity. Numerous Beethoven compositions were commissioned by and/or dedicated to Archduke Rudolph, including the Fourth Piano Concerto; the Fifth Piano Concerto, known as the "Emperor"; the Missa Solemnis, which was intended for the installation of Rudolph as Archbishop of Olmutz, but was not finished in time; the

Piano Sonata in E-Flat Major; and the Trio in B-Flat Major for Violin, Cello, and Piano (also called the "Archduke" Trio).

When Beethoven was in his late twenties, he began to hear noises that were symptoms of his ensuing deafness. He sought medical help, but to little avail. Around 1810 he found that he could no longer perform as a pianist, and by 1822 he was completely deaf. Beethoven wrote of his anxiety over his disability in a letter to his brothers that is referred to as the *Heiligenstadt Testament*. Plagued as he was, it is perhaps not surprising that Beethoven was an extremely temperamental individual. He did not, however, allow his frustration and bitterness to affect the mood of his majestic music, nor did he let it prevent him from working.

The nine symphonies, for instance, were written by Beethoven as his hearing was deteriorating, starting in the late 1790s and climaxing in 1823 with the premiere of the Ninth. The moods of the symphonies alternate between stormy and tranquil, with the odd-numbered works generally being the most blustery. The Third, known as "Eroica," was inspired by Napoleon Bonaparte (1769–1821), who, as a seeming advocate for democracy, was admired by Beethoven. The composer followed the revolution in France with approving interest, but became disenchanted when Napoleon set himself up as emperor. Beethoven altered the dedication of "Eroica" accordingly: "To the memory of a great man."

Symphony No. 5, perhaps the best known of Beethoven's works, opens with the familiar four notes—three short and one long, which in Morse code (developed some time after the piece was written) happens to stand for the letter V. Interpreted as "V for victory," this combination of sounds became used by the Allies in World War II. Later, at the 1967 victory concert in Jerusalem signaling the end of the Arab-Israeli War, the Israel Philharmonic Orchestra followed up the tradition by performing Beethoven's Fifth Symphony.

No. 9, known as the "Choral" Symphony, ends in a rousing finale incorporating the words of the German poet Friedrich von Schiller's "Ode to Joy." Originally Beethoven

MUCH LIONIZED BOTH IN HIS TIME AND IN THE ENSUING CENTURIES, LUDWIG VAN BEETHOVEN IS PROBABLY BEST REMEMBERED FOR HIS NINE SYMPHONIES, THE LAST OF WHICH WAS WRITTEN AFTER HE HAD ENTIRELY LOST HIS HEARING.

was going to use this poem as a concert aria, but upon consideration he decided that it would be a fitting climax for his Ninth Symphony.

Of course, Beethoven also wrote symphonies that he titled instead of numbering. Among these is *Wellington's Victory*, which is not fully accepted by Beethoven purists, many of whom have suggested that it should be labeled a symphonic poem (descriptive or picturesque orchestral music). *Wellington's Victory* was written for inventor Johann Nepomuk Maelzel's Panharmonicon, a many-instrument orchestral machine operated by air pressure. Maelzel, who had been involved in the development of the metronome, had also devised a primitive hearing aid for Beethoven, and he prevailed upon the composer to write a composition utilizing the Panharmonicon. The piece was duly written, but it was never performed with Maelzel's contraption. A lawsuit ensued over rights, but it was settled out of court.

String quartets represent some of Beethoven's most important compositions, and the quartets written in October 1826 were his last works. When he died the following March, Beethoven was given a grand funeral, but only his last name and dates of birth and death appear on the simple tombstone.

While Beethoven composed five piano concertos and one for violin, an assortment of overtures, thirty-six sonatas, numerous ensembles, and the nine symphonies, *Fidelio*—his one opera, said to be his favorite among his many monumental compositions—sums up his underlying ideal of majesty with equality. The opening sung dialogue consists of household small talk; it seems out of place and not at all like Beethoven. Moments later, however, the conversation turns to more weighty matters—with music to match—and rarely lets up after that. ♩

CARL (1786–1826) MARIA VON WEBER

A SORT OF MUSICAL CHAIRS GAME WAS PLAYED BY CARL MARIA VON Weber when, as conductor at the Breslau Opera in Germany, he devised a new plan for sectioning the orchestra at concerts, rearranging the instrumentalists' seating for acoustical reasons. Some colleagues resented this, along with other reforms he was introducing—requiring more rehearsals, ridding the repertoire of certain works, and recommending the severance of elderly, no-longer-qualified singers—perhaps because Weber was only eighteen years old.

Weber had grown up in the world of musical theater. Born in Eutin, Germany, in 1786, he was taken along with the traveling Weber Theatre Company, which was operated by his father and performed in by his mother. As a result, he received a strong musical education at a very young age, and at the age of thirteen his opera *Das Waldmädchen* ("The Forest Maiden") was successfully produced. By the time he was engaged as kapellmeister at Breslau, Weber had written three operas. Unfortunately, not long after Carl began in his new position, he had an accident that ruined his singing voice for two months, making him unable to fulfill his duties as kapellmeister: the elder Weber had gone into the lithography business and one day Carl drank from a wine bottle in which his father had stored engraving acid. When he returned to his post, Weber found his reforms had been undone. He resigned.

Soon after, he was hired as house musician for Duke Eugene Württemberg-Ols and was encouraged to compose. One composition in this period was an orchestral piece favoring the oboe—not a bad idea, considering the duke played oboe. In February 1810 gross mismanagement of funds by Weber's father reflected on the son, and Carl Maria was imprisoned and then banished from Württemberg for the rest of his life.

When his singspiel—the initial form of eighteenth-century German opera, which used considerable amounts of spoken dialogue—*Abu Hassan* played to great sucess in 1811, Weber became convinced his forte was opera. This did not, however, deter him from continuing to write instrumental music, although he was somewhat sidetracked from composing during the time he worked as opera director in Prague (from 1813 to 1816). Always conscientious, Weber involved himself as consultant on sets and costumes, tightened up rehearsal schedules, recatalogued the music library, and took a stand for employee benefits. In search of new talent for the Prague company, he journeyed to Vienna to audition singers. As he had found in Breslau, there was again opposition. In order to answer the critics in his new home, Weber learned to speak Czechoslovakian. To incite the public's interest and attendance, he wrote program notes and had them published in the newspapers in advance of performances.

After his time in Prague, Weber went to Dresden, where he worked as director of the German Opera. To Dresden, Weber brought his bride, the singer Caroline Brandt. En route, Weber, a highly regarded pianist, and Caroline performed in concert.

Through all this time and all these positions, Weber continued to write music. The Weber catalog contains concertos for various instruments and for orchestra, chamber music, piano sonatas, and two symphonies. The most memorable work in the instrumental category is probably *Invitation to the Dance*, a delightful work originally written for piano and orchestrated much later by Berlioz.

It is, however, his opera *Der Freischütz* ("The Free-Shooter"), based on a ghost tale he had discovered years before, for which Weber is best remembered. Premiering in Berlin in 1821, the opera was tremendously successful from the outset. There were other operas by Weber, notably *Euryanthe* and *Oberon,* which was commissioned by Covent Garden in London. At this time, Weber was suffering from tuberculosis and his health

was at a very low point; his wife counseled him not to accept the assignment. In view of the large fee, however, he was adamant: he would write the piece. *Oberon* was to be in English and, although Weber was not writing the libretto, he took 153 English lessons so that he could be fluent. He conducted the premiere on April 12, 1826. Plans were made to go home to Dresden on June 6, but Weber died in London on June 5.

Born twenty-seven years before Richard Wagner (see Chapter 4, page 75), Weber has unfortunately been overshadowed by the giant of German opera. It is Weber, however, who has the distinction, thanks primarily to *Der Freischütz,* of being the founder of German Romantic opera. ♫

OPPOSITE: WEBER USED RECURRING MUSICAL THEMES IN ASSOCIATION WITH EACH PERSONA IN HIS OPERAS TO SUGGEST A PARTICULAR CHARACTER'S PRESENCE WHENEVER HE APPEARED ONSTAGE. BELOW: THE MANY MOODS OF HIS OPERA *DER FREISCHÜTZ* ARE SHOWN BY THE COMPOSER'S VARIOUS STANCES WHILE CONDUCTING ONE OF HIS GREATEST WORKS.

LES HUGUENOTS

GIACOMO MEYERBEER (1791-1864)

GIACOMO MEYERBEER, ONE OF THE MOST INFLUENTIAL OPERA COM-posers of the first half of the nineteenth century, was a master at writing choruses and musically manipulating crowd scenes while giving finite attention to plot details and the music for solo voices. Born in Berlin, Meyerbeer, after writing several operas in the Germanic mode, went to Venice and studied Italian opera; with all he learned, he was able to weave the best of both those worlds into the French style.

Meyerbeer's given name was Jakob Liebmann Beer; his mother came from a prominent banking family and his father was an army contractor in Berlin and the owner of a number of sugar refineries in Germany and Italy. Jakob changed his given name to Giacomo when he became enamored of Italian opera. "Meyer" was added to "Beer" in response to his receiving a legacy from a relative. It is not certain whether the name change was done to honor the benefactor or to entice the legacy.

Early in his career, Meyerbeer was regarded as a better pianist than he was a composer. In fact, he was highly regarded from the time he was seven years old, when he first performed in public, playing Mozart's Piano Concerto in D Minor.

Meyerbeer's first attempts at opera, which he essayed while getting his music education in Darmstadt, were mostly ineffectual, but one piece, *Jephtas Gelübde* ("Jephta's Vow"), written in 1813, stood out. These pieces, however, were enough to arouse the attention of various important personages, and the following year Meyerbeer became court com-poser to the Grand Duke of Hesse-Darmstadt. Antonio Salieri, a leading composer of the day, advised Meyerbeer to study in Italy to absorb the Italian style of opera, which, more than any other style of opera, focuses on the facility of the human voice. Meyerbeer spent nine years, on and off, in Italy, and became enthralled by the operas of Gioacchino Rossini (1792–1868). Six operas, each one better than its predecessor, resulted from Meyerbeer's Italian sojourn; the series culminated with *Il crociato in Egitto* ("The Crusader in Egypt"), which had its 1824 premiere in Venice and soon thereafter was produced in London and Paris.

When Meyerbeer returned to Germany, he found there no professional or public interest in his operas. The composer seems then to have gone through a creative drought, but it was in that period that his two children and his father died.

Meeting Eugene Scribe (1791–1861) ushered in Meyerbeer's French phase. Scribe had written more than three hundred plays and a voluminous number of librettos for such composers as Vincenzo Bellini (*La Sonnambula,* "The Sleepwalker"), Gaetano Donizetti (*La Favorita*, "The Favorite"), and Giuseppe Verdi (*I Vespri Siciliani*, "The Sicilian Vespers"; see Chapter 4, page 73). In collaboration with Scribe, Meyerbeer wrote *Robert Le Diable* ("Robert the Devil"), which, enhanced by scenic effects that were extraordinary for the time, was a tremendous success in 1831. It started out as an

ALTHOUGH IN HIS YOUTH HE WAS BETTER KNOWN AS A PIANIST, GIACOMO MEYERBEER (ABOVE) LATER BECAME RENOWNED FOR GREAT OPERAS THAT COMBINED THE BEST ELEMENTS OF THE GERMAN AND ITALIAN SCHOOLS, INCLUDING *LES HUGUENOTS* (LEFT).

opéra comique but evolved into a more serious piece that emphasized the power of good over evil.

The collaboration, of course, did not end there. *Les Huguenots* by Meyerbeer and Scribe was premiered at the Paris Opera in 1836, and through its popularity it became the first opera by any composer to be performed at the Paris Opera more than one hundred times. One result of Meyerbeer's success with *Les Huguenots* was his appointment by the King of Prussia as Berlin's general music director. Another Meyerbeer-Scribe triumph was *Le Prophète* ("The Prophet"), written in 1849. *Les Patineurs* ("The Skaters"), a ballet with music by Constant Lambert, uses themes from *Le Prophète* and another Meyerbeer opera, *L'Etoile Du Nord* ("The North Star"). By the time he composed *Le Prophète*, Meyerbeer was able to custom-make arias to complement the artistic range of specific singers. This is particularly true of soprano Pauline Viardot and her origination of the role of Fides in *Le Prophète*. In *L'Etoile Du Nord*, Meyerbeer included six selections from the earlier opera or singspiel *Ein Feldlager in Schlesien*, which he wrote with the "Swedish Nightingale," Jenny Lind (1820–1887), in mind.

The Meyerbeer-Scribe relationship was weakened during the creation of *L'Africaine* ("The African Maid") because the composer kept wanting to make changes. The subject of this story is the Portuguese explorer Vasco da Gama (1460–1524), and Meyerbeer typically was careful about historical facts. Preliminary notes had been made by Meyerbeer more than twenty years before *L'Africaine* was completed—or nearly completed, inasmuch as he died in 1864 during rehearsals leading up to the world premiere in 1865 at the Paris Opéra.

Meyerbeer's operas were grandiose affairs with a definite theatrical flair, evidence that Meyerbeer believed in the entertainment value of his work rather than creating art for art's sake. ♪

GIOACCHINO ROSSINI IS BEST REMEMBERED TODAY FOR HIS OPERA *THE BARBER OF SEVILLE* (OPPOSITE), WHICH IS A STAPLE OF OPERA COMPANIES AROUND THE WORLD.

GIOACCHINO ROSSINI (1792–1868)

AT THE PINNACLE OF HIS SUCCESS AND MERELY HALFWAY THROUGH his seventy-six years, Gioacchino Rossini decided to stop writing opera. The reasons for this are still the subject of much debate.

Perhaps more than one reason impelled Rossini to deprive the musical world of more of his operatic genius. By the time he composed *Guillaume Tell* ("William Tell"), Rossini was a wealthy man who no longer had to "make a living." Both cultural tastes and the political climate were changing, and Rossini was not adapting well to the changes. The composer was suffering from a malady known as neurasthenia (an emotional-mental disorder characterized by lack of motivation, feeling of inadequacy, and psychosomatic symptoms). His mother, to whom Rossini was devoted, had died, possibly removing one source of inspiration from his life. And when *William Tell* premiered in 1830, it received mixed reviews, with the negative judgments outnumbering the positive.

DIX

SIR WILLIAM HERSCHEL (1738-1822)

Miranda, Ariel, Umbriel, Titania, and Oberon are not subtitles for Sir William Herschel's symphonies, but rather names of the moons surrounding Uranus, the planet discovered by Herschel. While scanning the vast sky one night in 1781, the English composer and amateur astronomer happened upon a pale greenish dot surrounded by faint parallel bands. Herschel was using a telescope with a design that he himself had perfected (logically, this device later became known as the Herschel Telescope). With George III (1738–1820) reigning in England at the time, the planet was designated *Georgium Sidus* ("Star of George"); it was subsequently renamed "Herschel" in honor of its discoverer; finally, the German astronomer Johann Elert Bode recommended "Uranus," the name of the oldest god in Greek mythology, which has been the accepted name of the planet since the late 1800s.

The discovery of Uranus, however, was not Herschel's only achievement. Herschel had a successful career as an organist and concert director, but in time the lure of astronomy took over and he set music aside, but not before he had composed twenty-four symphonies, several concertos, a number of chamber music pieces, and various anthems and selections for organ. In addition to the planet Uranus, the composer discovered two moons or satellites surrounding the planet Saturn and identified polar ice caps on the planet Mars.

Sir William Herschel was born in Germany but subsequently settled in England and became a British citizen in 1802; he was knighted in 1816. His father was a military musician and William, trained for his father's profession, became a proficient oboist and violinist.

Other members of the family also dabbled in the sciences: Sir William's sister Caroline discovered at least five comets and a number of star clusters. Sir William's accomplishments in astronomy resulted in his being named Astronomer Royal to King George III in 1781, the year that he discovered Uranus.

Regardless, Rossini was a renowned and respected composer. Even if he had written only *Il barbiere di Siviglia* ("The Barber of Seville"), his would have been a major contribution to world culture. Based on the play by the famous French writer Pierre Beaumarchais (1732–1799), Rossini's most familiar piece, a prime example of comic opera, premiered in 1816 and brought the twenty-four-year-old composer artistic and commerical success. (This may point to yet another factor in his decision to stop composing: too much success too soon.) Of course, Rossini was not the only composer to use Beaumarchais as a source of inspiration; *The Barber of Seville* also inspired three other composers: Georg Benda, Niccolo Isouard, and Giovanni Paisiello. Beaumarchais wrote three plays involving more or less the same characters and showing the evolution of French society in the decade leading up to the French Revolution. *Il barbiere di Seviglia* (1775) was first in the series; followed by *Le nozze di Figaro* ("The Marriage of Figaro," 1783), which inspired one of Mozart's most famous operas; and "The Culpable Mother" (1792) rounded out the trilogy.

Like Vincenzo Bellini and Gaetano Donizetti, Rossini composed in the manner of bel canto ("beautiful singing"), in which the musical writing focuses on vocal exactness and elegance without emphasis on drama and emotion. In Act II of *The Barber of Seville* for instance, there is a singing lesson scene which in itself possesses plenty of bel canto for the leading lady in the role of Rosina. But throughout operatic history, coloratura sopranos have elbowed-in minirecitals at that juncture. Marcella Sembrich, for instance, who was the Metropolitan Opera's first Rosina in 1883, was guilty of this embellishment and would interpolate such music as Johann Strauss's "Voices of Spring."

As young as Rossini was when *The Barber* premiered, he was even younger—barely twenty-one—and already idolized by the public when *Tancredi*, one of the earliest achievements of the boy genius, was first heard. In his early period, Rossini wrote about ten operas on commissions from various theaters in northern Italy. Both *Tancredi*, based on a play by Voltaire, and *L'Italiana in Algeri* ("The Italian Girl in Algiers") premiered in 1813. Rossini came out with *La Cenerentola* ("Cinderella") and *La gazza ladra* ("The Thieving Magpie"), both in 1817. Between 1810 and 1830, Rossini produced a total of forty operas. With this prodigious output, he often had to hire other composers to come up with minor arias or recitative; in these cases, he would rewrite these contributions when his schedule allowed.

Several Rossini operas, including the successful *Elisabetta,* were expressly written for one of the era's prima donnas, Isabella Colbran (1785–1845), who in 1822 became Rossini's first wife. Unfortunately, as the years progressed, their personal relationship cooled. When Isabella died, Rossini married Olympe Pelissier.

For the coronation of France's Charles X (1757–1836) in 1824, Rossini wrote *Il Viaggio a Reims* ("The Voyage to Rheims"). The king gave Rossini a ten-year contract to write and produce an opera every other year, after which he would have a pension for life. Unfortunately, however, Charles was forced to abdicate in 1830, and when his reign ended so did the agreement with Rossini. Only one opera—*William Tell*—was written under the terms of this contract. After Charles was overthrown, Rossini sued for his pension and won, but only after an extended legal battle.

When Rossini decided to quit writing opera, he continued to be prominent in music and social circles. He maintained a villa in Passy, and his luxurious apartment in Paris became a gathering place for the cultural elite. Although Rossini no longer wrote opera at this time, he still did some composing: he wrote his *Stabat Mater* in 1832 (it was first performed ten years later), a cantata for the Paris Exposition of 1867, and his *Petite Messe Solennelle* ("Little Solemn Mass") in 1864. In dedicating the last of these, Rossini wrote, "Thou knowest, O Lord, as well as I, that really I am only a composer of opera buffa."

One of Rossini's greatest compliments came from Giuseppe Verdi (see Chapter 4, page 73), who initiated a group composition of a requiem in honor of Rossini. In all, thirteen composers, including Verdi, wrote segments of this requiem, but it was not performed at the time. Rediscovered in the archives of the publishing firm Ricordi, the Requiem finally had its world premiere in 1988, 120 years after Rossini died. ♪

THE PROLIFIC GAETANO DONIZETTI DIED IN 1847 AFTER A PERIOD OF PROGRESSIVE PHYSICAL AND MENTAL DETERIORATION.

GAETANO DONIZETTI (1797-1848)

MASTER OF THE MAD SCENE, GAETANO DONIZETTI DIED IN THE SAME state of mind he portrayed so tragically onstage. Yet, this composer wrote some of the most delightfully comic operas in the repertoire.

Donizetti did not, however, write only comedies; he also worked in tragedy. Madness was brought to the opera house by Donizetti with *Lucia di Lammermoor*, based on the literary classic *The Bride of Lammermoor* by the Scottish writer Sir Walter Scott ((1771–1832). Donizetti was in his late thirties when this opera, considered his masterpiece, had its premiere in Naples. *Lucia* was sandwiched between his two major comedies, *L'elisir d'amore* ("The Elixir of Love") in 1832 and *La fille du regiment* ("The Daughter of the Regiment") in 1840.

No matter the subject matter, Donizetti was a specialist in writing in the bel canto style that was so popular in Italian opera at the time. Simply translated to "beautiful singing," bel canto shows off the exactness and elegance of the voice rather than using this "instrument" solely to express drama or emotion; bel canto is ornamental singing.

In his fifty-one years of life, Donizetti wrote about seventy operas, as well as string quartets, masses, cantatas, and songs.

His parents did not approve of their son taking on music as his profession, and to please his father Gaetano served in the army from about 1818 to 1822. His musical studies and his composing, however, continued apace, and his first major opera, *Enrico di Borgogna*, appeared in 1818.

His first well-known success—*Anna Bolena* ("Anne Boleyn"), Donizetti's thirty-third opera—did not appear until 1830. *Anna Bolena, Maria Stuarda* ("Mary Stuart"), and *Roberto Devereux* form a trilogy of operas based on people who were instrumental in the life and reign of England's King Henry VIII (1491–1547). Soprano Beverly Sills and the New York City Opera made cultural headlines reviving this trilogy in the 1970s.

During the years when Donizetti wrote those operas (1830–1837), he suffered tremendous personal losses. Two children were stillborn, a son died in infancy, both his parents died, and finally his wife, Virginia, whom he adored, also passed away.

In 1837 Donizetti, who had been schooled in the ways of Haydn, Beethoven, and Mozart and had had formal training with instruments and in conducting, was appointed director of the Naples Conservatory. He held this position for two years, until he left Italy over a censorship battle surrounding his opera *Poliuto*. After leaving his homeland, the composer traveled to Paris, where he assisted in the performance of several of his operas, including premieres of *La fille du regiment* and *La favorita*, and to Vienna, where he was present

for the successful premiere of *Linda di Chamounix*.

In addition to writing wonderfully melodic music and having a tremendous theatrical flair, Donizetti worked well under pressure. *L'elisir d'amore*, for instance, was composed in eight days to replace an opera undelivered by someone else. The comedy *Don Pasquale*, Donizetti's last major opera, was completed in eleven days in 1843 while the composer was on the verge of mental collapse. Two years later, Donizetti was committed to an asylum near Paris. At the end of 1847, his condition somewhat improved, and he was allowed to leave under the care of his brother and return to their native home of Bergamo, where the composer died in 1848.

Donizetti was a highly regarded composer during his lifetime and since. Asked which of his operas he favored, Donizetti modestly replied, with a certain poignancy, "How can I say which? A father always has a preference for a crippled child, and I have so many." ⸘

ABOVE: *ANNA BOLENA*, AN OPERA BASED ON THE LIFE OF HENRY VIII'S SECOND OF EIGHT WIVES, WAS ONE OF DONIZETTI'S MASTERPIECES. OPPOSITE: THE GREAT AUSTRIAN COMPOSER FRANZ SCHUBERT, WHO CAME FROM A FAMILY OF ESTABLISHED MUSICIANS, WAS A MASTER OF MELODY AND AN INSPIRED CREATOR OF *LIEDER*, OR GERMAN SONGS.

FRANZ (1797–1828) SCHUBERT

THE SYMPHONY THAT MADE FRANZ SCHUBERT FAMOUS IS THE SUBJECT of some debate. This work, one of Franz Schubert's most familiar, is the so-called "Unfinished" Symphony in B Minor. The tag "unfinished" was applied—after Schubert's death— because there are only two movements rather than the customary three or four. There also exist, at the end, nine bars of a scherzo—possibly the start of a third movement, possibly not. It is not true, however, that this was Schubert's last work and that he died before completing it; this piece is actually the eighth of nine symphonies composed by Schubert. It has been argued for decades whether or not Schubert planned to expand No. 8, but today scholars and critics generally agree that he intended only two movements.

As the centennial of Schubert's death approached in 1928, the Columbia Phonograph Company devised an international contest to complete the "Unfinished" Symphony. When the concept was criticized, the rules were altered, calling instead for a composition in the style of Schubert. The contest was won by one Kurt Atterberg of Sweden.

The strength of Schubert's "Unfinished" Symphony does not lie in the paradox, of course, but in its beauty. His reputation was at its height when he started the composition in 1822. When he was done, he set the piece aside; it was not performed until 1865.

As was typical of composers of this period and earlier, Schubert began his musical education in the bosom of his family. Born in Lichtental, outside Vienna, in 1797, Schubert,

the twelfth of fourteen children (nine of whom died in infancy), learned the piano from his older brother, Ignaz, and the violin from his father, a schoolmaster. When he outdistanced them in musical ability, young Schubert studied with Michael Holzer of the Lichtental parish church. The next step was candidacy for the Konvikt, the Imperial Court Choir School, for which one of the faculty-judges was composer Antonio Salieri. Accepted into the Konvikt at the age of eleven, Schubert had the advantage of studying with Salieri (see page 39). And at the same time that he received schooling for voice and various instruments, he also started his tremendous yield of compositions. It is said that, because of the Schubert family's limited finances, Franz had to turn to a fellow student for the music manuscript paper he needed. Schubert remained at the Konvikt for about five years, then trained to be a teacher and taught for a while in his father's school.

When Schubert was in his late teens, he moved to Vienna; he soon became known in the musical community there and in the cities of Linz, Steyr, and Graz. Fortuitously, he met Michael Vogl, leading baritone of the Court Theatre. Vogl became not only a good friend but also a promoter of Schubert's songs. More than once Schubert accompanied Vogl to the baritone's childhood home in Steyr, in the beautiful mountains of upper Austria; these experiences motivated the philosophy of many of Schubert's songs. On one of these mountain sojourns, Schubert is said to have been inspired with the idea for his Symphony No. 9 in C Major, also known as "The Great."

Among Schubert's most enduring songs are "Ave Maria," "Serenade," and "Who Is Sylvia?" With more than five hundred songs credited to him, it is not surprising that Schubert is regarded as one of the most prolific songwriters in the history of music. This composer, who himself possessed the aura and sensibilities of a poet, adapted the poetry of many great writers, including Johann Wolfgang von Goethe. He often grouped songs of like interest into cycles of a dozen or more tunes. Outstanding song cycles include *Die Schöne Müllerin* ("The Fair Maid of the Mill") and *Winterreise* ("Winter's Journey"), both with lyrics by poet Wilhelm Müller. Schubert's songs are termed Lied, defined in the *Harvard Dictionary of Music* as "a song in the German vernacular"; according to *Harvard,* the greatest era of German Lied was launched by the seventeen-year-old Franz Schubert with his "Gretchen am Spinnrad" ("Gretchen at the Spinning Wheel").

While scholars and enthusiasts often focus their attention on Schubert's songs and his symphonies, one must not overlook his other contributions, especially his chamber music and piano sonatas. Even though writing for the stage was not his forte, Schubert did become successful with incidental music to the play *Rosamunde*, which was written by Wilhelmina von Chezy and premiered at Vienna's Theater an der Wien in 1823. As a play, *Rosamunde* was found unacceptable, and it fell into oblivion until 1867, when the music was discovered by Schubert scholar Sir George Grove (1820-1900) and composer Sir Arthur Sullivan, who were seeking lost Schubert manuscripts.

Thirty-one years on this earth did not give Schubert much time to be recognized, and consequently the majority of his success was posthumous. Of Schubert's seemingly premature death in Vienna in 1828, composer Hugo Wolf (1860–1903) said, "A man is not taken away before he has said all he has to say."

PAINTER GUSTAV KLIMT PORTRAYED SCHUBERT AT THE PIANO OVER SEVENTY YEARS AFTER THE COMPOSER DIED, A TESTIMONY TO THE MUSICIAN'S LONG-LASTING PRESENCE IN THE WORLD OF THE ARTS.

VINCENZO BELLINI (1801-1835)

VINCENZO BELLINI AND HIS LIBRETTIST, FELICE ROMANI (1788–1865), the Rodgers and Hammerstein of their day, collaborated on six operas, including Bellini's best-known, *Norma* and *La Sonnambula* ("The Sleepwalker"), both written in 1831. Romani, who was considered the top Italian librettist of his time, also worked for Rossini (*Il Turco in Italia*, "A Turk in Italy"), Donizetti (*L'elisir d'amore* ["The Elixir of Love"], *Anna Bolena*, and *Lucrezia Borgia*), and Verdi (*Un giorno di Regno*, "King for a Day"). Romani's librettos were generally adaptations of established literary works. The librettist also made a name for himself as a poet and as a critic and editor in Milan.

Bellini was born in 1801 in Catania, Sicily. He died in 1835, joining the ranks of other musical well-knowns who died in their thirties, Wolfgang Amadeus Mozart (see page 40), Franz Schubert (see page 55), and George Gershwin (see Chapter 7, page 159) among them.

For Bellini, music was a part of his heritage—both his father and his grandfather had been composers. Bellini's early musical training took place within the family, and at the age of seventeen he attended the Naples Conservatory on a scholarship. As part of his conservatory curriculum, he wrote his first opera, *Adelson e Salvina*, and a cantata, *Ismene*, as well as some nonoperatic compositions. A second opera written during Bellini's conservatory days, *Bianca e Fernando*, was produced at the San Carlo Opera in Naples in 1826. This so impressed impresario Antonio Barbaja that he commissioned Bellini to prepare an opera for La Scala; the result of this commission was *Il Pirata* ("The Pirate"), which was staged at La Scala in 1827.

Bellini's operas attracted some of the greatest singers of the era, including tenor Giovanni-Battista Rubini and sopranos Maria Malibran, Giuditta Pasta, and Jenny Lind. These performers all excelled in the florid style of singing known as bel canto, of which Bellini was a master of composition. In these operas, the story and settings often take a back seat to the singing. Around 1850, bel canto opera lost its prominent place in the repertoire. It was kept alive in the late 1800s and early 1900s by such singers as Marcella Sembrich and Lilli Lehmann and experienced a resurgence, including the operas of Bellini and his ilk, in the late 1940s. The latter-day equivalents of Malibran, Sembrich, and the others, who have achieved greatness in the Bellini operas, include Maria Callas, Joan Sutherland, and Renata Scotto.

Unquestionably, the masterpiece among Bellini's eleven operas is *Norma*. This opera is particularly noteworthy because the top two female roles are of near-equal importance. At *Norma's* world premiere at La Scala in 1831, the great soprano Giuditta Pasta sang the title role and Giulia Grisi sang Adalgisa. Opening night received mixed reviews, but by the third performance *Norma* had unanimous and enthusiastic approval.

THE STATUS OF VINCENZO BELLINI AS A YOUNG MASTER OF THE ITALIAN OPERATIC *BEL CANTO* WAS SOLIDIFIED WITH THE SUCCESS OF HIS OPERA *NORMA*.

With fame came travel and with travel came adulation for Bellini in the capitals of Europe. Two years after the premiere of *Norma*, Bellini was feted on a visit to London, where several of his operas were then being performed. His popularity was enhanced by accompanying Pasta when she sang her London salon recitals.

Of all Bellini's operas, *Norma* became the favorite of the concertgoing public as well as of the composer. "If I were

MARILYN HORNE (LEFT) AND JOAN SUTHERLAND (RIGHT) PERFORMED AS ADALGISA AND AS THE TITLE CHARACTER OF *NORMA* IN A METROPOLITAN OPERA PRODUCTION.

shipwrecked at sea," Bellini said, "I would leave all the rest of my operas and try to save *Norma*."

Toward the end of his life, when Bellini was working on *I Puritani* ("The Puritans"), Gioacchino Rossini, composer of *The Barber of Seville*, suggested that the composer put greater emphasis on orchestral passages in order to achieve more dramatic contrast. Following the success of *I Puritani's* January 1835 world premiere in Paris, Bellini went to work on two new operas, which were never finished. Stricken with some sort of intestinal affliction, Bellini declined rapidly and died in September 1835. ♫

CHAPTER 4

The Romantic Era

HECTOR BERLIOZ
FELIX MENDELSSOHN
FRÉDÉRIC CHOPIN
ROBERT SCHUMANN
FRANZ LISZT
GIUSEPPE VERDI
RICHARD WAGNER
CHARLES GOUNOD
JACQUES OFFENBACH
CÉSAR FRANCK
BEDRICH SMETANA
ANTON BRUCKNER
JOHANN STRAUSS, JR.
JOHANNES BRAHMS
CAMILLË SAINT-SAËNS
LÉO DELIBES
GEORGES BIZET
PYOTR ILYICH TCHAIKOVSKY
ANTONÍN DVOŘÁK
SIR ARTHUR SULLIVAN
JULES MASSENET
EDVARD GRIEG
LEOS JANÁCEK
SIR EDWARD ELGAR
GIACOMO PUCCINI
VICTOR HERBERT

*L*udwig van Beethoven stood with one foot in the Classical period and the other in the Romantic. This kind of overlap is true of several composers, as it is of the phases in the history of music. The Classical period, for instance, did not end abruptly, with the Romantic commencing where it left off—they overlap, they blend.

The term "romantic" as it pertains to music, and to the arts in general, does not allude to decades of love songs—although there are those—but to a certain spirit and attitude. The roots of romanticism can be traced to late-eighteenth–century Germany, when a "school" of writers became disenchanted with their lot and sought to restore the chivalrous aura of the Middle Ages and its knights in shining armor and revered ladies. Certainly, these restless writers did not want to put on cumbersome armor or give up their modern comforts, but they were seeking the more aesthetic side of life that they believed had existed in the eleventh and twelfth centuries. The aesthetic reawakened by these writers was soon taken up by composers as well.

In music, Romanticism bypasses some of the technique and rigidity of earlier periods to allow for more emotion and imagination, which is a good idea for any artistic endeavor. Running from the early 1800s to the very early 1900s, the Romantic timeline covers slightly more than one hundred years. Of course, as with any era or movement, the Romantic period can be subdivided: composers in the first third are sometimes referred to as Viennese Classicists and those in the last as Post-Romanticists, leaving a middle third of supposedly pure Romanticists.

Thoughout the Romantic period, the world became more international with the opening of the Suez Canal, the invention of the telephone by Alexander Graham Bell (1847–1922), Commodore Matthew Perry (1794–1858) opening up trade between Japan and America, Thomas Edison (1847–1931) perfecting the light bulb and other uses of electricity, and Orville (1871–1948) and Wilbur Wright (1867–1912) pioneering the age of aviation. The Romantic era was also a period of great conflict, coming on the heels of Napoleon's empire-building and encompassing the American Civil War, the Spanish-American War, and the Russo-Japanese War.

In the first third of the Romantic era, Queen Victoria was crowned and married to Prince Albert, and Benjamin Disraeli was a successful author before turning to politics and becoming British Prime Minister. Great writers of this period (not all of them Romantic in orientation) included Victor Hugo (1802–1885) and Gustave Flaubert (1821–1880) in France, Henrik Ibsen (1828–1906) in Norway, and Edgar Allan Poe (1809–1849) in the United States; among the painters of this era were Eugène Delacroix (1798–1863) in France, J.M.W. Turner (1775–1851) in England, and Gilbert Stuart (1755–1828) in the United States.

In the middle part of the era, journalism and entertainment entrenched themselves—between 1850 and 1890, both *The New York Times* and P.T. Barnum's Greatest Show on Earth came into being. It was also during this time that the English author Charles Dickens (1812–1870) rose to prominence and the American satirist Mark Twain (1835–1910) brought his brand of humor and criticism to the world of letters.

In the final third of the Romantic period, the Klondike had its gold rush, Freud was interpreting dreams, and Einstein was theorizing on relativity. Writers at the end of the era included George Bernard Shaw (1856–1950) in the British Isles, Anton Chekhov (1860–1904) in Russia, and Rudyard Kipling (1865–1936) in England and India; among the painters were Paul Gauguin (1848–1903) and Henri Matisse (1869–1954) in France, and John Singer Sargent (1856–1925) in the United States.

These authors, poets, artists, and inventors are just a few of the many movers and shakers who were active during this period, an exciting time that was further enhanced by the composers known as the Romanticists.

OPPOSITE: THE CREATOR OF AN OVERTURE, A SYMPHONY, AND AN OPERA BASED ON SHAKESPEARE'S WORKS, HECTOR BERLIOZ PROBABLY DISCOVERED THE BARD AFTER FALLING IN LOVE WITH HARRIET SMITHSON, WHO PLAYED OPHELIA IN AN 1827 PRODUCTION OF HAMLET.

Among Hector Berlioz's strongest influences were the Roman poet Virgil (70–19 b.c.), William Shakespeare (1564–1616), and the inimitable German man of letters Johann Wolfgang von Goethe (1749–1832).

While Berlioz was certainly smitten by Shakespeare, this may have been less a result of the Bard's creative powers than an effect of Berlioz's infatuation with actress Harriet Smithson, who played Ophelia in a production of *Hamlet* that Berlioz saw when he was about twenty-four years old. An English company was performing at the Odeon Theatre in Paris while Berlioz was attending the Paris Conservatory. The production was in English and, although he knew little of the language, he was struck by the drama and emotion of Shakespeare's play. He adored Harriet from afar, met her five years later, and married her in 1833. But his fantasies about Harriet and an idyllic relationship did not match up with reality and they separated about nine years later.

His love of Shakespeare, however, remained strong, and Berlioz wrote a *King Lear* Overture in 1831, a symphony inspired by *Romeo and Juliet* in 1839, and the opera *Béatrice et Bénédict*, inspired by *Much Ado About Nothing,* in 1862; there are also several compositions that are said to have been suggested by his reading and seeing *Hamlet*.

Hector Berlioz, the oldest of six children, was tutored in his early years by his father, and this education included reading Virgil, a pleasure that stayed with the composer throughout his lifetime. Virgil's *Aeneid* became the source of Berlioz's mammoth opera, *Les Troyens* ("The Trojans"). Setting aside all other endeavors, Berlioz spent two years writing this opera and another five years try-

ing to get it produced. Finally, it was divided in two—with Acts I and II renamed *La Prise de Troie* ("The Trojan Prize") and Acts III and V called *Les Troyens à Carthage* ("The Trojans at Carthage")—and Berlioz settled for having the first half staged at the Théâtre-Lyrique in Paris in 1863. It was never produced in its five-and-a-half-hour entirety during Berlioz's lifetime.

HECTOR BERLIOZ
(1803–1869)

As for Goethe's influence on Berlioz, the composer became aware of the writer's *Doctor Faustus* in 1827, around the same time that he was moved by Shakespeare (and Harriet Smithson). Almost twenty years later, Berlioz composed *The Damnation of Faust*; written as a cantata, it was more successful when it was presented as an opera long after Berlioz's death.

The effect of Shakespeare, Virgil, and Goethe on Berlioz is interesting to examine, for the composer was himself a highly regarded writer. This talent was apparent in the letters he wrote to family and friends while he was in Rome furthering his musical education. This sojourn in Italy was a direct result of his studies at the Paris Conservatory. Berlioz had been enrolled in medical school in Paris in 1821, but he quit after two years, overpowered by his desire to pursue music. For some time he was alienated from his mother and father, a well-regarded physician, for having taken this course of action. Following his departure from medical school, Berlioz enrolled in the Paris Conservatory, where one of his teachers was the revered Jean-François Le Sueur (1760–1837). After several attempts, Berlioz won the Conservatory's Prix de Rome, which enabled him to study in Italy. While there is evidence that Berlioz was composing

LA PRISE DE TROIE

OPÉRA EN TROIS ACTES

HECTOR BERLIOZ

MEMBRE DE L'INSTITUT ETC

music at the age of thirteen or fourteen, we definitely know that he was composing during his time at the Paris Conservatory, although most of his early manuscripts have been lost. Only fragments survive of *La Mort de Sardanapale* ("The Death of Sardanapalus"), the cantata which won him the Prix de Rome, a scholarship to study in Italy, in 1830. Berlioz eventually was hired as librarian at the Paris Conservatory, but he was never granted the professorship he had hoped for.

The 1840s and 1850s were financially lean for Berlioz the composer, and he was forced to earn a living in journalism. As a music critic he wrote for several prestigious French publications, and for a time he was held to be a better critic than he was composer. Berlioz's *Memoirs* is considered one of the very best autobiographies by a composer.

Berlioz's career as a successful orchestral conductor was launched after he became established as a composer. Leading concerts of his own works promoted his compositions, and he kept extending his itinerary farther and farther throughout Europe. On these tours, Marie Recio was the soprano soloist. She was much more than that to Berlioz, however—he married her four months after Harriet died in 1854.

Berlioz was daunted by the fact that his operas were not more successful, but he need not have felt that way about his orchestral compositions. Added to those already mentioned, his *Symphonie Fantastique*, which Berlioz subtitled "Episode in the Life of an Artist" (1829), the "Harold in Italy" Symphony (1834), and the *Roman Carnival* Overture (1843) have given Berlioz a firm hold on the concert hall. ♪

OPPOSITE: BERLIOZ WAS SUCCESSFUL IN SEVERAL CAREERS: COMPOSER, WRITER, AND CONDUCTOR. AN 1850 CARICATURE SHOWS HIM AS A CONDUCTOR. INSET: THE FRONTISPIECE FOR *THE TROJAN PRIZE*, PART OF BERLIOZ'S EPIC OPERA BASED ON VIRGIL'S *AENEID*, ILLUSTRATES THE WORK HE SPENT TWO YEARS WRITING. RIGHT: UNLIKE MANY OF HIS PREDECESSORS AND CONTEMPORARIES, FELIX MENDELSSOHN BASED SOME OF HIS MASTERWORKS ON PERSONAL EXPERIENCE RATHER THAN DRAWING THEM FROM HIS IMAGINATION OR TURNING TO LITERATURE FOR INSPIRATION.

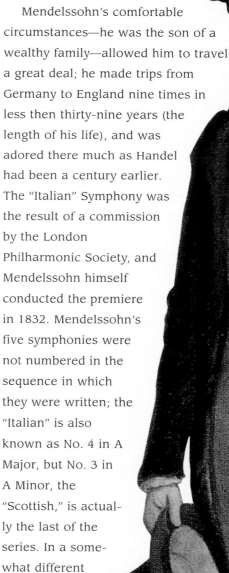

FELIX MENDELSSOHN (1809–1847)

FELIX MENDELSSOHN'S EXPLORATION OF THE RUINS OF THE CASTLE IN Scotland where Mary Stuart lived and the chapel where she was crowned Queen of Scotland, and his sightseeing tours through Italy, which included visits not only to Rome and Naples but also to Amalfi, Sorrento, and Capri, inspired two outstanding symphonies. The timbre of his "Scottish" and "Italian" Symphonies are outstanding because the works are based not on supposition but on personal experiences.

Mendelssohn's comfortable circumstances—he was the son of a wealthy family—allowed him to travel a great deal; he made trips from Germany to England nine times in less then thirty-nine years (the length of his life), and was adored there much as Handel had been a century earlier. The "Italian" Symphony was the result of a commission by the London Philharmonic Society, and Mendelssohn himself conducted the premiere in 1832. Mendelssohn's five symphonies were not numbered in the sequence in which they were written; the "Italian" is also known as No. 4 in A Major, but No. 3 in A Minor, the "Scottish," is actually the last of the series. In a somewhat different

The Romantic Era

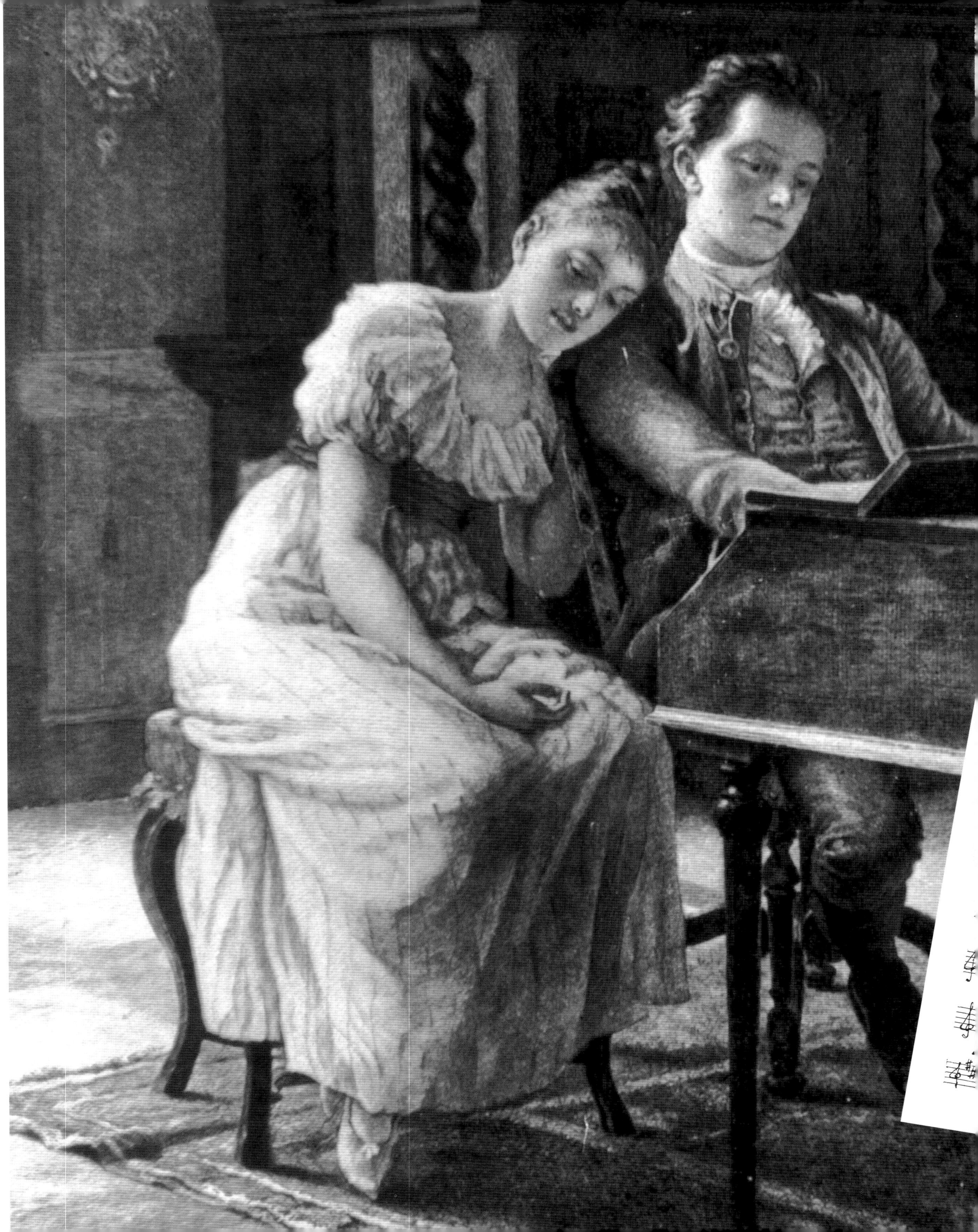

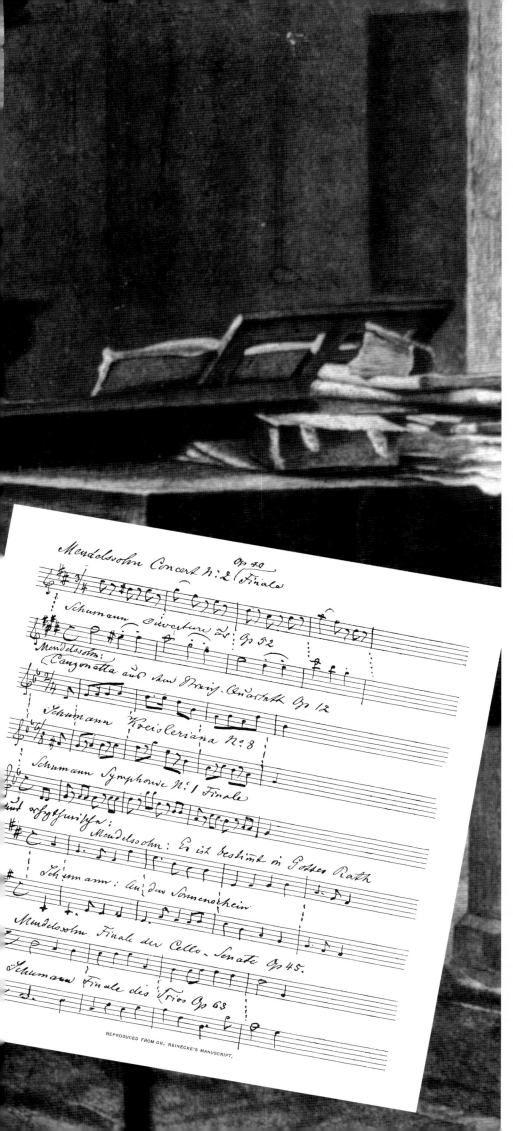

category, Mendelssohn also composed a dozen symphonies for string orchestra when he was in his early teens.

Born in Hamburg, Germany, in 1809, Mendelssohn, the grandson of the respected philosopher Moses Mendelssohn (1729–1786) and the son of a successful banker, grew up in a comfortable atmosphere. When Felix was about three years old, the family left Hamburg due to adverse business conditions, as well as general unrest, triggered by a French blockade. The Mendelssohns settled in Berlin, which was flourishing as a city of culture, and Felix grew up in comfortable circumstances where his talent was encouraged. Sunday evening musicales at home were a regular part of the family routine. The composer Carl Maria von Weber, an occasional guest at the Mendelssohn home, had praise for Felix's piano prowess, and poet and writer Johann Wolfgang von Goethe, another sometime visitor, also expressed his enthusiasm for the talented youth. Mendelssohn received his education from tutors, and then attended the Singakademie and Berlin University.

It was at the Singakademie in 1829 that Mendelssohn launched a revival of the works of Johann Sebastian Bach by conducting a performance of the *St. Matthew Passion*. This was the first time it had been performed since Bach's death in 1750. From then on, interest in the works of Bach never again diminished.

Although he was only twenty years old at the time of the *St. Matthew* performance, Mendelssohn was already a well-established composer. One of his most famous works—the Overture to *A Midsummer Night's Dream*—was written when he was seventeen years old. Sixteen years later, Mendelssohn added twelve selections of incidental music to the Shakespeare classic.

At the age of twenty-four, Mendelssohn became music director in Düsseldorf, where his responsibilities included writing and directing music for the church, opera, and several

A PORTRAIT OF MENDELSSOHN AT THE PIANO WITH HIS SISTER FANNY, A TALENTED PIANIST IN HER OWN RIGHT. <u>INSET:</u> MENDELSSOHN AND SCHUMANN, WHOSE WORKS ARE SHOWN ON THE SAME MANUSCRIPT PAGE HERE, WERE BOTH FACULTY AT THE LEIPZIG CONSERVATORY OF MUSIC, WHICH MENDELSSOHN ORGANIZED IN 1842.

The Romantic Era

NICCOLÒ PAGANINI (1782–1840)

Weird tales surround Niccolò Paganini, one of the most astounding violin virtuosos of all time. Many of them deal with magic and the supernatural, which most modern people, with all our scientific advances, reject. Some of these tales were spread by strangers who were envious of Paganini's talent or couldn't believe the virtuoso could have come by his talents naturally; Paganini himself related an anecdote concerning a know-it-all individual who melodramatically described a performance in which Paganini impeccably played *La streghe* with the Devil standing by his side. Enhancing the story is the translation of *streghe*: "witches." And Paganini's appearance—his gaunt face, flowing black hair, and out-of-date frock coat—certainly didn't help lay these rumors to rest. On the other side of the spiritual spectrum, when Paganini was a child, his mother told him that an angel had come to her in a dream prophesying a great career for the boy.

One of five children, Niccolò was taught the violin and the mandolin by his father, a shipping clerk on the wharfs of Genoa. After progressing from teacher to teacher, the thirteen-year-old went to Parma, accompanied by his father, to audition for the master violinist Alessandro Rolla, who proclaimed that Niccolò had learned all he could as a string player, and advised only that the prodigy have further study in composition and counterpoint.

Around 1800, Paganini played at the Festival of Santa Croce in Lucca; the following year he was appointed concertmaster of the National Orchestra, also based in Lucca. In the ensuing years he held a number of various musical positions in the royal court at Lucca through 1809.

Paganini's appearance at the Santa Croce festival signaled the start of his bombastic career as a violin soloist, obliterating all the competition. Fame accompanied him throughout Italy, into Germany, Austria, France, and Great Britain. Paganini's flair for showmanship in no way masked his supremacy on the violin. Except for a few seasons in the 1820s when ill health forced him to cancel, Paganini toured voraciously until around 1834, all the more remarkable considering the limited means of travel in those days. His health problems centered on a serious jaw condition and throat ailment, and by 1838 he could not speak at all and was forced to rely on his teenage son to intercede for him in conversation.

Paganini's virtuosity and his compositions for the violin presented a dilemma for Franz Liszt, Frédéric Chopin, Hector Berlioz, and Robert Schumann. While extraordonarily talented at composing for orchestra and other single or grouped instruments, when they were confronted with compositions like Paganini's "24 Caprices for Solo Violin" and *La streghe*, they were seriously challenged.

LEFT: DURING HIS LIFETIME, THE ASTOUNDING NICCOLÒ PAGANINI WAS SAID TO HAVE MADE A DEAL WITH THE DEVIL. OPPOSITE: FRÉDÉRIC CHOPIN WAS AS POPULAR AMONG WOMEN AS AMONG MUSIC CRITICS; IN 1848 A PARIS MUSIC MAGAZINE REPORTED THAT "THE FINEST FLOWER OF FEMININE ARISTO-CRACY...FILLED THE SALLE PLEYEL TO CATCH THIS MUSICAL SYLPH ON THE WING."

choral groups. After six months in Düsseldorf, he became music director of Leipzig's celebrated Gewandhaus Orchestra, a position he held for five years. The concertmaster was the acclaimed violinist Ferdinand David, and between the two of them the performance level of the orchestra was raised to new heights. They had originally met when they were in their midteens; interestingly, they realized that they had been born in the same house in Hamburg, only a year apart. It was for David that Mendelssohn composed his brilliant Concerto in E Minor for Violin, and David was the soloist at the concerto's world premiere in Leipzig in 1845.

When a new Academy of Arts was proposed for Berlin in 1840, Mendelssohn was invited to take charge of the orchestral and choral concerts. Put off by the bureaucratic difficulties that ensued, he took the job on the condition that it was for only one year. Little came of all this except for Mendelssohn's formation of the Domchor, or Cathedral Choir. So Mendelssohn redirected his expertise, enthusiasm, and energy elsewhere and organized the Leipzig Conservatory of Music. Around this time, he was also designated honorary kapellmeister (court orchestra director) to the King of Prussia.

Mendelssohn wrote in a variety of musical forms, but had only a brush with opera, perhaps because, as has been suggested, he could not find a literary work or libretto to suit him. Although he dabbled with several operas, the only one he completed was *Die Hochzeit des Camacho*, based on Cervantes' *Don Quixote*.

Particularly noteworthy among his other compositions is his *Songs Without Words*, a title which reflects the nature of his work, a collection of Mendelssohn's piano fantasies.

One of the most highly regarded oratorios by any composer is Mendelssohn's *Elijah*, which ranks with Handel's *Messiah* and Haydn's *Creation*. There were two other Mendelssohn oratorios—*St. Paul* and *Christus*—but *Elijah*, Mendelssohn's last major musical effort, was his finest. He died in 1847 in Leipzig from what is now thought to have been a series of strokes. Married for only ten years at the time of his passing, Mendelssohn had five children with his wife, Cecile (née Jeanrenaud). Six months before Mendelssohn's demise, the composer's sister, Fanny, died suddenly. The eldest of four siblings, Fanny had also excelled at the piano and had been an occasional composer; she was married to the painter Wilhelm Hensel. Felix's deep depression over the loss of Fanny, whom he loved deeply, was contrary to his generally ebullient personality. ♪

FRÉDÉRIC CHOPIN
(1810–1849)

THE ULTIMATE VIRTUOSO, FRÉDÉRIC CHOPIN WAS HERALDED BOTH AS one of the finest piano soloists and as a talented composer who wrote almost solely for the piano.

At the age of nine, Chopin was acclaimed for his piano recitals in Warsaw, Poland, near where he was born in 1810. Frédéric's mother was Polish and his father was French; both of these national connections would influence Chopin as he grew into a composer.

The second of four children, the boy showed an exceptional aptitude for the keyboard from a very early age, leading his parents to hire the esteemed keyboard teacher Adalbert Zywny to give piano instruction to their seven-year-old son. The youngster had barely started his lessons when his talent for composition became evident and he wrote his first known work, the Polonaise in G Minor. Chopin subsequently pursued his musical studies at the Warsaw Conservatory.

Gradually, his renown spread and he began regularly playing the concert halls of Germany. In 1832, he settled in Paris following his first concert there. Around that time, Chopin also began to decrease his public concertizing and to concentrate on composing. His reputation made it easy for

Chopin to collect high fees for teaching, freeing him from financial worries.

Chopin composed almost exclusively for the piano; even his two concertos for piano and orchestra minimize the use of the ensemble. Mazurkas, sonatas, nocturnes, preludes, scherzos, waltzes, études, and polonaises were all in Chopin's repertoire. The best known of his compositions are probably his Polonaise in A, the "Military," and his Polonaise in A-Flat, the "Heroic."

In Paris, Chopin fit in quite comfortably with the intellectual crowd. The musicians, painters, poets, and other artists who became his acquaintances and friends were often privately treated to his superb piano artistry at salon gatherings. There were also recitals for the royalty of Europe in their chateaux and palaces.

Among the intelligentsia with whom Chopin associated was Aurore Dudevant, the author who was better known as George Sand (1804–1876). In 1836, when Chopin was introduced to Dudevant, he was engaged to Maria Vodzinska, for whom he wrote his Waltz in A-Flat Major. This engagement, however, was broken off around the time when he met Aurore. Chopin's relationship with Aurore, which lasted for about a decade, has become one of the greatest love affairs in history. She was a radical social activist, seeking equal rights for women—to the extent that she actually dressed like a man (which was extremely radical in the mid-nineteenth century). Chopin was reserved, tended to be shy, and was a passive exponent of the arts. Their alliance seems to have gone through various stages—from passionate to platonic and from sweet to stormy. In 1849, two years after their alliance ended, Chopin died, having been plagued for years by tuberculosis.

Chopin attracted the attention of numerous writers who took it upon themselves to craft biographies of the pianist-composer or to write of him in other ways. One of these biographers was fellow pianist-composer Franz Liszt. Although these two men were contemporaries who sometimes performed together at concerts, their personalities were quite different—Liszt enjoyed being in the public eye, for instance, while Chopin was a very private person. Not

CHOPIN SITS AT THE PIANO, PERHAPS CONTEMPLATING HIS COMPOSITION *IMPROMPTU*, THE WORK FEATURED ON THE MANUSCRIPT PAGE SHOWN (INSET).

surprisingly, one of the writers who wrote about Chopin was George Sand. In her novel *Lucrezia Floriani*, she cast herself as Lucrezia and, indirectly but negatively, portrayed Chopin as Prince Karol. This negative portrayal was probably the result of their waning relationship; her earlier novel *La Mere au Diable* ("The Devil's Mother") was lovingly dedicated to Chopin.

In spite of his ties to France, Poland always remained at the core of Chopin, for he always honored the country of his birth. When the time had come to pursue his studies and his career elsewhere, Poland was in a state of political turmoil. Chopin left in the autumn of 1830, soon after a concert in Warsaw that turned out to be his last in that city; he took with him a silver cup containing Polish soil. Chopin played his final concert—for the benefit of Polish refugees—in London in 1848. He died the following year; his body was interred in Paris, but his heart was placed in Warsaw at the Church of the Holy Cross.

Much as Chopin always had a special place in his heart for Poland, his native land has always held Chopin up as one of its most revered citizens. When Warsaw fell to Germany in World War II, the final music heard on the radio in the Polish capital was the familiar opening notes of Chopin's "Military" Polonaise. ♪

ROBERT SCHUMANN (1810–1856)

ROBERT SCHUMANN'S LIST OF TOP TEN ARTISTS WOULD PROBABLY include Johann Sebastian Bach, Wolfgang Amadeus Mozart, Ludwig van Beethoven, Franz Schubert, Frédéric Chopin, Felix Mendelssohn, Hector Berlioz, Lord Byron, Johann Wolfgang von Goethe, and Friedrich von Schiller (1759–1805). True, the last three are authors, not composers, but when it came to the arts Robert Schumann was never one to limit himself to music.

In fact, Schumann's early childhood in Zwickau, Saxony, where he was born in 1810, provided more of a literary than musical environment. Father Schumann was a bookseller, author, and publisher, and at the age of thirteen Robert, the fifth and youngest child, wrote his first articles for a volume printed by his father. At this time, Robert had already been performing as a pianist and dabbling in composition. When Robert was about fifteen years old, his passion for societies and clubs was sparked when he helped organize one group devoted to fencing and another entrenched in German literature. At the age of eighteen, after his preliminary education, Schumann enrolled as a law student at the University of Leipzig—but he was absent from most of the lectures. Transferring to the university at Heidelberg, then back to Leipzig, he found that he had trouble attending classes no matter where he was. The distraction was his talent for music—he spent huge blocks of time composing and practicing piano, sometimes for seven hours a day.

Also in his eighteenth year, Schumann began piano study with Friedrich Wieck and met Wieck's nine-year-old daughter, Clara, who would later be courted by Schumann. Having boarded with the Wieck family for a time, Schumann moved elsewhere when Clara, a piano prodigy, was taken on one concert tour after another, chaperoned by her father.

Schumann was not destined to attain his fame at the piano keyboard—any idea of a career as a concert pianist was dashed when Schumann crippled one hand while experimenting with a mechanical device that was supposed to strengthen his fingers. Fortunately, this did not cripple his ability to compose.

Around 1837 Schumann, Wieck, and several of their friends founded the biweekly newspaper *Neue Zeitschrift für Musik* ("The New Music Journal"). Schumann had written for other publications, but *Neue Zeitschrift* gave him an assured place where his literary efforts would be seen, although he sometimes used the pseudonyms Eusebius or Florestan. *Neue Zeitschrift* changed hands several times, but Schumann was associated with the publication until 1844, serving as editor and in various other literary capacities.

The first kiss between Schumann and Clara Wieck took place on November 25, 1835, according to the *New Grove Dictionary of Music and Musicians.* Clara's father tried to thwart the relationship's development, and not entirely without reason. Schumann was a heavy drinker and was well known as a ladies' man; he had even been treated for syphilis. Papa Wieck's attitude at times forced the lovers to conduct secret rendezvous, and there was a point at which Clara was negotiating to wed Schumann legally without her father's consent. In the end, the whole matter was taken to court. To make himself more acceptable in the eyes of his would-be father-in-law, Schumann obtained an honorary degree. Finally, in August 1840, the court overruled Wieck's objections, and Schumann and Clara wed in September.

All this took its toll on Schumann's composing. Blissfully, his first composition after the wedding was the vocal duet "Wenn Ich Ein Voglein War" ("If I Were A Little Bird"), which was later interpolated into his only opera, *Genoveva.* In time the couple had eight children and eventually made peace with Papa Wieck.

After the marriage, Clara continued her career; at times, her popularity was greater than that of her husband, a fact of which he was painfully aware. Schumann was prone to bouts of depression, at least once to the point of attempting suicide. During one period of depression, Schumann

---

ABOVE: ROBERT SCHUMANN, WHOSE LOVE FOR LITERATURE WAS PERHAPS AS GREAT AS HIS LOVE OF MUSIC, FOUNDED THE BIWEEKLY NEWSPAPER *THE NEW MUSIC JOURNAL* AROUND 1837 WITH HIS PIANO TEACHER FRIEDRICH WIECK AND OTHER FRIENDS. OPPOSITE: CLARA WIECK WED ROBERT SCHUMANN IN 1840, BUT DID NOT LET HER MARRIED LIFE INTERFERE WITH HER CAREER AS A PERFORMER, COMPOSER, AND TEACHER.

exclaimed that listening to music "cut into my nerves as if with knives." Throughout his life, the composer suffered from a fear of going insane, and when the end did come, in 1856, it was in fact in an asylum.

Despite his mental troubles, this man composed beautiful and uplifting music. There was a great deal of piano music, including Fantasia in C, *Carnaval*, and *Fantasiestücke* ("Fantasy Pieces"), along with two collections for children, *Kinderscenen* ("Scenes from Childhood") and *Album für die Jugend* ("Album for the Young"). Schumann's Lieder included the cycles *Dichterliebe* ("Poet's Love") and *Frauenliebe und Leben* ("Women's Love and Life"). He also wrote chamber music, concertos for piano, violin or cello and orchestra, and four symphonies.

The 1848 revolutionary upheaval in Dresden, where the Schumanns lived, inspired his five "barricade" marches. Soon after, Schumann accepted the post of municipal music director at Düsseldorf. He and Clara were welcomed with concerts in

CLARA WIECK-SCHUMANN (1819–1896)

Clara Wieck was sixteen years old when composer Robert Schumann, a former student of the girl's father, earnestly began their romantic relationship. Not unlike Gigi, the title character in the Lerner and Loewe musical, Clara, no longer an awkward little girl, was suddenly seen quite differently by the gentleman who had observed her proverbial transformation from the ugly duckling into the swan. There was an added dimension: as a child, Clara had been a piano prodigy and had been much admired by Schumann.

As soon as Clara had begun to show signs of proficiency on the piano, she was no longer allowed a normal childhood. When she was six years old, her parents were divorced; her mother remarried the same year and her father three years later, in July 1828. In October of that year, Clara, who had just turned nine years old, made her debut as a pianist—she was enthusiastically applauded and gave her first complete recital two years later. The tremendous acclaim of his daughter spurred Wieck to manage tour after tour of European concert halls for her. Around 1839 Clara broke from her father and began to manage her own intense schedule of recitals and concerts.

Parallel with her remarkable professional calendar was an equally remarkable domestic life. Clara and Robert, having wed in 1840, had eight children between 1841 and 1854, during which time she kept up her public performances, composed, and taught. While it is true that the Schumanns had servants and that at various times the children were in boarding schools or staying with rel-

atives or friends, Clara was always in control. Maria, the eldest child, became a part-time "mother" to her siblings when she was not touring with Clara as an all-around assistant. Robert, who often joined his wife in the concert tours, was a loving father, but Clara was clearly head of the household.

Life took an odd turn for Clara in March 1854: having shown increasing signs of mental illness, Robert was sent to a hospital for the insane; for two and a half years following, Clara was not permitted to see Robert. In June 1854, their eighth child was born and, soon after, Clara resumed her concert tours. There are a number of different theories as to why Clara was kept away, while certain other relatives and friends were allowed to visit. One theory, for instance, holds that Robert's condition improved every once in a while, and doctors feared that seeing his wife might trigger whatever it was in the past that had caused his mental disturbance. In July 1856, Clara was summoned to her husband's bedside, where she stayed for the last two days of his life.

Clara's concert tours continued and continued until March 1891, when she played in public, in Frankfurt, for the last time.

their honor, a banquet, and a ball. Things went well at first, but Schumann's effectiveness as director deteriorated and ended.

In the last three years of his life, Schumann met Johannes Brahms. Even though Schumann was then in physical and creative decline, Brahms recalled, "To me, Schumann's memory is holy. The noble, pure artist forever remains my ideal. I will hardly be privileged ever to love a better person."

FRANZ LISZT
(1811–1886)

THROUGHOUT HIS LIFETIME, FRANZ LISZT WOULD POINT TO HIS FOREhead with pride and tell people that was where he was given a congratulatory kiss by Beethoven. The occasion was a recital by Liszt when he was twelve years of age and Beethoven was past fifty. Of course, Liszt knew of the older man's greatness and was duly impressed. Some years later, Liszt helped raise money through his concert tours for the Beethoven monument in Bonn, Germany, where Beethoven was born.

Regarded as the greatest pianist of his time, Liszt was adored by the public, whether he was performing on the European continent or in Iceland, England, or Portugal.

As a composer, Liszt wrote mostly for the piano; he is perhaps best known for the *Hungarian Rhapsodies*, of which there are fifteen. Liszt was born in Raiding, Hungary, in 1811 but was so deeply involved in the musical life of Germany that his Hungarian heritage is thin. His given name was Ferenc and he was baptized Franciscus, but he adopted the Germanic name Franz later in life. He did not speak Hungarian fluently, but from 1869 on he visited his homeland every year; in 1875 he became director of the Music Academy in Budapest.

His primary interests or motivations in life seem to have been threefold—music and the arts, of course, religion, and female companionship—and he was fervent about all three.

When it came to the arts, his interests extended well beyond music: while he was friendly with the composers Hector Berlioz, Frédéric Chopin, and Richard Wagner, he also associated with the artist Eugène Delacroix and the writers Victor Hugo and George Sand.

For Liszt, religious involvement went well beyond that of the ordinary worshiper: with the blessing of Pope Pius IX, he took the four minor orders of the Catholic Church in 1865. These vows taken, he could be addressed as Abbé Liszt and he wore the traditional Roman frock. Strangely, however, he was also involved in Freemasonry.

ABOVE: THE MOST TALENTED PIANIST OF HIS TIME AND A GENIUS INNOVATOR OF MODERN PIANO TECHNIQUE, FRANZ LISZT CREATED THE SYMPHONIC POEM. OPPOSITE: THE EVER-DASHING GIUSEPPE VERDI WAS PERHAPS THE ONLY CLASSICAL MUSICIAN WHO WAS SO POPULAR IN HIS OWN LIFETIME THAT HE BECAME RICH FROM HIS ART—HIS FORTUNES RIVALED, AND IN SOME CASES SURPASSED, THOSE OF THE NOBILITY.

Two women figured prominently in the life of Liszt, although he wed neither of them. Between 1833 and 1844, he took up residence in Geneva with Countess Marie d'Agoult, and from 1848 until he died in 1886, he lived with Princess Carolyne Sayn-Wittgenstein. Marie was a gifted writer who worked under the pen name of Daniel Stern; in fact, most of Liszt's biography of Chopin was written by her. In time, she became impatient with Liszt frequently being away on concert tours and she ended the relationship. Carolyne, on the other hand, convinced Liszt to cease touring and settle in Weimar as a full-time conductor and composer. In 1848 he became the kapellmeister (orchestra director) at the court in Weimar, where he remained until 1861.

During their time together, Liszt and d'Agoult had three children: two daughters and a son. Their daughter Cosima eventually married Hans von Bülow, a student of Liszt's who later became famous as pianist and conductor. While she was married to von Bülow, Cosima had an affair with Richard Wagner (see page 75), whom she married after obtaining a divorce from her first husband. Because Wagner was in political exile from Germany in 1850 when his opera *Lohengrin* was due for its first performance, Liszt conducted the premiere at the Court Theatre in Weimar.

As his reputation grew, Liszt was besieged with potential piano pupils. He worked with many of them, but refused payment, perhaps remembering that the renowned instructors Carl Czerny (1791–1857) and Antonio Salieri (see Chapter 3, page 39) had accorded him the same generosity on his way to fame.

Liszt is important as a composer not only for the specific pieces he wrote, but also for his achievements in musical theory. Liszt developed the concept of descriptive orchestral music and coined the term "symphonic poem" (also known as "tone poem") and the form it describes. *Les Préludes, Mazeppa,* and *Hamlet* are examples of Liszt's symphonic poems. Among his approximately four hundred compositions are two symphonies, *Faust* and *Dante;* the oratorios *Christus* and *St. Elizabeth;* two piano concertos; and, for the organ, Prelude and Fugue on (the name) B-A-C-H. To this were added many transcriptions, such as the adaptation of Paganini's *La Campanella* for piano. ♩

GIUSEPPE VERDI
(1813–1901)

It's a lively, happy place where Giuseppe Verdi is buried. Casa Verdi, where the composer and his wife are entombed in the chapel, is home to ninety dynamic musicians who are performing the last act of their lives in harmony and with a crescendo. The residents of Casa Verdi are retired singers and others from the field of opera, who live and work at the Casa.

As a composer, Verdi's success was so great that he became fabulously wealthy—the equivalent of a modern-day multimillionaire—and lived his later years in as grand a style as he desired. He was, however, a magnanimous benefactor as well as an astute businessman, and—undoubtedly motivated by his awareness of how poorly musicians were paid in his era, with no pensions, plus memories of his own lean years—he provided for "musicians less fortunate than I" by having Casa Verdi (Casa di Riposo per Musicisti) built in Milan. Construction of this grand structure began in 1889 and was completed in 1900, but the Casa did not become functional until 1902. Verdi had stipulated that it not be opened until

after his death (Verdi died on January 27, 1901); he did not want attention focused on his generosity. For sixty years, the Casa operated on royalties from Verdi's twenty-eight operas. But in 1962 the royalties ran out; today, the home is comfortably financed by a variety of sources, including contributions from residents according to their means. More than a thousand singers, conductors, composers, and instrumentalists have benefited from Verdi's legacy.

Born in 1813, Verdi quickly outgrew the musical opportunities of his hometown of Le Roncole and moved to Busseto to study at the modest conservatory there. While in Busseto, he worked in the provisions store of Antonio Barezzi to pay his room and board. When he had learned all he could at this small school, funds were raised by townspeople in Busseto for Verdi to study at the Milan Conservatory. Unfortunately, Verdi was rejected—although only in his late teens, he was considered by the conservatory to be too old and lacking in training and talent. So he went back to Busseto, where he married the boss's daughter, Margherita Barezzi, in 1836.

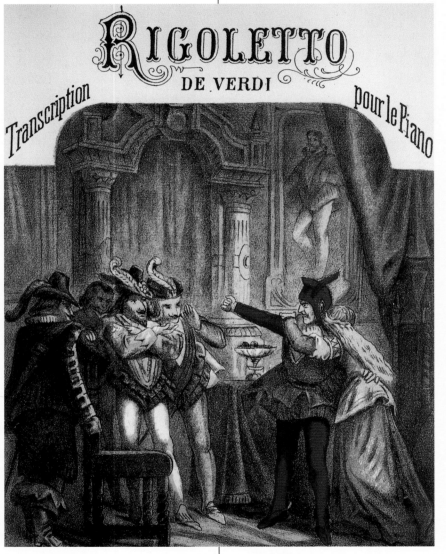

Three years later, he made a triumphant return to Milan when his opera *Oberto* was produced at La Scala; following this performance, the world-renowned opera house commissioned three more operas. Within the year, however, tragedy stepped in, with events more crushing than even the most devastating opera plots. In a period of three months in 1840, Verdi's wife, son, and daughter all died. The young composer was devastated and found it difficult to resume composing; when he did start again, the opera, strangely enough, was a comedy, *Un Giorno di Regno* ("King for a Day"). Considering Verdi's emotional state, it is understandable that this comic opera was unsuccessful. He did not attempt comedy again until his last opera, *Falstaff.*

In 1842 the course of Verdi's life was again changed: his opera *Nabucco* was released and was a tremendous success. The leading soprano was Giuseppini Strepponi (1815–1897), who would become Verdi's second wife seventeen years later. In the interim, they lived together, often in seclusion because public knowledge of Verdi having a mistress might damage his career.

Musicologists generally divide Verdi's operas into three categories. Phase one consists of rather thunderous works such as *Ernani, Macbeth,* and *I Lombardi.* In the second phase, which begins around 1851, Verdi's operas—*Rigoletto, La traviata* ("The Erring One"), *Il trovatore* ("The Troubadour"), *Un ballo in maschera* ("A Masked Ball"), and *Aïda* among them—take on more individual personality. The final phase is made up of only two works: *Otello* and *Falstaff.* As is apparent simply from looking at the titles, Verdi based the librettos of many of his operas on works by some of the greatest authors in history, including Victor Hugo's *Le roi s'amuse,* which became the opera *Rigoletto;* Alexandre Dumas' *La dame aux camelias,* which inspired *La traviata,* and several Shakespeare works, including *Macbeth,* which inspired the eponymously titled opera.

Verdi had to be talked into writing what many opera buffs consider his masterpiece, *Aïda*. Commissioned by the Egyptian government, *Aïda* was intended to inaugurate a new opera house in Cairo to coincide with the opening of the Suez Canal. Preparations were stalled, however, by the Franco-Prussian War and the canal began operating without benefit of *Aïda*. When the world premiere did take place in Cairo in 1871, the composer was absent—Verdi did not like to travel, although he and Giuseppina did journey to Russia when *La forza del destino* ("The Force of Destiny") had its premiere in St. Petersburg, having been commissioned by the opera there.

The time lapse between the premiere of *Aïda* (1871), the last opera in phase two, and *Otello* (1887) and *Falstaff* (1893), which solely comprise phase three, may seem strange, but when one considers the composer's other interests the picture begins to come clear. By the time *Aïda* was first produced, Verdi was a gentleman farmer actively involved in the maintenance of his estate, Sant' Agata, located outside Busseto. Verdi also had become involved in government: speaking out on issues resulted in his being elected to the Italian Parliament. Concerned for the future of his country, Verdi advocated Italian unification, which he lived to see.

Most of Verdi's musical genius was put into opera, although there are songs and a string quartet in the Verdi repertoire, as well as the *Hymn of Nations*, a choral work which he was invited to write for the London Exhibition of 1862. There is also the frequently performed Verdi Requiem in memory of the poet-patriot Alessandro Manzoni (1785–1873). Perhaps Verdi composed a sort of requiem for himself in the provisions in his will for Casa Verdi, which carries his memory on in others' music. ♪

RICHARD WAGNER (1813–1883)

THE PREMIERE OF RICHARD WAGNER'S OPERA *LOHENGRIN* TOOK PLACE in 1850, but its composer, the giant of German opera, did not get to hear a performance of the work until nine years later because he had been forced out of his homeland into exile by the German government.

During this period, political unrest was festering throughout Europe. When the 1848 Revolution spread to Saxony, in the spring of 1849, Wagner, music director of the Dresden Opera, was one of the insurrectionists. He took to the streets distributing antigovernment pamphlets and making instigative speeches. When the revolution was suppressed, arrest warrants were issued for the radical leaders, including Richard Wagner. Clandestinely, he fled the country by way of Paris and went into exile in Switzerland, where he mostly remained until 1861. Not only did Wagner remove himself from Germany but also from music; for several years, he composed no music, but wrote only prose. Often, he would corner his friends and force them to listen as he read his latest libretto or treatise stating what course music and art should take.

Wherever Wagner went, he lived extravagantly, in luxury that he could not afford. He often

borrowed money, and rarely paid his debts. Wagner had many affairs, and some of his benefactors were the husbands of his mistresses. Minna Planer, an actress who was married to Wagner, mostly unhappily, for thirty years, was aware of most of these affairs. Minna and Richard had no children, but Wagner had three offspring with Franz Liszt's daughter Cosima, whom he married in 1870, after Minna died. These children, all born out of wedlock, included two daughters, Eva and Isolde, and a son, Siegfried, all named for characters in Wagner's operas.

Wagner's childhood, it seems, was as convoluted as his adult life. Wagner's father, for instance, may have been either Karl Wagner or Ludwig Geyer. Historians have speculated that Richard's mother and Ludwig Geyer, an accomplished actor, painter, and playwright, were having an affair while Karl Wagner was alive. The confusion over Richard Wagner's paternity arises from this speculation and from the fact that six months after Richard was born in Leipzig in 1813, Karl Wagner died and his widow soon married Geyer. Although he died when Richard was eight years old, Geyer seems to have had a positive influence on the boy, who developed an affinity for Shakespeare and Beethoven during this early part of his life.

Rienzi, which premiered in Dresden in 1842, was the first of Wagner's operas to be produced. It was an immense success, not only because of the work itself but because of the magnificent production, which required five hundred costumes and never-before-seen special effects. Up until this point, Wagner had struggled along in two-bit conducting jobs in Magdeburg (in Germany), Königsberg (now in Russia), and Riga (now in Latvia). After he set out for Paris in 1839, hoping to find greater success there, Wagner negotiated to have composer Giacomo Meyerbeer (see Chapter 3, page 49) read his score and libretto for *Rienzi*. Meyerbeer offered little more than a compliment on the fine copying of the manuscript. It was, however, accepted by the Dresden Opera, and its success led to a six-year conducting post for the composer. Wagner, however, felt somewhat stifled by

A PIVOTAL SCENE FROM THE SAN FRANCISCO OPERA'S 1988 PRODUCTION OF WAGNER'S *PARSIFAL* SHOWS THE DRAMA OF THE COMPOSER'S WORK.

this, especially after his second opera, *Der Fliegande Höllander* ("The Flying Dutchman"), made a poor showing at its Dresden Opera premiere in 1843. The music and story of this work were radically different from *Rienzi*, and the public was taken aback. Only after audiences became accustomed to Wagner's style in his subsequent operas did *The Flying Dutchman* gain acceptance. After *The Flying Dutchman* came *Tannhäuser* (1845), *Lohengrin* (1850), *Tristan und Isolde* (1859), *Die Meistersinger von Nürnburg* ("The Mastersingers of Nuremburg," 1868), the four operas of *Der Ring des Nibelungen*, and *Parsifal* (1882).

Because of Wagner's radical ways and antagonistic attitude, socially and professionally, the press often presented an additional detriment to his artistic progress and success. One Viennese journalist who was particularly critical was Eduard Hanslick, of whom Wagner created an obvious caricature—the bumbling fool Beckmesser—in *Die Meistersinger*.

According to Wagner, his stage works were not operas but music dramas, a term he used most especially for the Ring Cycle. The composer looked upon this monumental work as a trilogy with a prologue. Founded on German mythology, the Ring evolved from the character Siegfried; Wagner fully developed the libretto before he attempted the music. *Das Rheingold* (1869), the prologue, was followed by *Die Walküre* ("The Valkyrie," 1870), *Siegfried* (1876), and *Die Götterdämmerung* ("The Twilight of the Gods," 1876). The most familiar of these is probably *Die Walküre*, which contains the familiar "Ride of the Valkyries" and the very descriptive "Magic Fire" music.

In Wagner's estimation, no ordinary opera house was good enough for the presentation of his Ring, and so he arranged for the construction of the Festspielhaus, or Festival Theatre, at Bayreuth. Wagner supervised its creation every step of the way, as he did the premiere productions of his operas. Much of the Festspielhaus was paid for by King Ludwig II of Bavaria, but the tremendous cost of the initial production of the Ring led to financial disaster and the theater shut down for six years. It reopened with the July 1883 premiere of *Parsifal*, produced five months after Wagner died of a heart attack while in Venice; his body was interred in the garden of his Bayreuth home, which was known as Wahnfried. The Festspielhaus, which has been run for generations by the Wagner family, remains in operation to this day, but only Wagner's operas are performed there.

Wahnfried was a gift from Ludwig II, who came into Wagner's life around the time of *Die Meistersinger*. The nineteen-year-old king, who was fanatical about Wagner's music, showed his esteem by paying Wagner's voluminous debts, bankrolling his operas, and by generally showing public favor to the composer, for instance, by inviting Wagner to join him in the royal box when *Die Meistersinger* premiered in Munich.

In a lengthy essay on Wagner in *The Music Lovers' Encyclopedia*, compiled by Rupert Hughes, the late composer, critic, and commentator Deems Taylor called Richard Wagner a "monster." After citing Wagner's egotism, selfishness, lack of responsibility, and faithlessness, however, he goes on to say that Wagner was "one of the world's great dramatists; he was a great thinker; he was one of the most stupendous musical geniuses that...the world has ever seen." Taylor concludes, "The miracle is that what he did in the little space of 70 years could have been done at all, even by a great genius. Is it any wonder that he had no time to be a man?" ♪

CHARLES GOUNOD
(1818–1893)

ON OCTOBER 22, 1883, IN ONE OF THE MOST OUTSTANDING EVENTS IN musical history, the Metropolitan Opera in New York City had its first performance: Charles Gounod's opera *Faust*. This was Gounod's first great honor at the Met; the second was his name being woven into the decor of the proscenium above the great stage when the Metropolitan Opera House was remodeled in 1903, an honor he shared with Ludwig van Beethoven (see Chapter 3, page 44), Christoph Willibald Gluck (see Chapter 2, page 30), Wolfgang Amadeus Mozart (see Chapter 3, page 40), Giuseppe Verdi (see page 73), and Richard Wagner (see page 75).

When Gounod was a small child, the family lived at Versailles because the father was engaged as a drawing teacher for the royal staff. Perhaps visual art was an inherited

RIGHT: TEN YEARS BEFORE HE DIED, GOUNOD WAS HONORED BY HAVING HIS OPERA *FAUST* CHOSEN FOR THE METROPOLITAN OPERA HOUSE'S VERY FIRST PRODUCTION.

talent, since Charles worked with the artist Jean Ingres (1780–1867), copying about one hundred pieces of the painter's artworks. There is also an Ingres portrait of the composer Luigi Cherubini (1760–1842) for which Gounod's hands were used as models.

In addition to his artistic skills, Gounod's father was also musically talented—he had earned a Prix de Rome, something Charles would do twice over. However, it was Gounod's mother, an accomplished pianist, who gave Charles his early musical training, inasmuch as her husband died when Charles was five.

Gounod, who was a student at the Paris Conservatory, had his first success as a composer with religious music: a mass that he wrote when he was in his early twenties was enthusiastically received when performed by the Vienna Philharmonic in 1842. He also served as a church organist, and the church influence led him to study for the priesthood from 1846 to 1848; he was sometimes referred to as l'Abbé Gounod. While not a practicing clergyman, his religious fervor was applied to music and peaked with the "Ave Maria." Independent of opera and church music, he wrote the "Funeral March of a Marionette." A popular concert offering, this piece is a movement from his unfinished *Suite Burlesque*.

In 1849 Gounod was introduced to prima donna Pauline Viardot; she and her sister, Maria Malibran, also a singer, were the well-known daughters of the equally well-known tenor and teacher Manuel Garcia. Gounod's first experience with opera, which occurred when he was barely a teenager, was hearing Malibran in Gioacchino Rossini's *Otello*. Viardot secured Gounod a commission to write an opus for the Paris Opera, which became *Sapho* (1851) and starred Viardot herself. However, it was not until he finished Faust, his fourth opera, in 1859 that Gounod made his operatic mark. *Faust* and *Romeo and Juliet* (1867) are Gounod's claims to operatic fame, although he wrote about a dozen operas in total, including *Philémon et Baucis* (1860) and *Mireille* (1864).

Whether romance flourished between Gounod and Viardot is not certain, but the year after *Sapho*'s premiere Gounod wed Anna Zimmermann, daughter of his piano teacher. The couple had two children, but the marriage was not a happy one. Gounod was linked with Georgina Weldon, a sometime singer, some years later when he and his family lived in London for about five years, around the time of the Franco-Prussian War.

Faust is unquestionably Gounod's masterpiece. More than twenty operas or operalike works have their roots in the German legend concerning the exchange of one's soul for eternal youth; only Berlioz's *The Damnation of Faust* and Boito's *Mefistofele*, however, approach the level of Gounod's treatment of the legend. Writers throughout the centuries have also latched onto the legend, most notably the literary genius Johann Wolfgang von Goethe. It was in fact Goethe's *Doctor Faustus* that provided the basis for Gounod's opera. The *Walpurgis Night* ballet music that emerged in Faust gave Gounod entry into yet another dimension of music: dance.

Gounod's extended fascination with the *Faust* story is evident in his *Memoirs*, in which he wrote, "This poem [Goethe's] was never out of my possession. I carried a copy of it everywhere and recorded in scattered notes the different ideas that might be of use someday when I should attempt this subject as an opera." That "someday" became Gounod's heyday. ♩

JACQUES OFFENBACH (1819–1880)

CARICATURES OF JACQUES OFFENBACH SEEM TO PREDOMINATE IN ILLUS-trations of the "Father of French Operetta." The cartoon approach, better than formal paintings and photographs, conveys the image of this angular man with craggy features as adventuresome, energetic, and full of good cheer.

Jacques' father, Isaac Juda Eberst, was born in Offenbach am Main, and after he migrated to Cologne and became a cantor in the synagogue, the family name evolved into Offenbach. Jacques, who was given the name Jacob when he was born, was Isaac's second son and the seventh of ten children; he was born in 1819 in Cologne, near the square that has since been renamed in his honor. (In adulthood, he sometimes signed his name as O. de Cologne.) Jacques took easily to the cello, and with professional instruction he became a virtuoso, performing in Paris with Polish pianist Anton Rubinstein (1829–1894) and in Cologne with Franz Liszt. In their youth, he and his siblings Julius and Isabella played in the cafés of Cologne as a trio consisting of cello, violin, and piano. After a year at the Paris Conservatory and

various small orchestra jobs, young Offenbach was engaged as a cellist in the Opéra-Comique orchestra.

Even though Offenbach had his theater work *Pascal et Chambord* staged when he was twenty years old, for a while afterward he could not interest anyone in producing his operettas. With the Paris Exhibition of 1855 attracting large numbers of tourists, he decided to present his own shows—he rented a minute theater, the Marigny, on the Champs-Elysées, created his own company, the Bouffes Parisiens, and delighted Parisians and visitors alike with the shows they performed. At the same time, Offenbach resigned as conductor at the Théâtre Français, a post to which he had been appointed in 1850, and devoted himself to his own successful enterprise; he operated the Marigny until 1866. The musical concoctions offered there included not only Offenbach's own operettas, but also pieces by other composers, including the lighter works of Mozart and Rossini (see Chapter 3 for more information on these composers).

In 1856, Offenbach sponsored a composition contest for young people. Seventy-eight aspiring composers entered, and the six finalists were given a libretto called *Le Docteur Miracle* ("The Miracle Doctor"), written by Ludovic Halévy and Léon Battu, to set to their original music. The result: a tie for first place with *Le Docteur Miracle* by Georges Bizet (using the original libretto's title), and *La Fille de Mme. Angot*, by Charles Lecocq, as the winning compositions. Offenbach produced both works at the Marigny in April 1857.

A peculiar law governed Offenbach's license to run his theater: Only four performers could be hired for each pro-

duction. Offenbach, however, tested the authorities. *Croquefer* (1857) had a cast of five, one of which played a mute. After this, Offenbach maneuvered for a license allowing larger casts...and got it!

In the early days of the Bouffes Parisiens, the operettas were one-act offerings. In the late 1850s, however, Offenbach decided to present a full-length piece: *Orphée aux Enfers* ("Orpheus in the Underworld"). Newspaper reviews after the October 21, 1858, opening were sensational. Short or long, most Offenbach operettas were satires on current events, classics, and famous people; some were racy and all were melodious. As the years unfolded, the Bouffes Parisiens had its ups and its downs; many of the downs were quite serious, for despite all his artistic talent, Offenbach was not an astute businessman.

Orphée, of course, was not Offenbach's only grand-scale success, nor was the Marigny the only venue in which his works were produced. His other noteworthy works include *La Belle Hélène* ("Beautiful Helen"), *Barbe-Bleue* ("Bluebeard"), *La Vie Parisienne* ("Parisian Life"), *La Grande Duchesse de Gerolstein*, and *La Périchole*. The leading lady in several Offenbach hits was Hortense Schneider (1833–1920), who was the "toast of" wherever she happened to be. *Gerolstein*, in which she played the title character,

---

TREATING CLASSICAL MYTHOLOGICAL CHARACTERS WITH GREAT IRREVERENCE AND SEASONING HIS WORKS WITH ROLLICKING MELODIES, IRONIC HUMOR, AND EXTRAVAGANT BURLESQUE, JACQUES OFFENBACH BECAME A POPULAR MASTER OF THE OPERETTA.

opened in April 1867, the same month as Paris' Exposition Universelle. On her way into the Exposition, the diva's carriage was stopped at the gate, for only royal vehicles were allowed beyond that point. Schneider advised the guards that she was the Grande Duchess of Gerolstein—she was not only admitted but also saluted on her way in.

The only time Offenbach visited the United States was for a concert tour during that country's centenary year, 1876. The condition of his health was precarious, and his family—his wife, four daughters, and a son—urged him not to go. Offenbach did go, however, and his motivation was at least partly financial. The composer conducted concerts in New York and in Philadelphia, where the Centenary Exhibition took place. In his memoirs of the trip, Offenbach expressed admiration for Niagara Falls—although he was surprised there were no Indians there—American railroads, New York newspapers, and American women, who were "handsome in a proportion wholly unknown in Paris."

Offenbach composed for the theater into 1881, creating a total of more than one hundred works. He did not live to see and hear the premiere of the most monumental of his compositions: *Les Contes d'Hoffmann* ("The Tales of Hoffmann"), his only true opera. Upon Offenbach's death, composer Ernest Guiraud was assigned the task of completing the orchestration; it is likely that Guiraud also contributed the recitatives, although there is some debate over this. This opera, based on stories by the German composer, writer, and illustrator E.T.A. Hoffmann (1776–1822), has gone through some evolution since its premiere at the Opéra-Comique. A fire at Vienna's Ring Theatre in 1881 and at the Opéra-Comique in 1887 destroyed some of Offenbach's score. As recently as 1988, and before that in 1972, notes by the composer concerning *Hoffmann* were found at the Offenbach homestead and have been incorporated into certain productions. In spite of some loss and some gain, *The Tales of Hoffmann* continue to be told. ♩

THOUGH HE WAS NOT A PROLIFIC COMPOSER, CÉSAR FRANCK WAS EXTREMELY INFLUENTIAL—HIS EMPHASIS ON THE ORGAN HELPED TO LEAD A WHOLE GENERATION OF FRENCH COMPOSERS AWAY FROM OPERA AND BACK TO THE IDEA OF MUSIC FOR ITS OWN SAKE.

CÉSAR FRANCK (1822–1890)

CÉSAR FRANCK, AN OUTSTANDING ORGANIST AS WELL AS COMPOSER, was a gentle man who went about his business, leaving his critics to themselves. He often retreated to the sanctuary of Saint Clotilde Church to play the organ in a tranquil atmosphere devoid of the jealousies of the outside world. Always receptive to his students' ideas, Franck easily won their affections, as evidenced by their tender pet name for him: Father Franck.

Franck was quite unlike his own father, who sought to manipulate the lives of his two sons. César, the elder son, was born in 1822 in Liège, Belgium. Enrolled in the Liège Conservatory, the eight-year-old boy was soon winning awards for his piano ability. As his father saw progress, he also saw the financial possibilities in his son's abilities and soon took young César on a recital tour of Brussels, Aachen, and Liège, promoting him as a keyboard prodigy, much as Leopold Mozart exploited the talent of his young son, Wolfgang Amadeus (see Chapter 3, page 40).

In 1835 the family moved to Paris, where César studied with Anton Reicha, who also taught Gounod, Liszt, and Berlioz. Franck's Paris debut, arranged by his father, was hardly noticed. Once the older Franck secured naturalization papers in 1837, César started at the Paris Conservatory. After five years, however, he withdrew at his

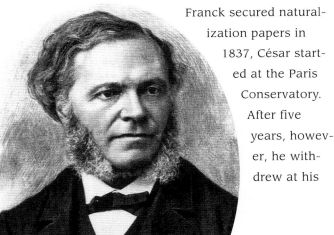

father's behest to focus on a career as a piano virtuoso. There was, however, a good deal of tension between the father and the son, and eventually César called a halt to their working together. Now on his own, César Franck earned his way by teaching music lessons and serving as an organist at the small Church of Notre-Dame de Lorette.

The gap between father and son widened when César married Felicité Saillot Desmousseaux, a young woman whom his parents frowned upon because she was part of a theatrical family—hardly a worthy profession in their eyes. However, they did agree—reluctantly—to attend the 1848 wedding at Notre-Dame de Lorette.

In time César Franck's reputation as an extraordinary organist spread. After services, he would play extemporaneously, drawing enthusiastic crowds; his first major work, *Six Pièces* (1862), developed from these sessions. In 1853, he went from Notre-Dame de Lorette to the Church of St. Jean-St. François du Marais. In 1858 he became the organist at Saint Clotilde Church, where he remained for thirty-two years. As something of an artistic representative of the organ designer and builder Aristide Cavaille-Coll, Franck inaugurated the Cavaille-Coll organ in the new basilica of Saint Clotilde in 1859 and the organ at the Paris Trocadero in 1878, for which occasion he composed *Trois Pièces*.

Franck was appointed organ professor at the Paris Conservatory in 1872; he also taught elsewhere and was a well-regarded teacher. A number of his many students, such as Paul Dukas (see sidebar below) and Vincent d'Indy, became composers of note. His pupils were his disciples and one of them, composer Henri Duparc, introduced Franck to Alexis de Castillon, first secretary of the Société Nationale de Musique; through this contact, Franck was able to have his compositions performed at the Société's concerts. In 1886, Franck was elected the Société's president.

PAUL DUKAS (1865–1935)

Mickey Mouse has been cast in many varied screen identities, from cowboy to astronaut, but his most prestigious part, dramatically speaking, was the title role in *The Sorcerer's Apprentice*, the best-known work of French composer Paul Dukas.

Dukas, a professional music critic for several publications, was highly self-critical—he set very high standards for his own music, and destroyed any compositions that did not meet his standards. Perhaps this accounts, in part, for his limited catalog of music. Dukas wrote orchestral pieces (Polyeucte Overture), ballet (*La Péri*, his last major published work), cantatas (Velleda), and one successful opera (*Ariane et Barbe-Bleu*). Dukas dedicated his Piano Sonata to Camille Saint-Saëns (see page 92) in appreciation for being asked to share in orchestrating Ernest Guiraud's unfinished *Frédégonde*. During his lifetime, Dukas taught at the Paris Conservatory, where he had studied, served as inspector of musical education in the provincial conservatories, and was elected to the Académie des Beaux Arts. He is best known, however, for *The Sorcerer's Apprentice*.

Based on Goethe's *The Apprentice Magician*, which in turn had been founded on a 2,000-year-old tale by the ancient Greek writer Lucian, this most descriptive of symphonic poems had its premiere in Paris in 1897. In 1937 American animator and filmmaker Walt Disney, who was well aware of Dukas's music and the story, obtained the rights to use the work. *The Sorcerer's Apprentice* was "father" to Disney's *Fantasia*, a milestone in animated films. Originally intended as an independent cartoon, *The Sorcerer's Apprentice* was discussed by Disney during a chance meeting with renowned conductor Leopold Stokowski (1882–1977). With composer-commentator Deems Taylor, Disney and Stokowski expanded the concept of animating classical music into a full-length film. A program was assembled of eight musical masterpieces by Bach, Beethoven, Modest Mussorgsky, Amilcare Ponchielli (1834–1886), Schubert, Stravinsky, Tchaikovsky, and Dukas. Stokowski made the soundtrack for *The Sorcerer's Apprentice*, the first section of the film, with a Hollywood studio orchestra, but recorded the other seven compositions with the Philadelphia Orchestra in its home concert hall, the Academy of Music. Through the cartoon medium of *Fantasia*, countless people were exposed to classical music for the first time.

Fantasia had its New York premiere in 1940 at the same theater—the Broadway, formerly the Colony—where twelve years earlier Mickey Mouse had made his debut as Steamboat Willie.

With an intense routine of teaching and organ playing, Franck had to schedule his composing time in the mornings,, from 5:30 to 7:30, and during summer holidays. Twice, however, he spent ten-year periods without composing anything. Franck's output was greatest in the latter part of his life. His masterpiece oratorio, which was finished in 1879 after ten years of work, is *Les Beatitudes*. Other oratorios include *Ruth, Redemption,* and *Rebecca.* Franck also composed numerous tone poems, among them *Le Chasseur Maudit* ("The Accursed Huntsman"), *Psyche*, and *Les Eolides.* Other outstanding works include the Quartet in D Major and the Quintet in F Minor for Piano and Strings.

Less than two years before Franck died in 1890, he heard his only symphony premiered. Reviews could not have been more mixed. In time, however, the Symphony in D Minor became known as his masterpiece and, moreover, a masterpiece in the catalog of symphonies by all composers. ♪

BEDRICH SMETANA (1824–1884)

THE SETTING OF THE CORNERSTONE FOR THE NATIONAL THEATRE IN Prague was symbolic in the life of Bedrich Smetana, for he is the cornerstone of Czechoslovakian music. When the building's foundation was set in place in 1868, Smetana's *Dalibor*, his third opera, was produced to mark the event.

In 1866 Smetana had become principal conductor of the Provincial Theatre, the National Theatre's predecessor, and within six months of reorganizing the theater, he had raised performance levels and revised the repertoire to present the best in classical music. This was not without loud opposition from Jan Mayr, the man he had succeeded, and others. The time was one of political turmoil, including a campaign for freedom in Czechoslovakia which called for more nationalism in the arts.

Love of country became ingrained in Smetana at an early age. The family moved a lot, depending on the father's work, and Bedrich, born in Litomysl in southern Czechoslovakia (then controlled by Austria) in 1824, was exposed to many different regions and absorbed the many beauties of the Bohemian countryside. His father, a brewer of beer, was brewmaster on the estate of Count Waldstein at the time of Bedrich's birth. He was also an amateur musician, and Bedrich learned quickly from his father; by the time he was eighteen years old, Bedrich excelled at the piano and was writing piano compositions on commission for private gatherings and parties.

Shortly before his twentieth birthday, Smetana went to Prague to be on his own; there he suffered the typical problem of a struggling musician—lack of money. While he studied composition, harmony, and counterpoint, he gave piano lessons for his upkeep, and was fortunate in being employed as music teacher in the household of Count Leopold Thun for four years. Life was not limited to routine, however, for Prague in the 1840s offered the best in theater and in music— the young Smetana heard Liszt playing recitals and Berlioz conducting concerts.

In 1848 revolution was in the air throughout much of Europe. In Czechoslovakia the rule of the Hapsburgs—and along with it the entire feudal system—was threatened. Smetana allied himself with the cause for national freedom. Besides becoming physically involved in the fight, he was inspired by the political scene to write several nationalistic compositions, including "The Song of Freedom," which became a rallying cry of the freedom fighters. The Austrians put down the Czech revolution, but unrest continued.

Although he had not met Franz Liszt, Smetana wrote to him for financial assistance in starting a music school. Impressed by the young composer, Liszt helped him, enabling Smetana to open his school in Prague in 1851. Subsequently, Smetana and Liszt became friends. Beginning in 1856, Smetana spent five years in Sweden as the director of the Philharmonic Society in Gothenburg, and during that time, he occasionally visited Liszt in Weimar. In Sweden, Smetana wrote the first of his three descriptive symphonic poems: *Richard III,* based on Shakespeare's play; *Wallenstein's Camp*, inspired by a play by Friedrich von Schiller; and *Haakon Jarl*, from a work by a Danish poet. It was during the years in Sweden that Smetana's first wife, who had been a strong influence on her husband in keeping his musical career alive, died. His second wife could not cope with the cold climate in Sweden and urged their return to Prague.

Smetana, however, had been somewhat forgotten in his five-year absence from Prague, and he had to reestablish

With no pension from the National Theatre and no royalties from his operas, Smetana was forced to leave Prague and live in an isolated area of Czechoslovakia. Frustration from deafness led to a deep change in his personality. He began to show signs of madness and was admitted to a mental hospital in the spring of 1884; he died there on May 12. Smetana was buried in Prague alongside Czech national heroes, and a memorial performance of *The Bartered Bride* took place at the National Theatre soon thereafter.

Remarkably, considering his hearing loss, Smetana learned to visualize music and kept composing during the last ten years of his life, writing the last three of his operas, a number of string quartets, a work called *The Czech Dances*, and what is undoubtedly his best-known work, the symphonic poem cycle *Má Vlast* ("My Country"). In this last piece, which consists of six segments, Smetana musically illustrates his native land. The most famous section is *Vltava* ("The Moldau"), in which the composer characterizes the river and its activities as it flows through his beloved Czechoslovakia.

himself in that city's cultural circles. The first step in this process was his being hired as music critic for the newspaper *Narodny Listy*. This gave him an opportunity to editorialize in favor of the arts, and the defeat of Austria in the Austro-Hungarian War opened up many opportunities. In 1863 Smetana's *The Brandenburgers in Bohemia*, full of revolutionary references, was entered in a contest to find a Czechoslovakian national opera. While Smetana's work was judged somewhat lacking in its national fervor, it did win and was soon produced at the Provincial Theatre to enthusiastic public acclaim.

The Bartered Bride, Smetana's second opera, is his most popular and enduring. There followed six more operas, some serious and some at least partially comedic. His critics often accused the composer of writing too much in the Wagnerian—that is, German—style. Opposition to Smetana for this and other reasons built to the point of his offer in the spring of 1874 to resign as conductor of the National Theatre (a post he had taken in 1866). Before political factors could force the theater to decide, however, Smetana stepped down because of a sudden loss of hearing that became total deafness in October of that year.

ANTON BRUCKNER (1824–1896)

ANTON BRUCKNER WAS A PERPETUAL STUDENT WHO, WELL INTO ADULThood, sought to refine his musical abilities and couple them with his natural talent. The feeling of inadequacy that prompted him to do so also slowed recognition of him as a composer, but fame eventually did come to him.

Bruckner was born in 1824 in Ansfelden, Austria, to musical parents. By the age of ten, Anton was sufficiently proficient at the organ to substitute for his father at church services. He was thirteen when his father died, and although Anton was the eldest child, his mother did not want him to bear the burden of family support. Enrolled as a chorister at the St. Florian monastery, Anton was educated there for

PERHAPS THE MOST INFLUENTIAL COMPOSER IN THE HISTORY OF CZECHOSLOVAKIAN MUSIC, BEDRICH SMETANA IS BEST REMEMBERED FOR THE SYMPHONIC POEM CYCLE *MY COUNTRY*, AN ODE TO HIS HOMELAND.

The Romantic Era

three years. His devotion to the institution that gave him his education was steadfast, and the composer would return there later in life.

In time Bruckner decided on a career as a schoolmaster and took teacher training in Linz. There, in the capital of Upper Austria, the young man was exposed to finer music than he had ever experienced. In spite of that, he accepted assignment as an assistant schoolmaster in Windhaag, a post that carried with it menial farm chores and little money. After a while, Michael Arneth, prior at St. Florian's and Bruckner's mentor, had him reassigned to a better teaching position in Kronstorf. When Bruckner was twenty-one years old, he was moved into the position of first assistant teacher at St. Florian's, where he remained for ten years, becoming organist at the monastery. This was the point at which he turned away from teaching and turned toward composing.

Bruckner was an outstanding organist, but he composed very little for the instrument. Improvisation was his forte at the organ. He received great acclaim as an organist and was invited to various European capitals to perform on the very finest organs.

During his time in Linz, Bruckner was employed as organist at the Linz Cathedral. Seeking further education, Bruckner engaged in a correspondence course through the Vienna Conservatory. After earning his diploma as a counterpoint and harmony instructor, he went on to further study in symphonic structure and orchestration. During his thirteen years with the cathedral, Bruckner was also conductor of the Liedertafel Frohsinn choral society; in this position he led the first performance of the closing passages of Richard Wagner's *Die Meistersinger*, two months prior to the opera's premiere. This involvement had the blessing of Wagner, whom Bruckner revered. They had met in Munich in 1864, at the first performance of Wagner's *Tristan und Isolde*. Wagner was apparently impressed by Bruckner, especially with his

Symphony No. 3, which Bruckner dedicated to the elder composer, calling it the "Wagner Symphony." In that gesture, Bruckner, who was struggling to have his symphonies accepted, did himself a disservice because there was vociferous conflict at the time between the followers of Johannes Brahms and the fans of Wagner. The sad tale is often told of Bruckner conducting the premiere of his Symphony No. 3 and being unaware of the audience members walking out in mid-performance; when Bruckner turned to the audience after the final movement, there were a mere dozen of his supporters present. Eduard Hanslick, a contemporary influential critic, was anti-Wagner and so became anti-Bruckner. When Bruckner applied for a position at the Vienna Conservatory, Hanslick, dean of the music faculty, protested. Hanslick was overruled, and in 1875 Bruckner received an honorary appointment; two years later he became a salaried employee.

Bruckner's music met with much criticism. "Wild," "nonsense," and "unplayable" were adjectives used to describe his symphonies. Well-meaning friends took it upon themselves to temper his music for presentation, and the ever-humble Bruckner felt helpless to intervene.

Bruckner was sixty years old before he enjoyed success, whereas now he is considered one of the "Magnificent Seven" Viennese symphonists—the others being Haydn, Mozart, Beethoven, Schubert, Brahms, and Mahler. Bruckner composed some well-regarded religious choral music, but he is best known for his nine well-known symphonies. (He actually wrote eleven symphonies, but he did not number the first two, and they are rarely performed.) No. 7 is considered by some aficionados as Bruckner's masterpiece, whereas No. 4 ("Romantic") and No. 8 are Bruckner's most popular. The ninth was left unfinished when the composer died, and conductors have occasionally used his choral Te Deum as a fourth movement.

In his sixties and seventies Bruckner received a number of well-deserved grants, honors, and accolades, and his work came to be performed with increasing frequency. When he died in 1896, his remains were buried beneath the organ at St. Florian's, as he had wished. ♩

JOHANN STRAUSS, JR. (1825–1899)

JOHANN STRAUSS, JR., WAS CALLED THE "WALTZ KING"—IRONIC, SINCE he never learned to dance.

Strauss gained his title in competition with his father, who preceded Johann Jr. as an internationally known violinist, composer, and conductor. The waltz was all the rage in Europe during the nineteenth century, in concert halls and dance halls, and the two Johanns were in the midst of it; so, to a lesser degree, were Johann Sr.'s other sons, Josef and Edouard (see "Other Strausses" sidebar, page 89).

Johann Sr. (1804–1849) was certainly used to competition— his main rival was Joseph Lanner, the first major composer to write waltzes. These two composers were contemporaries who met as violinists in a Vienna orchestra and individually churned out waltzes to satisfy the public demand. Coincidentally, Lanner had a son who also followed in his father's dancesteps.

Although Johann Sr. attempted to discourage his namesake's pursuit of a musical career, the young man persisted. Because of his father's popularity, and not wanting to offend him, managers were hesitant about hiring the son. One was willing to take the risk, however, and engaged Junior at age nineteen to conduct a program of his father's waltzes and some of his own at Dommayer's Café. Johann Jr. was an instant hit.

In fact, the handsome, gallant, and talented younger Strauss became an idol not unlike Frank Sinatra, the Beatles, Elvis Presley, or Michael Jackson in the twentieth century. One story in particular illustrates this popularity: during one concert tour, Strauss's valet was selling swatches of fur snipped from a dog, a black Labrador retriever, as samples of Strauss' dark, shiny hair. When the composer learned of this, he called an immediate halt to the operation.

In 1876 Strauss went to the United States for a concert tour in conjunction with that country's centennial. On all his tours, he was greeted by exuberant audiences consisting of adoring ladies. At receptions and parties, Strauss would demur from dancing. He was reportedly engaged to be married thirteen times; he had three marriages: Henriette (Jetty) Treffz, Angelika (Lili) Dittrich, and Adele Deutsch.

The so-called rivalry between father and son was overblown by outsiders. With the frenzied modishness not only of the waltz, but also of polkas, mazurkas, and quadrilles, there was in fact room for both Strausses. Their

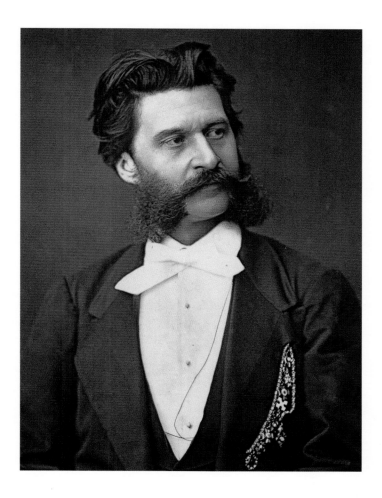

OPPOSITE: ANTON BRUCKNER, SEATED AT HIS PIANO, DID NOT ACHIEVE SUCCESS UNTIL MUCH LATER THAN MANY OF HIS CONTEMPORARIES: HE WAS SIXTY YEARS OLD BEFORE ACCLAIM FOUND HIM. ABOVE: JOHANN STRAUSS, JR., WAS FAMOUS NOT ONLY FOR HIS MUSIC BUT FOR THE WAY HIS POPULARITY MANIFESTED ITSELF; HE WAS SUBJECT TO MOBS OF FANS AND WILD RUMORS, MUCH LIKE THE POP MUSIC STARS OF THE TWENTIETH CENTURY.

The Romantic Era

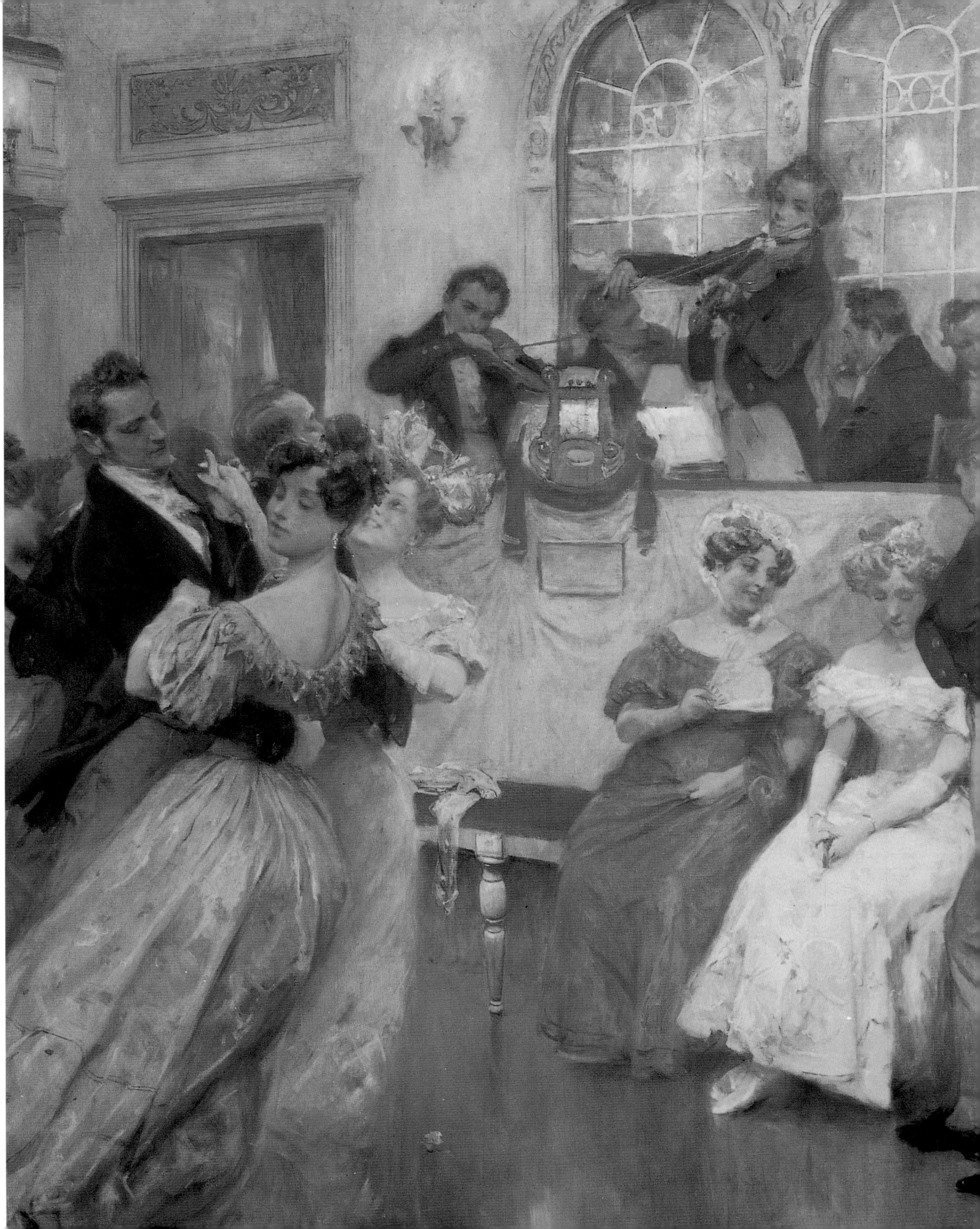

era was a period of political upheaval in Vienna, and the two did come down on different sides of the political fracas. The father's allegiance was with the old order, whereas the son sided with the revolutionaries. Marches were also popular (Papa Strauss, for instance, composed the well-known "Radetzky March"), and both led military bands.

Strauss's compositions were often commissioned by organizations. There was a "Fast Pulse Waltz" for a medical society and a "Jurists' Ball Waltz" for a legal association. For various manufacturers, there were the "Electro-Magnetic Polka" and the "Motors Waltz." Once, when he was late in fulfilling a particular contract, Johann Jr. hurriedly made notations on a restaurant menu—these notes became the "Acceleration Waltz."

Strauss the younger was well into his career before he began composing for the theater. He was led into this field at the suggestion of Jacques Offenbach, the outstanding composer of French operetta. Others urged the same thing and, fortunately, Strauss heeded the advice. His first operetta, although only mildly successful at the time, was *Indigo and the Forty Thieves*, produced in 1871. Although he was particular about his music, Strauss never insisted on having a good libretto. In fact, so many people had a hand in writing *Indigo and the Forty Thieves* that a joke arose around Vienna:

OTHER STRAUSSES

Johann Strauss, Sr., had thirteen children: six with his wife, Anna Streim, and seven with Emilie Trambusch. Johann Jr., Josef, and Eduard's mother was Anna, and all three boys were born in Vienna.

Josef Strauss (1827–1870), brother to Johann Jr., was a reluctant composer, even though his famous sibling said that Josef had superior talent. The title "The First and Last Waltz" suggests that perhaps this composer did not want to write this work at all; apparently, however, he relented, for he wrote a waltz titled "The First After the Last," and in the end there were more than two hundred compositions credited to him. Interestingly, while waltzes were popular as both dance and listening music, his approach to the form was styled more for the concert auditorium than for the dance hall.

Though Josef wrote many fine works, composition was an avocation not a profession—to make money, he worked as an architect and engineer, designing the waterworks in Trumau and working on inventions that included a street-cleaning machine. Josef knew enough about the music business to take over his brother's orchestra when Johann was ill in 1853. Persuaded by the need, he not only conducted the orchestra but also augmented his knowledge of harmony and orchestration and learned to play the violin, a Strauss trademark. With Johann recovered, the two brothers—and subsequently the third, Eduard—shared the responsibilities of the great Strauss Orchestra.

Josef did not enjoy the limelight, for he was a reserved person. His sense of tranquility lapped over into his happy marriage. He and his wife, Karoline, had a daughter, but their time as a family was cut short when Josef died at the age of forty-three.

While Johann Jr. and Josef had a mutually caring relationship, their brother Eduard (1835–1916) was egotistical and antagonistic. He toyed with the idea of going into the diplomatic service, but was lured into music because of family musical tradition. Following his brothers, he became an outstanding violinist and conductor. Although Eduard kept up with Johann and Josef in those capacities, he lagged significantly behind them in composing. He knew it and let his jealousy show.

A good businessman, Eduard arranged for the Strauss Orchestra to be sudivided so that they could accept simultaneous engagements. For more than thirty years, he wielded the baton and brought the famous orchestra to the United States while touring internationally. Josef died in 1870 and Johann in 1899, and Eduard maintained the Strauss Orchestra until 1901.

this play was written by forty librettists, they said. The two most popular of Strauss's fourteen known operettas were, and are, *Die Fledermaus* (1874) and *The Gypsy Baron* (1885). The charming quality of *Die Fledermaus* even led to its translation for the Broadway stage.

Perhaps Strauss's best-known compostion is "The Blue Danube," which was written for the Vienna Men's Choral Society; the title was derived from the last line of a poem by Karl Isidor Beck. Considering its later phenomenal success, the response to this waltz's 1867 premiere was rather tepid. In time the text was revised and "The Blue Danube" gradually caught on. Apparently, this work had the respect of critics and other composers, as well as of the general public. Critic Edward Hanslick said to Strauss, "Your melody has become a quotation." When composer Johannes Brahms was asked by Strauss's wife, Adele, to autograph her fan, he complied by writing a few bars of "The Blue Danube" and the notation "unfortunately not by Johannes Brahms."

On June 3, 1899, a concert of Strauss's works was held in Vienna. Strauss was not there, and the public knew that this was because their idol was ill. Suddenly, during the playing of "The Blue Danube," the orchestra was stopped. Without an announcement, the audience knew that Johann Strauss, Jr., had died. ♩

JOHANNES BRAHMS (1833-1897)

JOHANNES BRAHMS' PERSONALITY WAS NOTHING LIKE THE FREE-FLOWing, sensitive-yet-dynamic music he composed—he was brusque, tightfisted, ornery, and rude—but friends apparently overlooked his faults and accepted him on his merits. Among his peers, Johannes Brahms was one of the best-loved composers of his time.

Musically, Brahms's merits were many. He composed in all forms except opera with rarely a flop. It was not, however, his own writing but Robert Schumann's that certified the young German as the bright light on the musical horizon. Schumann wrote an article, "Neue Bahnen" ("New Paths"), published in *Neue Zeitschrift für Musik* ("The New Music Journal"), the newspaper he had founded, in which he

extolled Brahms. Already a highly regarded composer, Schumann first encountered Brahms in 1853 via a letter of introduction from Hungarian violin virtuoso and conductor Joseph Joachim (1831–1907). At the time of the meeting, the twenty-year-old Brahms was on tour as piano accompanist to violinist Eduard Remenyi. Within a few months of the newspaper story by the respected Schumann, Brahms was able to have three piano sonatas accepted and published.

Brahms had had some piano lessons during his childhood in Hamburg, where he was born in 1833. His family was not poverty-stricken, but neither were they well off, and his earliest music lessons were given him by his father, who played bass in theater orchestras and eventually became a member of the Hamburg Philharmonic. Young Brahms's academic education was negligible, and he earned his keep playing piano in taverns around the city's docks.

Brahms's relationship with Schumann and his wife, Clara, an exceptional piano artist, went well beyond the professional level—according to legend, the three were the closest of friends. For some time about a year after meeting each other and for two years prior to his death, Schumann was in an insane asylum, and Brahms's attention to Clara was steadfast. After Schumann died in 1856, Brahms's concern for Clara endured. She died forty years later, and Brahms died the following year, in 1897. Whispers of a love affair between Clara and Brahms persist to this day.

The year after Schumann died, Brahms accepted the position of music director and teacher in the court of Prince Lippe-Detmold, but his duties were minimal enough to allow him to freelance. Brahms went from city to city teaching, composing, and conducting. With the artistic and financial success of *Eine Deutsches Requiem* ("A German Requiem") in 1868 at the Bremen Cathedral, Brahms gave up teaching. Among his compositions after the requiem was the 1870 work *Triumphlied,* which paraphrased the Bible's Book of Revelation.

As Brahms's fame grew, he was hailed as successor to Beethoven for his prowess as a composer; this accomplishment was all the more impressive because it occurred with the simultaneous popularity of Wagner. During his career, Beethoven had written nine symphonies; when Brahms' Symphony No. 1 premiered, the eminent conductor Hans von Bülow referred to it as the "Tenth"—as if one champion (Brahms) had taken over for another (Beethoven).

Brahms was forty-three years old when Symphony No. 1 came before the public; there were reports that he had written it much earlier but had been hesitant to bring it forth. Brahms's four symphonies are quite distinctive; the critic W. J. Henderson (1855–1937) differentiated them with specific descriptive words: No. 1—grandeur, No. 2—charm, No. 3—magisterial, and No. 4—melancholy.

Cambridge University wanted to confer an honorary doctor of music degree on Brahms, but he was concerned about seasickness and refused to make the journey across the English Channel to receive the award. He did, however, accept an honorary doctor of philosophy degree from the University of Breslau, and in response composed the *Academic Festival Overture* in 1880. A popular composition, this overture uses familiar themes of German student songs. The same year, Brahms wrote his *Tragic Overture*. *The Hungarian Dances* is also a popular concert piece; originally written for piano(s) and four hands, this composition later evolved into a piece for piano and violin and then into a work for full orchestra.

A leader in lied, Brahms wrote approximately two hundred songs. "Serenade" is a misleading word with this composer, for the two that Brahms wrote-No. 1 in D and No. 2 in A Major-are not simple songs, but monumental orchestral works. Among his concertos is a unique piece for cello and violin that has been tagged the "Double Concerto"; this was Brahms's last orchestral work. At the Double Concerto's 1887 world premiere in Cologne, Brahms conducted, the cello soloist was Robert Hausmann, and the violin soloist was Joseph Joachim. When the concerto was published, Brahms presented the score to Joachim with the inscription "To him for whom it was written"; this was a tribute to the musician-who, in introducing the newcomer to Schumann years earlier, had first perceived the greatness of Brahms and had been instrumental in his success. ♩

THE THIRD OF THE SO-CALLED THREE B'S, AFTER BACH AND BEETHOVEN, JOHANNES BRAHMS BEGAN HIS MUSICAL CAREER PLAYING PIANO IN TAVERNS AND RESTAURANTS, NOT, AS SOME HAVE SUGGESTED, IN BROTHELS.

CAMILLË SAINT-SAËNS (1835–1921)

WHILE HE FORBID ITS PERFORMANCE IN ITS ENTIRETY DURING HIS LIFE-time, Camillë Saint-Saëns's *Carnival of the Animals* has become one of the Frenchman's most popular compositions. He silenced this work, except for the segment "The Swan," because he had written it as a sort of musical joke and apparently regarded it as below his dignity. The cuckoo, elephants, and kangaroos had to wait to be heard until Saint-Saëns died in 1921.

Camillë Saint-Saëns was born in Paris in 1835. His father died a few months later, and the boy was raised by his doting mother and her aunt, Charlotte Masson, who gave the toddler his first piano lessons. Like many of history's great composers, Saint-Saëns was a prodigy. He performed in public a number of times before his tenth year, but it was not until 1845 that he made his formal debut—playing Mozart and Beethoven at Paris' Salle Pleyel.

Saint-Saëns was not only a virtuoso pianist, but also one of the most praised organists of his time. Franz Liszt dubbed Saint-Saëns the greatest organist in the world. His studies at the Paris Conservatory, which he entered at the age of thirteen, included organ, and in his late teens Saint-Saëns served as organist for two Paris churches. From 1857 to 1876, he was organist at the Madeleine, one of the city's most prestigious churches.

The only teaching he did was at the Ecole Niedermeyer, a school dedi-cated to improving the level of church music. His pupils included André Messager and Gabriel Fauré (1845–1924), both of whom would go on to become well-known organists, directors, and composers.

Fauré was more than a prize student—he was a protégé of Saint-Saëns and a friend. Fauré, his wife, and children filled a void for Saint-Saëns, who had lost his own young sons. In 1880, Saint-Saëns married a woman twenty years his junior and they had two sons. When very young, both boys died within six weeks of each other. Saint-Saëns withdrew from the marriage via a legal separation, and he and his wife never saw each other again. As a welcome visitor to Fauré's home, Saint-Saëns assumed the "favorite uncle" role.

At a time when German classics were prominent on concert programs in France, it was a boon to French composers to have the support of the Société Nationale de Musique, which was founded in 1871 by Saint-Saëns and Romain Bussine, professor of singing at the Paris Conservatory. The original governing committee included composers Alexis de Castillon, César Franck (see page 82), Edouard Lalo, and Fauré. They and other French composers had the advantage of often having their works premiered by the Société Nationale. Saint-Saëns wrote in almost every musical form: five symphonies, thirteen operas, ten concertos, oratorios, chamber music, more than one hundred songs, and the first film music by an established composer. Saint-Saëns did much to popularize the descriptive orchestral compositions known as symphonic poems, of which he wrote four, among them the celebrated *Danse Macabre*. He also wrote poems, books, articles, and plays.

Saëns par Fauré

Of his thirteen operas, only one remains in the popular repertoire: *Samson et Delilah*. A premiere was hard to arrange because managers felt that the biblical theme was risky. Through the efforts of Liszt, *Samson et Delilah* was first heard at Weimar in 1877; it did not come to the Paris Opéra until 1891.

Saint-Saëns was idolized in England and the United States long after his popularity in his native land began to wane. Two visits were made to America, and he often went to Great Britain, where he was made Commander of the Victorian Order in gratitude for the march he composed for the coronation of Edward VII.

Saint-Saëns was an avid traveler, and he would often arrange concert tours to coincide with an anticipated eruption of Mount Etna or a solar eclipse somewhere in the world. He enjoyed Africa—his Piano Concerto No. 5 is known as the "Egyptian"—and he traveled to Uruguay and wrote a national anthem for that South American country. One of his favorite places was Algeria, for which he wrote his *Suite Algérienne* in 1880. Forty-one years later, when he was eighty-six, he died suddenly while in Algiers. ❧

OPPOSITE: WHEN CAMILLË SAINT-SAËNS WAS ONLY EIGHTEEN YEARS OLD, HE RECEIVED A LETTER FROM FELLOW COMPOSER CHARLES GOUNOD THAT WARNED HIM OF THE "OBLIGATION OF BECOMING A GREAT MASTER." BELOW: PRODUCERS WERE RELUCTANT TO PRESENT *SAMSON AND DELILAH* WHEN IT WAS FIRST WRITTEN BECAUSE THEY WERE FEARFUL THAT THE BIBLICAL THEME WOULDN'T BE COMMERCIALLY VIABLE; HOWEVER, IT WAS PRODUCED SUCCESSFULLY AND REMAINS A PART OF MODERN OPERA COMPANIES' REPERTOIRE.

The Romantic Era

LÉO DELIBES
(1836-1891)

SPARKLING THOUGH THE MUSIC OF *COPPÉLIA* IS, A SHADOW FELL OVER Léo Delibes's highly acclaimed ballet within months after its world premiere on May 25, 1870. The Franco-Prussian War forced the closing of the Paris Opéra, where *Coppélia* had first been enthusiastically applauded by an ardent audience that included Napoleon III (1808–1873) and Empress Eugènie. Within a year, the first man to dance the Coppelius role, Francois Dauty, died, and the leading ballerina, seventeen-year-old Giuseppina Bozzachi, succumbed to smallpox; furthermore, the choreographer of *Coppélia*, the renowned Arthur Saint-Léon, suffered a fatal heart attack.

When *Coppélia* premiered, Delibes was thirty-four years old. He was also not the only successful and popular composer working that year— Tchaikovsky released his *Romeo and Juliet Overture* and Richard Wagner the second of his Ring operas, *Die Walküre*.

Four years earlier, while serving as organist at the Church of St. Jean et St. François, a post he held for approximately ten years, Delibes had collaborated with Ludwig Minkus on the ballet *La Source*. Perhaps Delibes's affinity for ballet was sparked at the Paris Conservatory, where in his teens he had studied with Adolphe Adam, composer of the ballet *Giselle*. And this affinity was strong—despite the tragedies following the premiere of *Coppélia*, Delibes scored again in 1876 with *Sylvia*.

After his student days, Delibes was employed as an accompanist at the Théâtre Lyrique in Paris, where he worked in a high-level operatic atmosphere that included premieres of Gounod's *Faust*, Bizet's *Les Pêcheurs de Perles* ("The Pearl Fishers"), and Berlioz's *Les Troyens* ("The Trojans").

He first stage work to be produced, when he was just nineteen, was the operetta *Deux Sous de Charbon*. From then on, for more than a decade, Delibes had an operetta produced almost every year. This meshed into his most notable success as a ballet composer.

Delibes's career in ballet somewhat overlapped his years composing opera. In 1873 his *Le Roi l'a Dit* ("The King Said So") was produced by the Opéra-Comique. There followed *Jean de Nivelle* in 1880 and *Lakmé*, Delibes's best-known opera, in 1883. Around this time, Delibes returned to the Paris Conservatory as a professor of composition. Delibes's opera *Kassya*, which was left unfinished at the time of the composer's death, was orchestrated posthumously by Jules Massenet.

Lakmé remains Delibes's operatic masterpiece, and he reportedly had soprano Marie Van Zandt (1858–1919) in mind when he composed the piece. Van Zandt, an American by birth, sang in both the world premiere at the Opéra-Comique in Paris and the 1892 Metropolitan Opera premiere of *Lakmé*. ₰

A MASTER OF THE ROMANTIC TECHNIQUE OF COMPOSITION, LÉO DELIBES WROTE NUMEROUS OPERAS, INCLUDING *SYLVIA, OR THE NYMPH OF DIANE* (RIGHT), CULMINATING IN HIS TRIUMPHANT OPERATIC MASTERPIECE, *LAKMÉ*, A LYRIC EVOCATION OF INDIA.

GEORGES BIZET
(1838–1875)

He never knew what a success *Carmen*—one of the greatest operas ever written—would be, for Georges Bizet died exactly three months after the world premiere.

Bizet did not succumb, according to some melodramatic tales, to a broken heart because *Carmen* was not well received at its 1875 premiere; he died because his heart was diseased. Certainly, overwork from the preparation of *Carmen* may have accentuated his physical problem, for he kept fine-tuning his score throughout the rehearsal period— *Carmen*'s opening aria, for instance, known as the "Habanera," was rewritten by Bizet thirteen times for Celestine Galli-Marie, whom he personally had selected to play the dazzling gypsy woman in the premiere.

If multiple performances are any indication of success, then *Carmen* did not strictly fail when it was introduced at the Opéra-Comique in Paris, for it was given thirty-seven performances that season. (And that number resonates: Bizet died just short of his thirty-seventh birthday.) But its sensuous story, founded on a novella written by Prosper Mérimée (1803–1870) in 1845, offended the public and the critics. And that was not the only criticism—another complaint was that Bizet's opera sounded too "Wagnerian," particularly in the use of leitmotifs (repeated themes used to identify characters or situations); Bizet was a follower of Richard Wagner at a time when the German composer was not in favor in France.

Other composers—namely Fromental Halévy (1799–1862), composer of *La Juive*, and Charles Gounod (1818–1893), composer of *Faust*—also had an influence on Bizet's career. Bizet was only nine years old when he was accepted into the Paris Conservatory; the institute had to break the rules, for he was officially too young to enroll. His musical ability was encouraged, even pushed, by his parents; his father was a singing teacher and his mother a pianist. By the time he was in his late teens, Bizet had won the Conservatory's Prix de Rome, which enabled him to study for three years in Italy, and had composed his Symphony in C Major.

The Symphony did not premiere, however, until 1935, sixty years after Bizet died. Bizet's widow—Genevieve Halévy, with whose father Bizet had studied at the Conservatory—strangely refused performance of the Symphony during her lifetime; she died in 1926. Discovered in the library of the Paris Conservatory, the manuscript was brought forth and the Symphony had its world premiere in Basel, Switzerland.

Bizet's most popular orchestral work is *L'Arlésienne* ("The Girl from Arles"), which appeared in 1872 and earned Bizet his first acclaim as a composer. Initially written to accompany a play by Alphonse Daudet (1840–1897), it has become an oft-performed concert selection.

Opera was Bizet's primary output; he had six operas published and eight destroyed or left incomplete. *Les Pêcheurs de Perles* ("The Pearl Fishers") is Bizet's second best-known opera, following *Carmen*; this work premiered in 1863, and its popularity has grown through the years. His other four published operas are *Le Docteur Miracle* ("The Miracle Doctor," 1857), which won Bizet first prize in a competition sponsored by composer Jacques Offenbach, *Ivan IV* (1865), *La Jolie Fille de Perth* ("The Fair Maid of Perth," 1867), and

Djamileh (1872). Inasmuch as great success did not surround these operas, to supplement his income Bizet worked as an arranger, teacher, and accompanist.

Eight years after the world premiere of *Carmen*—eight years after the composer died—Bizet's masterpiece was again presented at the Opéra-Comique. As before, the leading lady was Celestine Galli-Marie. Certain revisions had been made, the most prominent of which were the recitatives composed by Bizet's colleague Ernest Guiraud to replace the spoken dialogue which had not set well in the original production. From that point on, *Carmen* has remained in the top echelon of opera. Musicologist Henry Simon has said, rightly or wrongly, that the reason *Carmen* has become more acceptable is that these days we have "hardier moral stomachs." ♫

GEORGES BIZET (ABOVE) BEGAN HIS OPERATIC CAREER IN 1857 WITH A CONTEST PIECE CALLED *THE MIRACLE DOCTOR*; TODAY HE IS CELEBRATED FOR HIS MASTERWORK, *CARMEN* (OPPOSITE), WHICH WAS FIRST PRODUCED AT THE OPÉRA-COMIQUE IN PARIS IN 1875.

PYOTR ILYICH (1840–1893) TCHAIKOVSKY

IF YOU GO TO THE CONCERT HALL AND HEAR TCHAIKOVSKY'S FOURTH, Fifth, or Sixth Symphony, you will leave the place humming a melody. The same holds true if you attend the ballet for a performance of *Swan Lake* or *The Nutcracker*, if you go to the opera house to see *Eugene Onegin*, or if you join the throngs at an outdoor concert and listen to the *1812 Overture*. If you want melody, Pyotr Ilyich Tchaikovsky is your man.

All this melody and much more welled up in a person who was a nervous hypochondriac, suicidal, self-incriminating, and irritable much of the time. Tchaikovsky's problems were not due to a stark, struggling childhood. He was born in 1840, one of six children in an upper middle-class family in Kamsko-Votinsk, Russia, where the father was a mining inspector in the Ural Mountains. Unlike the many prodigies in the ranks of composers—Mozart, Schubert, and Mendelssohn among them—Tchaikovsky did not contemplate serious study of music until he was twenty-one years old. Trained for the legal profession, he was working as a government law clerk when his interest veered. He was accepted at a newly opened musical institute, the forerunner of the St. Petersburg Conservatory. After graduating, Tchaikovsky put his education to use by teaching harmony at the conservatory in Moscow and his talent into gear by composing.

Tchaikovsky's orchestral fantasy *Romeo and Juliet*, written when he was thirty years old, was the composer's first popu-

lar success. In the years immediately preceding, Tchaikovsky entered into a quasi-romantic relationship with Nadejda von Meck, a weathy middle-aged widow. He was experiencing financial difficulties at the time, and she substantially subsidized him between 1876 and 1890. Why the relationship was abruptly terminated, at her instigation, has been left to speculation: it may have been that she was embarrassed by the arrangement, she became bored, she was ill, or she had a family problem. Also odd was that, although the two exchanged more than a thousand letters, by mutual consent von Meck and Tchaikovsky never met.

Tchaikovsky's Symphony No. 4 was dedicated to von Meck. All of the six symphonies he composed were well received, but the Fourth, Fifth, and Sixth have remained the most popular. He wrote ten operas, two of which remain in the standard repertory: *Eugene Onegin*, which was based on Aleksandr Pushkin's poem of the same name and premiered in 1879, and *Pique Dame* ("The Queen of Spades"), which was first performed in 1890 (the story of *Pique Dame* is also attributed to Pushkin, but its libretto is by Tchaikovsky's brother, Modest).

Melodrama of the sort found in opera stalked Tchaikovsky's personal life. During his relationship with von Meck, he wed one of his former students, Antonia Miliukova; this marriage lasted only nine weeks. Why he married at all is another mystery in the saga of Tchaikovsky's life; some historians have speculated that it was to cover up his homosexuality. Distraught over the whole situation, Tchaikovsky tried to commit suicide in a river but was rescued. He quickly embarked on a European tour, supposedly for his health, and never returned to his wife.

This melodrama was continued in his death. In October of 1893 Tchaikovsky conducted the world premiere of his Symphony No. 6; less than two weeks later he was dead. It is understood that he died of cholera contracted from drinking unboiled water. The symphony's subtitle is "Pathétique," and while its last strains are quite sad, it would be too melodramatic to say that Tchaikovsky had had a premonition of his death. His own words, in fact, would indicate otherwise: "I have never felt such satisfaction, such pride, such happiness as in the knowledge that I myself am truly the creator of this beautiful work."

Of course, not all was doom and gloom in Tchaikovsky's fifty-three years. One of the brightest spots for him had to be conducting at the grand opening of New York's Carnegie Hall on May 5, 1891. Known then as the Music Hall, the prestigious concert space was renamed Carnegie Hall for its benefactor, Andrew Carnegie, in 1894. Tchaikovsky shared conducting honors that night with renowned conductor-musician Walter Damrosch (1862–1950); Tchaikovsky led the New York Symphony Society in his *Marche Solennelle*. Actually, Tchaikovsky participated in four concerts during the opening week celebration; in the end his visit to the United States lasted for four months, with conducting engagements in Philadelphia and Baltimore as well as New York.

Tchaikovsky was not in the United States, however, in 1875, when his Piano Concerto in B-Flat Minor had its world premiere in Boston. This composition was an instant success. The soloist was Hans von Bülow, to whom Tchaikovsky dedicated the concerto in appreciation for Bülow's frequently performing the Russian composer's piano works in Europe.

Toward the end of Tchaikovsky's career, he wrote *The Nutcracker*, his third ballet (*Swan Lake* and *The Sleeping Beauty* were the first two). *The Nutcracker*, based on a fairy tale by the German writer, illustrator, and composer E.T.A. Hoffmann, was composed for the Imperial Ballet in St. Petersburg. It is a prime example of Tchaiovsky's mastery of melody.

PERHAPS THE MOST FAMOUS RUSSIAN COMPOSER WHO EVER LIVED, PYOTR ILYICH TCHAIKOVSKY (OPPOSITE) COMPLETED HIS MOST SUCCESSFUL OPERA, *EUGENE ONEGIN* (LIBRETTO TITLE PAGE ABOVE), BASED ON A POEM BY PUSHKIN, IN 1878.

ANTONIN DVOŘÁK
(1841–1904)

"A Czechoslovakian in Spillville" may sound like an absurd title, but it would aptly describe Antonín Dvořák's summer sojourn during his years in the United States.

When Dvořák's secretary, Josef Kovarik, suggested a holiday in his Iowa childhood hometown of Spillville (named for its settler, Joseph Spielman), the composer welcomed the opportunity to see more of the United States. In Spillville's Riverside Park there is a monument to Dvořák commemorating his 1893 visit to the community. During his summer residency, he composed his String Quartet in F and String Quintet in E-Flat, both known as "The American." While on this holiday, Dvořák also visited Omaha, St. Paul, Buffalo, Niagara Falls, and Chicago, where he conducted a concert of his works during the Columbian Exposition.

Dvořák had come to America as the director of the National Conservatory of Music (a post he held from the autumn of 1892 through the spring of 1895) at the behest of its primary founder, Jeannette Thurber, the wife of a wealthy food wholesaler. Thurber had studied at the Paris Conservatory, and apparently this experience had triggered the idea of creating a similar institution in New York. Located on East 17th Street off Irving Place—in the vicinity of what was New York's cultural center in the mid- to late-1800s—the conservatory was near the Third Avenue elevated railway, which delighted Dvořák, who was a train enthusiast. Per Thurber's request, Dvořák arrived with a new composition, Te Deum, which he conducted, a month after his arrival, in New York's Music Hall (renamed Carnegie Hall, for its benefactor, Andrew Carnegie, in 1894).

It has been suggested that Thurber had a secondary purpose in having Dvořák come, namely to have him write an opera based on The Song of Hiawatha, by the American poet Henry Wadsworth Longfellow (1807–1882). Dvořák never wrote this opera, but many listeners believe that the symphony "From the New World" does have remote suggestions of American Indian themes. Other analysts, however, say that the symphony contains more hints of African-American themes than of Native-American ones. This makes sense, as

the conservatory was wide open to black pupils and Dvořák was exposed to a great deal of black musical literature—that is, spirituals—from student Harry T. Burleigh (1866–1949), who later became a noted baritone singer, as well as a noteworthy composer and arranger. Proposing that the piece could not contain Native-American themes, however, would be foolish, for Dvořák did see Indians perform tribal dances as they passed through Spillville and Jeannette Thurber did take him to Buffalo Bill's Wild West Show in New York.

Native-American and black aside, some critics think the strongest musical influence in "From the New World" is Dvořák's Czech roots. Dvořák originally labeled "From the New World" Symphony No. 9, but later disregarded the earlier ones and renumbered "New World" as No. 5. Appropriately, it had its December 16, 1893, premiere at the New World's Music Hall in New York.

Dvořák is considered, along with Leos Janácek and Bedrich Smetana, uppermost in the nationalist movement in Czech music. He was born near Kralupy in 1841 and had an unremarkable childhood. Following the family tradition, Antonín was trained as a butcher. This did not sit well with him, however, and, after much argument, he convinced his father to allow him to pursue music. From 1857 to 1859 he attended a church music school in Prague, where he became proficient on the viola; after graduation, he easily gained employment in various orchestras, spending seven years (1866–1873) as principal violist in the orchestra of the Prague National Theatre. During this time, Dvořák also composed a great deal. He entered fifteen compositions in the 1874

Austrian State Stipendium, for which one of the judges was Johannes Brahms, who became a lifelong friend and adviser. Brahms steered Dvořák to a publisher, which aided considerably in making his compositions known to the world.

A family man, Dvořák married in 1873 and had six children, who shared the Spillville summer with their father and mother. The loss of three other children seems to have inspired the writing of his *Stabat Mater*, a form of thirteenth-century Roman Catholic liturgy and a text used by numerous other composers. Following the successful performance of the *Stabat Mater* in London, the London Philharmonic Society invited Dvořák to come and conduct concerts of his own music. He accepted, and the subsequent trip was his first journey outside his homeland. Successful in London, Dvořák was invited to compose choral works for the Birmingham and Leeds festivals (*The Spectre's Bride* and *St. Ludmilla*, respectively). When Dvořák achieved the milestone of his one-hundredth opus, the Violin Sonatina, in 1894, he dedicated it to his children.

His foray into opera started with *Alfred*, written when Dvořák was not quite thirty years old. In his later years, the bulk of his compositions were operas. Some of these works were comic, such as *The King and the Collier*, and others were in a serious vein, like *Dimitrij*. During the first performance of his last opera, *Armida*, which did not turn out to be a success, Dvořák was stricken with pain and unable to stay through the finale; five weeks later, on May 1, 1904, the composer died. Dvořák's best-known opera is probably *Rusalka*, which was based on *The Little Mermaid*, by the Danish writer Hans Christian Andersen (1805–1875), and *Undine*, by the German author Heinrich Fouqué (1777–1843). *Rusalka* had a successful premiere in 1901 at Prague's National Theatre, which presented a cycle of Dvořák's operas to celebrate his sixtieth birthday (Dvořák was at that time director of the Prague Conservatory). ♪

OPPOSITE: ANTONÍN DVOŘÁK, WHO WAS A METICULOUS CRAFTSMEN WITH A MOST ECLECTIC MUSICAL STYLE, IS PERHAPS BEST REMEMBERED FOR THE INCORPORATION OF FOLK MUSIC INTO HIS CLASSICAL PIECES, SPECIFICALLY THE SLAVONIC DANCES. ABOVE: WITH SIR WILLIAM S. GILBERT AS LIBRETTIST, SIR ARTHUR SULLIVAN WROTE ELEVEN INNOVATIVE OPERETTAS.

SIR ARTHUR SULLIVAN (1842–1900)

QUEEN VICTORIA SAID, "YOU OUGHT TO WRITE A GRAND OPERA, SIR Arthur, you would do it so well." Knighted by the queen in 1883, Arthur Sullivan was one of Victoria's favorites, but she was quite wrong in her predictions about his success with grand opera. The only opera Sullivan wrote, *Ivanhoe*, was a dismal failure. A disappointment to its composer, it was also a letdown for the Royal English Opera Company, inasmuch as *Ivanhoe* was their initial production.

Sullivan achieved eminent success, however, with light opera, or operetta, expressly the ones he wrote with lyricist Sir William Schwenk Gilbert (see sidebar, page 103), which are unique unto themselves because of their unprecedented style. Gilbert and Sullivan worked together from 1875 to 1889, producing eleven operettas in that time; after a hiatus, they reunited to write two more works (in 1893 and 1896).

Prior to their partnership, Sullivan was already a prolific composer of sacred music, although his theatrical bent was

evident at age twenty when he wrote incidental music for a Crystal Palace production of Shakespeare's *The Tempest*. (He later did the same for other Shakespeare plays.)

Sullivan grew up in a musical environment—his father was an army bandmaster and clarinet professor at the Royal Military School of Music. Musical study for Arthur, born in 1842 in London, took a leap when, at fourteen, he was awarded the first Mendelssohn Scholarship at the Royal Academy of Music, which included attendance at the Leipzig Conservatory for further instruction in composition, conducting, and piano.

"Onward, Christian Soldiers" is probably the best known of Sullivan's sacred music; the words are by Sabine Baring-Gould. Other published hymns by Sullivan include "Angel Voices, Ever Singing," "Draw Thou My Soul, O Christ," and "Come, Ye Faithful, Raise the Strain." Sullivan's oratorios include *The Prodigal Son*, which premiered at the Worcester Festival in 1869; *Light of the World*, which was performed at the Birmingham Festival of 1873; and *The Martyr of Antioch*, which was written for the 1880 Leeds Festival. Sullivan also wrote a sacred overture, *In Memoriam*, when his father died. Later, when his brother Frederic, a gifted singer and actor, died at the age of thirty-nine, Sullivan wrote the song "The Lost Chord."

According to English music critic and editor Eric Blom (1888–1959), the music of Franz Schubert (see Chapter 3, page 55) held sway over some of Sullivan's writing. Certainly

LEFT: ONE OF THE UNIVERSAL FAVORITES AMONG THE WORKS OF GILBERT AND SULLIVAN IS THE VERY HUMOROUS *THE MIKADO*. INSET: *H.M.S. PINAFORE* OPENED IN LONDON ON MAY 25, 1878, AND WENT ON TO RUN FOR 700 CONSECUTIVE PERFORMANCES.

Sullivan had a keen interest in Schubert. Sir George Grove (1820–1900), editor-in-chief of the authoritative music dictionary that carries his name, accompanied Sullivan in 1867 on a search for missing Schubert manuscripts. Their efforts made a marked contribution to musical history: in Vienna they discovered several manuscripts, including *Rosamunde.*

Cox and Box (1867), sometimes considered a Gilbert and Sullivan operetta, actually had its music by Sullivan but its libretto by F. C. Burnand, who later became editor of *Punch* magazine. Sullivan did not meet Gilbert until 1869, when they were introduced while attending the rehearsal of a play by a mutual friend. Aware of their talents, John Hollingshead, founder of the Gaiety Theatre, commissioned them to write *Thespis*, which was produced in 1871. This operetta fizzled, but it was seen by impresario Richard D'Oyly Carte (1844–1901), who saw beyond the failure and four years later fostered Gilbert and Sullivan's collaboration on *Trial by Jury*, produced as part of a triple bill. This one was well received, and Gilbert and Sullivan were on their way to fame and fortune. Success followed success with *The Sorcerer, H.M.S. Pinafore, The Pirates of Penzance, Patience, Iolanthe, Princess Ida, The Mikado, Ruddigore, The Yeomen of the Guard,* and *The Gondoliers.*

In 1890, however, an unfortunate occurrence took place. D'Oyly Carte, who had gained fame along with the duo, decided that the Savoy Theatre, home to the Gilbert and Sullivan operettas since 1882, needed new carpeting. "Fine," Sullivan said, but Gilbert disagreed. They wrangled over the matter, and eventually went to court. By now, the relationship between Sullivan and his partner was strained. Each had been writing separately, and when they joined forces again three years after the court battle, the sparkle in their creativity was gone. Their final operettas, *Utopia Limited* and *The Grand Duke*, were unsuccessful. The D'Oyly Carte Company, which had presented all the Gilbert and Sullivan premieres, continued with revivals until 1982, having endured for 107 years.

Sullivan died in 1900 (Gilbert passed on in 1911), but three years earlier he had the honor of contributing to Queen Victoria's Diamond Jubilee by composing the Festival Te Deum, which was performed at the Chester Festival, and a ballet, *Victoria and Merrie England*, which was presented at the Alhambra Theatre. ♩

SIR WILLIAM SCHENCK GILBERT (1836–1911)

Gilbert without Sullivan, and vice versa, would be unheard of, yet both men also had independent careers. W. S. Gilbert earned a degree from the University of London while endeavoring to obtain a military commission during the Crimean War. Before that happened, the war ended and Gilbert took an assistant clerkship in a British governmental education department. Finding that distasteful after four years, he qualified as a barrister-at-law and worked as a journalist. In the early 1860s, he was on the staff of a periodical called *Fun*; he also contributed to other publications, including *Punch*, was drama critic for the *Illustrated Times* and eventually devoted all his professional self to writing. *Fun* magazine published his famous "Bab Ballads"—Bab was his nickname from childhood—which Gilbert also illustrated; the "Ballads" were also issued as books.

Through various connections, Gilbert became involved in writing for the theater. One of his earliest contributions was an 1866 satire on Gaetano Donizetti's opera *L'Elisir d'amore* ("The Elixir of Love"), which he titled *Dulcamara, or the Little Duck and the Great Quack.* When this work proved successful, he gave similar treatment to several other popular operas but then branched out to writing original texts. Early works included *No Cards, Our Highland Home,* and *Eyes and No Eyes.* His success as a playwright rolled on with such works as *Palace of Truth, The Wicked World,* and *Randall's Thumb,* which was commissioned for the opening of the Court Theatre. Around the time of *Randall's Thumb,* written in 1871, Gilbert had his earliest collaboration with Sullivan (*Thespis, or, the Gods Grown Old*), but the partnership did not blossom until 1875, with *Trial by Jury.* While Gilbert collaborated with Sullivan on thirteen stage productions, he also continued writing nonmusicals.

On the surface, Gilbert was a domineering individual, although friends and close colleagues recalled him in a warmhearted manner. When collaborating, he took over all aspects of production. Considering his potent personality, it is surprising that Gilbert was happily married. Four years after he was knighted in 1907, the librettist had a heart attack while rescuing a woman who thought she was drowning—she lived; he died.

The Romantic Era

JULES MASSENET
(1842-1912)

JULES MASSENET WAS A MARKET-DRIVEN COMPOSER: HE KNEW THE tastes of opera-goers of the late nineteenth century, and he was able to deliver what they ordered.

This Frenchman, born in Montaud in 1842, possessed more than a penchant for pleasing the public, for he was a fine musician. At age eleven Massenet entered the Paris Conservatory, where one of his instructors was Ambroise Thomas (1811–1896), composer of the opera *Mignon*. In 1878 Massenet returned to the conservatory as professor of advanced composition, a position he held for twenty years. One of his pupils was Gustave Charpentier, who would achieve fame for writing the opera *Louise*. While he was a student, the young Massenet supported himself by playing piano at cafes in town and worked as a percussionist at the Paris Opéra. His diligence at his studies was awarded with various prizes, including a Prix de Rome, which gave him the opportunity to travel to Rome.

In 1873, upon his return from Italy, Massenet composed the first of four oratorios, *Marie-Magdeleine*. Aided by the sponsorship of Pauline Viardot, one of the leading sopranos of the day, the work was a reasonable success; less so were Massenet's other oratorios: *Eve, La Vierge* ("The Virgin"), and *La Terre Promisé* ("The Promised Land").

While Massenet is best known for his operas, he also wrote three ballets, more than 250 songs, seven orchestral suites, a fantasy for cello and orchestra, and piano music, including solos, four-handed compositions, and a concerto. He also wrote incidental music for dramas, and one of his earliest successes was music for *Les Erinnyes*, by the French poet Leconte de Lisle (1818–1894). This was written in 1873,

after he served in the National Guard during the Franco-Prussian War. "Elegie," which subsequently became a popular Massenet solo, was derived from *Les Erinnyes*. Incidental music for another play, *Jerusalem* by Georges Rivollet, was Massenet's last composition, written the year he died.

Massenet had a profound sense of drama, and he applied this understanding to opera, establishing himself in that field with *Le Roi de Lahore* ("The King of Lahore") in 1877, followed by *Herodiade* four years later. In the interim, he was elected to the prestigious Académie des Beaux-Arts, the youngest man to be so honored.

Of all his twenty-seven operas, Massenet is best known for *Manon*, his third. *Manon* is one of the most effective of all French operas. The book on which it is based, *Histoire du Chevalier des Grieux et de Manon Lescaut*, by Abbé Prevost d'Exiles, was also translated into a major opera by Giacomo Puccini. *Manon* had its world premiere at the Opéra-Comique in Paris in 1884, when the composer was forty-one years old. A decade later Massenet composed the one-act piece *Le Portrait de Manon*, in which the aging hero, des Grieux, reminisces over his life with Manon. Part of Massenet's expertise was writing for the female voice. Marie Heilbronn played Manon in the world premiere of the opera, but for the Metropolitan Opera premiere in 1895, Massenet coached the American soprano Sybil Sanderson. Massenet was enamored with Sanderson, for whom he wrote two operas: *Esclarmonde*,

ABOVE: JULES MASSENET, THE SECOND-MOST POPULAR FRENCH COMPOSER OF OPERA, AFTER GOUNOD, EXERCISED A PROFOUND INFLUENCE ON THE FORM THROUGH HIS TEACHING AS WELL AS THROUGH HIS MUSIC. OPPOSITE: THE GRANDSON OF A SCOTS EMIGRÉ, THE NORWEGIAN EDVARD GRIEG, WHO OFTEN PERFORMED WITH HIS WIFE, NINA, IS PERHAPS BEST KNOWN FOR THE NATIONALISM OF HIS WORKS.

commissioned for the Paris Exposition of 1889, and *Thais*. Massenet's work was also noteworthy in its use of leitmotifs, themes identifying persons or situations

Of Massenet's other operas, the most familiar are *Werther, Le Cid, La Navarraise,* and *Cendrillon*. After 1900 he seemed to rest on his laurels. Rather than challenge himself, Massenet resorted to repetition of style and manner with few new exciting melodies. Operas including *Le Jongleur de Notre Dame, Thérèse, Cleopatra*, and *Amadis* did not fare well. He was also facing competition from Richard Strauss (see Chapter 7, page 137) and Claude Debussy (see Chapter 6, page 124). However, his dramatic flair brought audiences to see his work and earned him a place in the musical canon. ♩

EDVARD GRIEG
(1843–1907)

EDVARD GRIEG SEEMS A RATHER PARADOXICAL COMPOSER—A MINIMAL- ist who wrote monumental music. Most of what the Norwegian composer wrote were works in which one basic concept is repeated over and over—that is, minimalism—but his famous Piano Concerto in A Minor bursts with themes that are developed throughout the three movements. First heard in 1868, the concerto was revised numerous times by Grieg.

Grieg is considered Norway's foremost composer, but he could have been Scotland's. His great-grandfather, Alexander Greig, emigrated from Scotland to Norway around 1765 and, upon assuming Norwegian nationality around 1779, switched the vowels in his family name, changing it to Grieg.

Born in Bergen in 1843, Edvard showed aptitude as a pianist at an early age. When Edvard was in his early teens, Norwegian violinist Ole Bull (1810–1880) heard the young man play and persuaded Grieg's parents to send their son to the conservatory in Leipzig. Discontent in Leipzig after four years, Grieg returned to Norway and studied with Niels Gade (1817–1890) in Copenhagen. Gade, a Danish composer of chamber music, choral works, and eight symphonies, later became head of the Royal-Danish Music Conservatory. With Gade's encouragement, Grieg wrote his Symphony in C Minor, but upon being impressed by the First Symphony of

his peer Johan Svendsen, Grieg withdrew his symphony from further performances, and it was not heard again until 1981.

At the time Grieg was studying in Copenhagen, he met up with his cousin Nina Hagerup, who was a singer. They had a very special relationship, and were married in 1867. Throughout the years, they would perform joint recitals of songs he composed, and Nina was regarded as a fine inter- preter of her husband's music.

Another compatriot of Grieg's was Rikard Nordraak (1842–1866), com- poser of the Norwegian nation- al anthem, "Ja, vi elsker dette lan- det" ("Yes, We Love This Land"). It was Nordraak who heightened Grieg's awareness of folk music. When Nordraak died, Grieg wrote a funeral march in memory of his fel- low composer.

Grieg opened the Norwegian Academy of Music in 1867. With Svendsen, Grieg shared the direc- torship of the Christiania (now Oslo) Philhar- monic Society and with Nordraak he originated the Euterpe Society for the Promotion of National Scandinavian Music. While Svendsen and Nordraak wrote with nationalistic fervor, Grieg tended to incorporate the spirit of the country in his compositions rather than pointedly employ folk themes.

Despite his recurring respiratory problems, Grieg spent much of his career on tour as pianist and conductor. The last of his tours was to England in 1906, the year before he died. He established a routine in which the autumn and winter

The Romantic Era

were devoted to concert tours and the spring and early summer were dedicated to composing. The late summer was reserved for his walking vacations.

When author Henrik Ibsen completed his drama *Peer Gynt*, he invited Grieg to provide incidental music for the play. The result was Grieg's well-known pictorial music describing the adventures and misadventures of the title character. First performed in 1876, Peer Gynt was a great success for Grieg.

In celebration of the bicentennial of the birth of Norwegian philosopher and playwright Ludvig Holberg (1684–1754), Grieg was commissioned to write a musical tribute, resulting in five movements titled the *Holberg Suite*; Grieg originally created this piece for piano, but subsequently arranged the composition for string orchestra.

From 1885 until his death in 1907, Grieg made his home at Troldhaugen. Grieg was given a state funeral and his cremated remains were placed in a cliff overlooking the fjord at Troldhaugen.

The first Scandinavian composer to be internationally recognized, Grieg, sometimes called the "Chopin of the North," had various honors bestowed upon him. Honorary degrees were conferred by Cambridge and Oxford, and he was given membership in the Swedish Academy and the French Academy. One unique accolade was the creation of a musical play by Robert Wright and George Forrest, who adapted Edvard Grieg's life and music into a successful 1944 Broadway musical appropriately titled *Song of Norway*.

LEOS JANÁCEK
(1854–1928)

LEOS JANÁCEK'S OPERA *THE CUNNING LITTLE VIXEN*, A CHARMING CHILdren's story designed to also be enjoyed by adults, carries a hidden message. In this work, the composer proposes that cuteness in the animal kingdom can be calculating and that this behavior carries over to humankind—but, he says, that is all part of nature's blueprint. Janácek, who proclaimed himself to be an atheist, focused on nature as God.

Philosophical or not, *The Cunning Little Vixen* is a delightful opera based on a nineteenth-century Moravian folk fable that was detailed in nearly two hundred sketches by artist Stanislav Lolek. Cast aside by Lolek, the sketches were inadvertently rescued by a staff member of *People's News* in Brno. Author Rudolf Tesnohlidek was assigned to come up with a story to fit the sketches. Tesnohlidek had had more than his share of lifetime tragedy and so it was surprising that he wrote the sprightly saga of a fox, Vixen Sharp-Ears, and her forest friends. The illustrated stories ran twice a week for almost three months in 1920 in *People's News* and were published as a book the following year. Sensing the operatic possibilities, Janácek went to work on the music and the libretto, faithfully following Tesnohlidek's novel. Janácek was accustomed to writing down musical notations to simulate the sounds he heard in nature. Searching for specifics, the composer had a forester locate a den of foxes for him to observe; this was near Hukvaldy, Czechoslovakia, where Janácek had been born in 1854 and where he continued·to maintain a house. The opera was successfully premiered in Brunn, Bohemia, in 1924. Janácek left instructions that *Vixen's* final scene, an uplifting one, be played at his funeral, and his wish was granted when he died in 1928.

Contrary to *Vixen*, most of Janácek's other eight operas are ponderous and brooding. Janácek's era was a time of verismo—portrayal of realistic, everyday life that had been launched by the Italian composers. Janácek took verismo a step further, exploring his characters' emotional motivations. He manipulated his music so that the singers' performances were more like conversational speech; one result of this approach was that the orchestra carried the little melody that exists in Janácek's music.

This scholarly man had his early musical training in a children's choir, and when he was ten years old he auditioned and was accepted for the monastery choir at Brno. During his several years as a student there, he learned to play the organ and became a fine pianist. Journeying to Prague, Janácek was admitted to the College of Organists and earned a teaching certificate from the State Teachers Training College. In 1882 Janácek organized the College of Organists in Brno, the center of music education in Moravia, and for thirty-seven years was the leading teacher in the city.

The first success for Janácek was *Jenufa*, which continues to be regarded as his best opera. This work sprang from the play *Her Stepdaughter*, by Gabriela Preissova, who was a pioneer in women's liberation. Earlier operas included *Sarka*, which was written in 1887 but not performed until 1925, and *The Beginning of a Romance*, written in 1894. *Jenufa* premiered in 1904 in Brno, where Janácek lived for many years. To be truly successful, *Jenufa* would have to play at Prague's National Theatre, which was Czechoslovakia's leading opera house, but it was another twelve years before *Jenufa* made the grade. Obstacles were put in the way by Karel Kovarovic, artistic director and conductor at the National Theatre, who reportedly did not like Janácek's music; it might be noted that some years earlier, when Janácek had been working as a newspaper critic, the composer had negatively reviewed an opera by Kovarovic. When Janácek finally got the go-ahead

from the National Theatre, it was on the condition that Kovarovic make some revisions in the score.

Janácek was past middle age when success came, but making his mark with *Jenufa* gave the composer renewed energy and enthusiasm, and the last decade of his life represents Janácek's greatest musical accomplishment. There followed in Janácek's opera repertoire *Destiny, The Excursions of Mr. Broucek, Kat'a Kabanova, The Cunning Little Vixen, The Makropoulos Case*, and *From the House of the Dead*, inspired by Fyodor Dostoyevsky's semifictional memoirs of imprisonment in Siberia.

Janácek's unsteady marriage gradually worsened with the death of his two children—Vladimir at the age of two and a half and, much later, Olga at twenty-one. The beautiful Olga resembled the heroine in some of her father's operas. To break a romantic liaison of which Janácek did not approve, Olga was sent to live with relatives in Russia for a while. Afflicted with typhoid fever, she came home to Brno. Janácek composed parts of *Jenufa* near Olga's bedside and dedicated his opera to his daughter, who did not live to hear it publicly performed.

Among Janácek's few nonoperatic works are the *Lachian Dances*; the symphonic poem *Tara Bulba*, about the war between the Poles and the Cossacks; the five-movement *Sinfoniett*, and the Slavonic Mass, also known as the Glagolitic Mass. The title of the latter refers to the old Slavonic alphabet; the words of the mass are in archaic language that, according to Janácek, was meant to convey the aura of the ninth-century Greek apostles Kyrill and Methodius.

Perhaps it was the mass that prompted Janácek to verbalize a sort of credo: "I wanted to portray the faith in the certainty of the nation, not on a religious basis but on a basis of moral strength which takes God for witness." ♪

LEOS JANÁCEK, ONE OF CZECHOSLOVAKIA'S GREATEST COMPOSERS, WORKED IN NUMEROUS DIFFERENT COMPOSITIONAL STYLES, FROM ESTABLISHED ROMANTIC TECHNIQUES AND FORMULAS TO BOLD, DISSONANT COMBINATIONS.

The Romantic Era

SIR EDWARD ELGAR (1857–1934)

IF YOU HAVE GRADUATED HIGH SCHOOL OR COLLEGE, YOU KNOW SIR Edward Elgar's music. His most familiar composition is undoubtedly "Pomp and Circumstance" March No. 1, the theme of which, better known as "The Land of Hope and Glory," has unofficially become the traditional processional at many graduations.

Elgar composed five "Pomp and Circumstance" marches between 1901 and 1907, and Arthur C. Benson contributed the words in 1902 that gave No. 1 a double life as *The Land of Hope and Glory.* Earlier, Elgar had created the Imperial March for the Diamond Jubilee of Queen Victoria; in 1911 he composed *To the Memory of Edward VII* performed at the London Music Festival; and during World War I he wrote a cantata called *The Spirit of England.* These various nationalistic titles convey a mental picture of a classic distinguished British gentleman. Indeed, the adult Elgar did possess such a dignified, proper appearance and demeanor.

His early years were spent quite humbly; he lived with his parents and siblings above his father's music shop in Broadheath in Worcestershire, England. The father, besides being an instrument salesman, was a piano tuner, but young Elgar gravitated to the violin and took lessons from a local teacher. In other aspects of music, he was self-taught. Around the age of sixteen, he gave up his academic schooling and took a job in a solicitor's office to earn room and board while seeking a career in music. This career started with jobs arranging and composing for local orchestras, as well as being conductor and instrumentalist. One job, which lasted about five years, was at the Powick lunatic asylum, where Elgar was bandmaster for an ensemble of attendants in the institution.

The image of the British gentleman was enhanced by Elgar's marriage in 1889 to one of his piano pupils, the daughter of a British army major-general stationed in India. Although marrying Alice Roberts gave Elgar social status, she also became a valued personal critic of his work and a strong supporter of his career. In the interest of his career, the newlyweds moved to London, but when that proved to have no advantage, the couple returned to Worcestershire and settled in Malverne. A baby girl, Carice, their only child, was born in 1890.

National attention came to the forty-two-year-old Elgar in 1899 with his *Variations on an Original Theme* (generally known as the *Enigma Variations*), which had the distinction of being conducted at its London premiere by the eminent Hans Richter. Each of the fourteen variations is descriptive of one of Elgar's friends, to whom the composition is dedicated; the individual titles are the initials of each person. The "enigma" of the title is the hidden melody on which Elgar based the theme.

After Alice died in 1920, Elgar ceased composing, explaining, "I take no more interest in music...the secret of happiness for an artist when he grows old is to have a passion that can take the place of his art. I have discovered the joy that diatoms can give me." With that quote, Elgar offers us another puzzle—diatoms

LEFT: THE EMERGENCE OF SIR EDWARD ELGAR, WHO IS BEST KNOWN FOR "POMP AND CIRCUMSTANCE MARCH NO. 1," AS A MAJOR COMPOSER WAS REMARKABLE CONSIDERING THAT HE HAD VERY LITTLE FORMAL ACADEMIC TRAINING. OPPOSITE: THE ONLY FAMOUS MEMBER OF A FAMILY OF PROFESSIONAL MUSICIANS, GIACOMO PUCCINI IS PROBABLY BEST REMEMBERED FOR HIS OPERA *LA BOHÈME.*

are minute plankton-like algae, but how did they give him joy?—as he did with the hidden melody in his *Enigma Variations*. He continued to record and conduct at concerts, however, but only his own compositions.

For the two decades between the success of the *Enigma Variations* and Alice's death, Elgar composed copiously—he wrote two symphonies; several oratorios, including *The Light of Life* and *The Kingdom*; cantatas; the *Froissart, In the South*, and *Cockaigne* overtures; and several compositions for the violin, on which Elgar was proficient. His masterpiece is considered to be *The Dream of Gerontius*, an oratorio-style work for orchestra, chorus, and soloists, based on a religious poem by Cardinal John Henry Newman (1801–1890). The Church so enjoyed this piece that they created a memorial window in the Worcester Cathedral designed around *The Dream of Gerontius* and dedicated to Elgar. Surprisingly, considering Elgar's nationality and patriotism, this musical composition, like some of Elgar's other writing, demonstrates the influence of Mendelssohn, Brahms, Schumann, and other German composers. The Wagnerian aura enveloping *Gerontius* prompted George Moore to evaluate it as "Holy water in a German beer barrel."

The many honors bestowed on Elgar included being knighted in 1904, being named Master of the King's Music in 1924, and receiving numerous honorary doctor of music degrees by American and English colleges and universities—at which ceremonies the processional may well have been *Pomp and Circumstance*. ⸘

GIACOMO PUCCINI
(1858–1924)

"THERE IS NO COMPARISON BETWEEN MY LOVE FOR MANON, MIMI, AND Tosca and that love which I have in my heart for Butterfly for whom I wrote music in the night," noted Giacomo Puccini, composer of operas with the abovementioned women as the heroines. Puccini composed twelve operas, each of which is full of melody and plots entwined with drama, intrigue, and passion. Ironically, it because of this that Puccini is at times criticized by opera purists.

In most of his operas, the story revolves around a woman, and Puccini is said to have been "in love" with each of his heroines. The four heroines mentioned above represent his third through sixth operas; all have endured. Success was not immediate for Puccini: *Le Villi* and particularly *Edgar* did not go far in the opera world. His last six operas—*The Girl of the Golden West, Rondine, Il Tabarro, Suor Angelica, Gianni Schicchi*, and *Turandot*—were all successful to varying degrees.

Music was part of life for five generations of Puccinis—singers, teachers, and organists. None of these musicians, however, achieved the fame of Giacomo. Born in 1858 in Lucca, Italy, Giacomo was about five years old when his father died. At the time, his mother was pregnant with a second son. There were also five sisters, and raising seven children presented a rather sizable financial burden for Signora Puccini. Giacomo's mother recognized the inherent musical talent in her older son and prevailed upon a wealthy uncle and Queen Margherita of Italy for financial aid to send her son to the Milan Conservatory. Tuition money was provided, but Puccini had a stark existence outside the conservatory. Puccini roomed with Pietro Mascagni (1863–1945), the eventual composer of *Cavalleria Rusticana*, and the two young men shared a lifestyle that is mirrored in *La Bohème*, perhaps Puccini's best-known opera.

Le Villi, Puccini's first opera, was his entry into a contest in 1883, the year he graduated from the conservatory. The music publisher

The Romantic Era

Sonzogno was the sponsor of the competition, whose rules called for a one-act piece. Turning in his work at the proverbial last minute, Puccini had not allowed himself time to recopy the pages and they were abruptly dismissed as not legible. But his manuscript had been seen—and deciphered—by some knowledgeable and influential people, who arranged for a Milan performance in 1884. The struggling composer had to borrow money to send a telegram to his mother following the premiere. *Le Villi* showed promise for Puccini, but this was dragged down by the fiasco of *Edgar* in 1889.

Although Puccini's forte was opera, he did write in other musical forms. Many of his compositions—such as *Capriccio Sinfonico,* his graduation composition—were for courses at the conservatory. Themes from that work and from *Chrysanthemums*, written in 1890, show up in many of his operas. *Messa di Gloria*, composed in 1880, was rediscovered in 1951, and fourteen songs have been revived in recent years.

Puccini traveled to the United States twice. In 1907 he came to assist with rehearsals of the Metropolitan Opera premieres of *Madama Butterfly* and *Manon Lescaut*, but his ocean liner was fog-bound outside New York harbor and he did not arrive until the first performance was in progress. The world premiere of *La Fanciulla del West* ("The Girl of the Golden West") was scheduled for the Metropolitan in 1910, and for this one Puccini arrived on time. Puccini, however, did not come to New York for the 1918 world premiere of *The Triptych,* which comprises three one-act operas: *Il Tabarro* ("The Cloak"), *Suor Angelica* ("Sister Angelica"), and *Gianni Schicchi.*

It was on a trip to London in 1900 for preparations of *Tosca* that Puccini first encountered Butterfly. He attended a performance of the play *Madame Butterfly*, by David Belasco (1853–1931), and although Puccini understood very little English he was enthralled by the emotional aspects. Four

years later Puccini's *Madama Butterfly* had its world premiere at La Scala in Milan.

Though he "loved" all his leading ladies, Puccini certainly was not limited to experiencing his romance vicariously. Handsome and well dressed, the composer was very much a ladies' man. Puccini also enjoyed hunting fowl on his estate, and when automobiles and motorboats first began to be produced he decided that he would possess both. Linked with various women, Puccini had a lengthy relationship with Elvira Gemignani, with whom he had a son out of wedlock. Gemignani was married, and according to Italian law she could not be divorced. Nonetheless, the two kept their romance alive, and when her husband died, eighteen years after the start of her affair with Puccini, Gemignani and the composer were married.

Turandot was the last of Puccini's operatic loves. The opera bearing her name was not yet finished in 1924 when the composer entered a Brussels hospital to have surgery for throat cancer. He took along the *Turandot* manuscript—about three-quarters finished—expecting to work on it during his convalescence. A few days after the operation, Puccini died of a heart attack in the hospital. He never opened the briefcase containing the *Turandot* score. Composer Franco Alfano (1876–1954) was subsequently designated to complete Puccini's opera, but at *Turandot's* 1926 world premiere, conducted by Arturo Toscanini (1867–1957) at La Scala, the maestro put down his baton and ended the performance at the point where Puccini had written his last measures. ♪

ABOVE: GIACOMO PUCCINI'S OPERA *LA BOHÈME* SERVED AS INSPIRATION FOR THE HIT BROADWAY MUSICAL *RENT* IN THE 1990'S. OPPOSITE: IN TURN, PUCCINI'S *MADAMA BUTTERFLY* WAS BASED ON DAVID BELASCO'S PLAY *MADAME BUTTERFLY.*

VICTOR HERBERT
(1859–1924)

WHILE HIS FUTURE WIFE MADE HER DEBUT ON THE METROPOLITAN Opera stage, he played first cello in the Metropolitan orchestra. The year was 1886 and Victor Herbert was playing principal cello in the Court Orchestra of the Royal Opera of Stuttgart when he became enamored with Thérèse Forster, one of their leading sopranos. The two soon began a romantic relationship, and they were married in August. Almost simultaneously, Thérèse Forster was offered a contract with the Metropolitan Opera, and she and Herbert journeyed together to the United States. Her debut was in Goldmark's *Die Konigin von Saba* ("The Queen of Sheba"), and was followed by the title role in the Metropolitan Opera's premiere, in German, of Verdi's *Aïda*; other roles, at the Met or elsewhere, included parts in Wagner's *Lohengrin, Rienzi*, and *Tannhäuser,* Verdi's *Il Trovatore,* and Meyerbeer's *Les Huguenots.*

Although he was born in Ireland, Herbert and his sister grew up in Germany; after their father died, their widowed mother married a German doctor and the family was moved to the Continent. Just prior, a few years were spent in the household of his maternal grandfather, Samuel Lover (1797–1868), a well-known painter, novelist, poet, and writer of Irish songs. Educated in both music and academics in Germany, Herbert became regarded as a brilliant cellist; this reputation gradually led him to the Stuttgart Court Orchestra and the opera—and Thérèse Forster.

Herbert's career in the United States took him out of the orchestra pit and into directing the famed band of the 22nd Regiment of the New York National Guard. He next moved to Pittsburgh to serve as music director of that city's symphony orchestra from 1898 to 1904, after which he formed the Victor Herbert Orchestra and toured extensively, bringing a variety of music to grassroots America.

His conducting career overlapped his life as a composer and, although he was best known as the Dean of Operetta, Herbert received accolades as a "serious composer." Among his compositions are two concertos for cello and orchestra, the symphonic poems *Woodland Fancies* and *Panamericana*, a *Suite for Strings*, the *Irish Rhapsody*, and the oratorio *The Captive*. Herbert also composed piano pieces, one of which, "Indian Summer," became a popular song in 1939 with lyrics by Al Dubin. Herbert's *A Suite of Serenades* was on the program with George Gershwin's *Rhapsody in Blue* at the latter's 1924 premiere, launching something unique in concert hall music. Just a few months after the Gershwin premiere, though, Herbert died suddenly from a heart attack.

Of course, Herbert is most highly regarded for his operettas; he wrote forty of them between 1894 and 1924. The best known of these are perhaps *Mlle. Modiste* (1905), including songs like "Kiss Me Again"; *The Red Mill* (1906), with "Because You're You"; *Naughty Marietta* (1910), which featured "Ah! Sweet Mystery of Life"; *Sweethearts* (1913), and its title song; *Eileen* (1917) and "Thine Alone." These are the romantic legacy of Victor Herbert. As accomplished as he was with theater music, however, Herbert could not fulfill his ambition of writing a great American opera. Both his attempts—*Natoma* (1911) and *Madeleine* (1914)—were performed, respectively, by the Philadelphia-Chicago Opera Company and the Metropolitan Opera, but went no further.

Herbert's accomplishments didn't end with performance and composition. In the early part of the twentieth century, Herbert and his colleagues went to Congress hoping to establish copyright protection. Their efforts culminated in the founding of the American Society of Composers, Authors and Publishers. ♪

THOUGH BEST KNOWN AS A COMPOSER OF LIGHT OPERAS, VICTOR HERBERT WAS A SERIOUS MAN—HE ORGANIZED AND LED TWO HUGE BENEFIT CONCERTS FOR VICTIMS OF NATURAL DISASTER IN HIS ADOPTED HOMELAND, THE UNITED STATES.

The Romantic Era

CHAPTER 5

MIKHAIL GLINKA

ALEKSANDR BORODIN

MODEST MUSSORGSKY

NIKOLAI RIMSKY-KORSAKOV

RUSSIAN NATIONALISTS

RUSSIAN NATIONALISTS

It could be said that all composers are nationalists because of inborn pride in their native lands, pride that is frequently manifested in their music. Lots of composers have deliberately planted their roots in their music—Bedrich Smetana with *My Country*, Jean Sibelius with *Finlandia*, and Aaron Copland with *Appalachian Spring*, for example. Folk melodies or the mood of folk songs have influenced many composers throughout history.

But there is a category of Russians, specifically and intentionally nationalistic, that is concentrated in the nineteenth century. Mikhail Glinka is considered the "father" of the Russian nationalistic school of music. Along with Glinka, three of the most productive nationalists of the 1800s are presented in these pages—Aleksandr Borodin, Modest Mussorgsky, and Nikolai Rimsky-Korsakov.

After Glinka's death, Mily Balakirev (1837–1910), a mostly self-taught composer who made his debut in St. Petersburg as a pianist when he was in his late teens, took up the cause. Balakirev, who became a successful conductor, composed the symphonic poems *Russia* and *Tamara*, a piano concerto, various overtures and symphonies, and *Islamey*, a sonata-style Oriental fantasy for piano. Outside his own compositions, Balakirev's major contribution to the perpetuity and prominence of Russian nationalistic music was the organization of Borodin, Mussorgsky, Rimsky-Korsakov, and César Cui into a dedicated group, which came to be known as "Kutchka," "The Five," or sometimes as the "Mighty Handful." Cui (1835–1918), a professor at the St. Petersburg Engineering Academy and a critic with the St. Petersburg Gazette, was well known for his operas, including *William Ratcliffe*, *The Mandarin's Son*, *The Saracen*, and *The Captain's Daughte*r. Borodin, Mussorgsky, and Rimsky-Korsakov are discussed in this chapter. As each man died, the size of the group simply shrank, for there were no replacements. Individually and collectively, these five artists made a lasting and clear imprint on music in the name of Russian nationalism.

MIKHAIL GLINKA
(1804–1857)

"GLINKA'S OPERA IS ONLY A BEAUTIFUL BEGINNING," SAID FAMED Russian author Nikolai Gogol, predicting many successes for the composer after the premiere of his first opera, *A Life for the Czar*. But Glinka's second opera, *Russlan and Ludmilla*, was to be his last. Nevertheless—even though he did not have as many great achievements as the other composers discussed in this chapter—Mikhail Ivanovich Glinka is considered the father of Russian opera. The reason for "Father" Glinka's having only two operatic "children" was likely because he was creating something new—Russian opera—and was selectively finding his way. And in the end, Glinka has come to be seen not only as the father of Russian opera but also as the father of the nineteenth-century Russian nationalist school of music, for his successor in composing opera, Mily Balakirev, cofounded and headed up "The Five," a group of composers who brought the spirit of their homeland to music.

In spite of an overly protective grandmother who kept Mikhail close to her until her dying day (when he was about six), Glinka absorbed early on the folk songs of the Smolensk area. Glinka was born in Novospasskoye in 1804, and the town has since been renamed in Glinka's honor. The region is known for its church bells and the dissonant sound of their ringing, which is echoed in Glinka's early compositions.

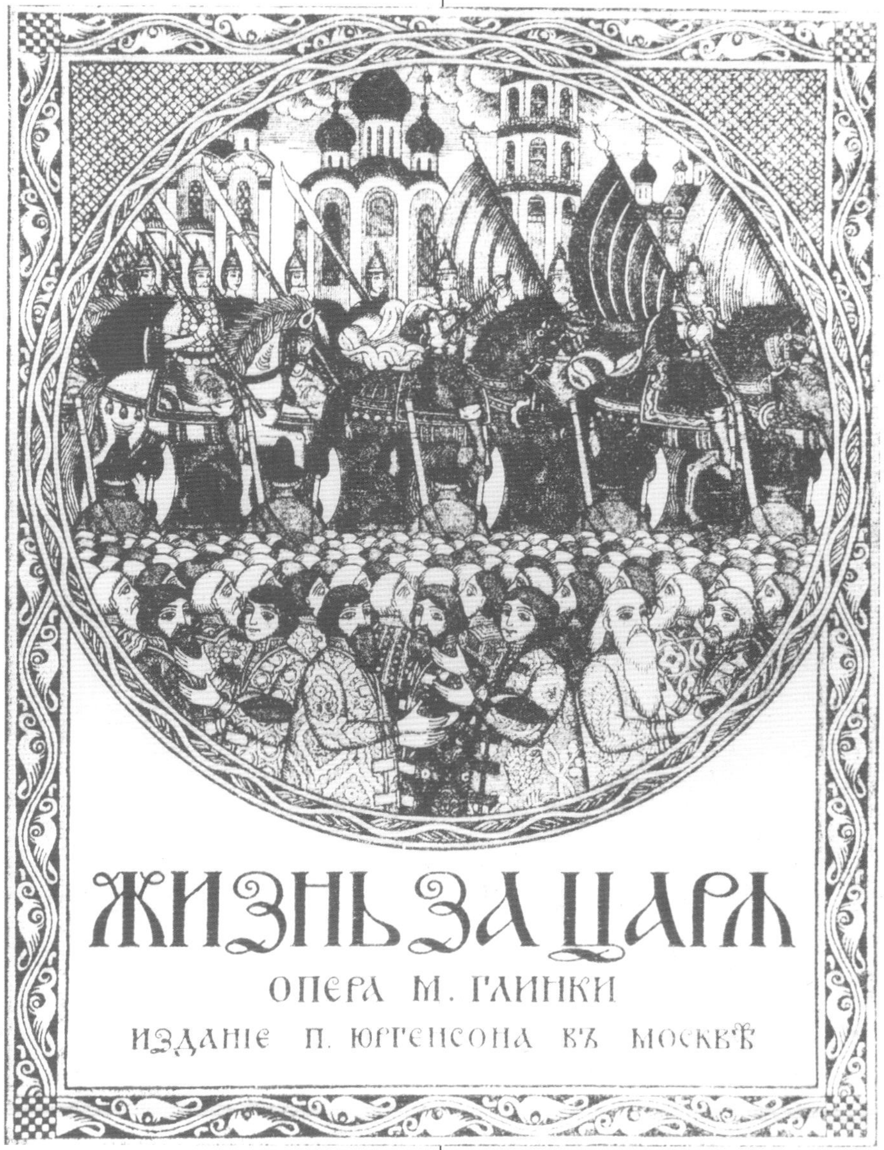

Glinka's parents gave the boy more freedom than his grandmother had, and at thirteen he was sent to school in St. Petersburg. When he left school five years later, he set himself up in St. Petersburg as a dilettante, making himself known in social circles for his artistry as a singer and pianist. In the 1820s, St. Petersburg ranked with other major European cities in offering the finest in visual and performing arts. Glinka dabbled at composing, but it soon became apparent that he needed a job, and he found employment as an under-secretary in the Council of Communications office from 1824 to 1828.

Faraway places held great appeal for Glinka. Leaving Russia in May 1830, for two years he traveled throughout Italy with aspiring tenor Nikolay Ivanov. Glinka took some instruction at the Milan Conservatory and Ivanov made his operatic debut in Naples. After spending some time in Venice, Glinka took the long way home, stopping to hear the famous orchestras of Johann Strauss, Sr. and Joseph Lanner in Vienna and pausing for five months to study composition in Berlin. This considered, it is not surprising that the symphony Glinka was working on at the time, although it contained two Russian themes, followed German musical structure. (Incidentally, this symphony was never completed.) Summoned back to Russia in 1834 when his father died, Glinka stayed put for a while and married the following year.

A Life for the Czar is based on the story of Ivan Susanin, a peasant who detained the Polish enemy, sacrificing his own life to save the Czar. Originally, the opera was to be called *Susanin*, but Glinka changed the title on the suggestion of the czar. (With the overthrow of the czar in the Russian Revolution of 1917, the title was changed back to *Susanin*.) A royal and wealthy audience attended the premiere in St. Petersburg's Imperial Theatre in 1836, and the opera was a tremendous success. Among the opera's outstanding elements were its mammoth chorus scenes and ballet, and the use of recitative instead of spoken dialogue between musical segments. Glinka also put leitmotifs into play for this work; he was ahead of his time in this use of specific theme music

ЖИЗНЬ ЗА ЦАРЯ

ОПЕРА М. ГЛИНКИ

ИЗДАНІЕ П. ЮРГЕНСОНА ВЪ МОСКВѢ

MIKHAIL GLINKA (LEFT), WHO WROTE ONLY TWO OPERAS—*A LIFE FOR THE CZAR* (TITLE ILLUSTRATION ABOVE) AND *RUSSLAN AND LUDMILLA*—CAME TO BE CALLED THE FATHER OF RUSSIAN NATIONALIST MUSIC FOR HIS PIONEERING CULTIVATION OF RUSSIAN FOLK STYLES.

RUSSIAN NATIONALISTS

to identify the various characters in the opera. One of Glinka's rewards was his appointment as music director of the imperial chapel, a post he held until 1839, when he tired of the commitment.

Russlan and Ludmilla, Glinka's second and last opera, did not attain the same heights. The composition of this work had plodded along for several years, and during that time the composer had dire marital problems—both Glinka and his wife had been unfaithful, and the marriage ended in divorce. Because of the greatness and the success of *A Life for the Czar*, the public expected too much of *Russlan and Ludmilla*. The fairy-tale story had little appeal, and Glinka hardly used recitatives and injected only one leitmotif. The reception at the premiere in 1842 was quite cool.

After the dismal reaction to his second opera, Glinka refocused his goals and set out to write *fantasies pittoresques* for orchestra, the equivalent of descriptive symphonic poems. With this goal in mind, he set out for Spain to absorb the country's sights and sounds. Glinka spent two years enjoying Valladolid, Madrid, Granada, and Seville, based on which he composed the First and Second Spanish Overtures.

Intermingled with his other works were numerous songs with wistful titles: "Disenchantment," "Heart's Memory," "A Voice from the Other World," and "I Recall a Wonderful Moment." His health declining, Glinka was buoyed when his colleagues, Berlioz and Meyerbeer among them, programmed his music in concerts they conducted. Following a successful concert of his music by the St. Petersburg Philharmonic Society in 1852, Glinka was elected an honorary member.

Glinka was in Berlin for a concert of his music in January 1857 when he caught a cold, which worsened. He died on February 15 of that year. While his compositions are limited in number, they possess great substance, making Glinka not only the musical father in his own country, but also the first Russian composer to be hailed outside his native land. ♪

ALEKSANDR BORODIN (1833–1887)

"ON THE ACTION OF ETHYL-IODIDE ON HYDROBENZAMIDE AND AMARINE" was one of Aleksandr Borodin's finest compositions. You can't hum it, but it was a hit with the Russian Academy of Sciences in 1858. "On the Action..." was the title of a paper Borodin presented to the physico-mathematical section of the academy in March 1858; this paper was his first published work—it appeared in the Academy's annual bulletin. In May of the same year, Borodin received his doctorate upon delivering his dissertation, "On the Analogy of Arsenical with Phosphoric Acid."

Aleksandr Borodin was the illegitimate son of an elderly Russian prince and, as was custom in such a circumstance, was registered as the lawful son of one of the prince's serfs, in this case Porfiry Borodin. Aleksandr, born in St. Petersburg in 1833, was brought up by his biological mother, a governess, and numerous tutors. Because of this, he was provided with all sorts of cultural perquisites and he became fluent in several languages. When he was eight years old, Borodin heard a military band play; this sparked his inter-

Russian Nationalists

est in music, and by the following year he was composing at the very same time he was tinkering with a child's version of scientific experiments. At seventeen, he was enrolled in the Medico-Surgical Academy, graduating *cum eximia laude* in 1856. As an extracurricular activity during his student days, he formed a chamber music ensemble, which gave him access to a larger, more experienced group of musicians.

Pursuing his career as a research chemist with further study in the field left Borodin little time for composing music. While working in Heidelberg, Germany, in 1861, he met Ekaterina Protopopova, who was there to be treated for tuberculosis. Protopopova was an outstanding pianist who loved the music of Chopin, Liszt, and Schumann. Borodin at the time was a Mendelssohn buff, but his musical tastes were converted by Ekaterina, who also eventually converted him from a bachelor into a husband. Soon after their engagement, they went to Pisa—she for health reasons and he to work with two eminent Italian chemists—where they shared the thrill of playing Bach on the organ in the Cathedral of Pisa. During their stay in Italy, Borodin was able to squeeze in some composing between chemistry projects; this resulted in his Piano Quintet in C Minor and the Tarantella in D Major.

In 1864 Borodin was awarded a full professorship at the Medico-Surgical Academy. An apartment at the academy came with the position, and it was in this apartment that he and Ekaterina lived out their happy marriage. They did not have any children of their own, but in 1869 they adopted a seven-year-old girl.

Borodin took to writing music on a large scale mostly as a result of the urging of composer Mily Balakirev. It was Balakirev who prompted Borodin's Symphony in E-Flat Major, which was first performed publicly in 1869. Other major influences on Borodin were Nikolai Rimsky-Korsakov, Modest Mussorgsky, and Cesar Cui. Borodin and these other four composers were known as "The Five" (or "Mighty Handful"), a label given them by writer and critic Vladimir Stasov. Upon the death of Mussorgsky—he was first of "The Five" to die—Borodin wrote a musical tribute based on Russian poet Aleksandr Pushkin's "For the Shores of Thy Far Native Land." Using an established poet's words for a musical piece was unusual for Borodin; for most of the songs he composed, he wrote the text himself.

Thanks mostly to Franz Liszt (see Chapter 4, page 72),

Borodin's music was gradually being heard in western Europe; as a token of his appreciation for Liszt's publicity efforts, Borodin dedicated *In the Steppes of Central Asia* to the Hungarian composer. This symphonic poem describing a caravan wending its way across the Russian terrain is part of a series of twelve compositions by different composers celebrating the first twenty-five years of the reign of Czar Alexander II. Written by Borodin in 1880, *Steppes* contributed substantially to his early fame as a composer.

Another of Borodin's European promoters was the Countess of Mercy-Argenteau, who helped popularize the Russian composer's music in her homeland of Belgium; to the Countess, Borodin dedicated a set of piano pieces later published as the *Petite Suite*.

In 1887, while attending a St. Petersburg fancy-dress ball (to which he wore nationalistic Russian attire, including a red shirt and high leather boots), Borodin collapsed and died instantly; some believe that his death was the result of his heart having been damaged two years earlier when he came down with a severe case of cholera. When death took him, his Symphony No. 3 in A Minor was still in progress. Ekaterina was severely ill at this time; she outlived her husband by only five months, but in that short period she was able to dictate reminiscences to augment Borodin's biography.

The opera *Prince Igor* is probably Borodin's best-known work. This piece was many years in the making; it was started by Borodin in 1869 and finished, after Borodin's death, by Rimsky-Korsakov and Aleksandr Glazunov (1865–1936); its world premiere was held in St. Petersburg in 1890. While the concertgoing public is familiar with the opera's Polovtsian Dances, the theatergoing public will recognize a theme from the Dances as "Stranger in Paradise" from *Kismet*, a Broadway hit of 1953–1954 for which Robert Wright and George Forrest transformed a variety of Borodin's melodies. *Kismet* also contained the song "This Is My Beloved," which was based on Borodin's Second String Quartet; this song earned Borodin a Tony Award in 1954, some sixty-seven years after he died. ♪

OPPOSITE: THOUGH HE WAS A FOUNDING MEMBER OF THE RUSSIAN NATIONALIST SCHOOL, MODEST MUSSORGSKY, PERHAPS THE MOST POTENT TALENT AMONG "THE FIVE," INFLUENCED MANY COMPOSERS OUTSIDE HIS HOME COUNTRY.

ARTIST-ARCHITECT VICTOR HARTMANN CREATED MANY FINE PAINTINGS, including *The Old Castle, The Hut on Fowl's Legs,* and *Tuileries.* After Hartmann died in 1873, he was honored by his friend Modest Mussorgsky with a musical interpretation of his works entitled *Pictures at an Exhibition.* Ten of Hartmann's paintings are represented in this symphonic poem, and they are connected by a theme called "Promenade," which represents the walk through the metaphoric gallery in which this exhibition is held. The finale to the piece is "The Great Gate at Kiev," the most musically familiar of the *Pictures,* based on Hartmann's sketches for a new entrance to the city. The "paintings" in *Pictures at an Exhibition* were originally composed by Mussorgsky as piano selections. The composition has been adapted for orchestra numerous times, and the most popular of these adaptations is by the French Impressionist composer Maurice Ravel (see Chapter 6, page 128); this adaptation was commissioned by Serge Koussevitzky, who conducted it at its premiere in Paris in 1923, nearly fifty years after Mussorgsky wrote the *Pictures.*

Mussorgsky was born in 1839 in Karevo into a family of wealthy landowners. In 1851, his parents decreed that he would go into the military, and so he was enrolled in the School for Cadets of the Guard. After graduation he began a short-lived military career. It was during this time that Mussorgsky started drinking, carousing with pals while off duty; his bouts with alcohol, which he referred to as "my nervous disorder," haunted Mussorgsky throughout his life, and led to many problems for the composer.

After serving as an officer for a short time, Mussorgsky resigned his commission so that he would have time to work

MODEST (1839–1881) **MUSSORGSKY**

on his music. (Some sources say that he resigned his commission for financial reasons: when the serfs who worked the land throughout Russia were liberated, Mussorgsky's family, like many other landowning families, was thrust into poverty, and young Mussorgsky found that he could earn more money as a government clerk than as a military officer.) He had been drawn to music upon meeting Aleksandr Dargomyzhsky (1813–1869), composer of the operas *Russalka* and *The Stone Guest*, and Mily Balakirev, organizer of the group of Russian nationalist composers known as "The Five." Although Mussorgsky foundered for a while as a composer, he eventually became one of the nationalistic "Five," along with Balakirev, Aleksandr Borodin, Cesar Cui, and Nikolai Rimsky-Korsakov. When Mussorgsky himself took to writing opera, he put much emphasis on making the music compatible with the inflections of the language.

Unfortunately, Mussorgsky let his talent and skill at musical description become consumed by his drunkenness. When he was sober, Mussorgsky could be described as charming, warmhearted, and scintillating; when he was drunk it was a different story. His friends sustained him through his difficult periods as best as they could. During one of Mussorgsky's alcohol-free periods, he served as piano accompanist on a recital tour by soprano Daria Leonova, who also sang in the world premiere of Mussorgsky's opera *Boris Godunov* (see below). Undoubtedly, she included some of his compositions on her program, for Mussorgsky wrote numerous songs. Probably the most popular is "The Song of the Flea" (1879), the last song he composed and one which has become a classic for bass singers in recital.

RUSSIAN NATIONALISTS

In the end, Mussorgsky lost his war with alcoholism. There was little help for alcoholics in nineteenth-century Russia, and Mussorgsky, while he often had the strength to shake himself out of his drink-induced stupors, was finally unable to help himself—he died in a St. Petersburg military hospital at the age of forty-two.

Mussorgsky may not have been as good a composer had it not been for Nikolai Rimsky-Korsakov. While Mussorgsky was still alive, Rimsky-Korsakov provided professional and technical guidance, for Mussorgsky had little musical training. After Mussorgsky died, Rimsky-Korsakov was responsible for completing, or at least polishing, a number of his colleague's works. Rimsky-Korsakov's reworking of Mussorgsky's *Boris Godunov*, the only opera of seven that Mussorgsky finished on his own, became quite controversial. The subject of the opera, Czar Boris, who died in 1605, was himself rather controversial. Boris was accused of arranging the murder of Czarevitch Dimitri, younger brother of Czar Feodor, leaving no heir to the throne; Boris had been a minister in the czar's court, and when Feodor died, in Mussorgsky's interpretation, Boris manipulated the people to name him czar. In real life, Boris was eventually cleared, but he was the subject of much speculation throughout the ordeal.

In 1872 Mussorgsky submitted his opera to the directors of the Imperial Theatre in St. Petersburg. The directors rejected *Boris Godunov* because of its controversial subject matter, the omission of ballet, and the lack of love-interest and the consequent lack of a substantial female lead. With musical revisions, *Boris Godunov* had its world premiere two years later at the Maryinsky Theatre in St. Petersburg. The costumes and sets used for the opera were drawn from an earlier production of Alexandr Pushkin's play of the same name, on which Mussorgsky had based his libretto. *Boris* was reasonably successful, but nonetheless fell into oblivion. After Mussorgsky's death, Rimsky-Korsakov came up with an orchestration that screened out some of Mussorgsky's raw musical style; in 1908 he revised the score even further. In more recent years, some opera companies have reverted to Mussorgsky's original. Rimsky-Korsakov's first version marked the point at which Boris Godunov achieved genuine success, an accomplishment enhanced by the portrayal of the czar by bass Feodor Chaliapin (1873–1938), who was synonymous with the role for three decades.

Rimsky-Korsakov's improvements (or meddling, depending on who you ask), did not stop with *Boris*—he also polished the Mussorgsky opera *Khovanshchina* and fine-tuned the symphonic poem *A Night on Bald Mountain*, a fantasy that paints a picture of weird doings on St. John's Eve (June 23) on Mount Triglaf in the vicinity of Kiev (in yet another illustration of the adaptation of classical pieces for pop culture audiences, this piece was brought to life in stunning full color in the 1940 Disney animation masterpiece *Fantasia*). And Rimsky-Korsakov was not the only composer to step in and have a go at Mussorgsky works: *The Fair at Sorochinsk* received finishing touches in no fewer than four versions by no fewer than four composers: Cui, I. Sakhnovsky, Vissarion Shebalin, and Nicolai Tcherepnin. ♪

NIKOLAI RIMSKY-KORSAKOV (1844–1907)

SOME SAY HE MEDDLED, OTHERS CLAIM THAT HE MADE IMPROVEMENTS; in either case, the fact is that Nikolai Rimsky-Korsakov revised several operas written by his colleagues Aleksandr Borodin, Aleksandr Dargomyzhsky, Mikhail Glinka, and Modest Mussorgsky, in addition to composing fourteen operas of his own.

Three of the above composers—Rimsky-Korsakov, Borodin, and Mussorgsky—along with Mily Balakirev and César Cui, were known as "The Five" or the "Mighty Handful," a group of nineteenth-century Russian composers whose premise in composing was to write music entrenched in their national heritage.

A few years younger than each of his four compatriots, Rimsky-Korsakov was seventeen years old when, having shown some musical aptitude, he was sent to Balakirev for

OPPOSITE, INSET: THE YOUNGEST MEMBER OF "THE FIVE," NIKOLAI RIMSKY-KORSAKOV FOUGHT GOVERNMENT CENSORSHIP OF HIS OPERA *LE COQ D'OR* AND MADE REVISIONS OF OPERAS WRITTEN BY BORODIN, ALEKSANDR DARGOMYZHSKY, GLINKA, AND MUSSORGSKY. OPPOSITE: PEEPING OUT FROM BEHIND THE CURTAINS, HE IS SEEN AS A WIZARD OF THE STAGE.

guidance. The teacher was so impressed with his pupil that he skipped over the rudiments of composing and assigned young Nikolai a symphony to write. But Rimsky-Korsakov was about to graduate as a midshipman from the College of Naval Cadets in St. Petersburg and embark on a two-and-a-half-year worldwide cruise. The aspiring composer took along his unfinished musical manuscript, but soon lost interest in it.

Renewing his association with Balakirev after his tour of duty, Rimsky-Korsakov finished his Symphony No.1 in E-Flat Minor, which was performed in December 1865, conducted by Balakirev, and was well received. It was at this time that the young composer joined the "Five." After several more successful orchestral compositions, Rimsky-Korsakov felt he was ready for opera, and he chose serious historical dramas for his inspiration. *The Maid of Pskov* (also known as *Ivan the Terrible*), written in 1873, was his first operatic achievement.

The following year, apparently recognizing that Rimsky-Korsakov's musical talent was important to Russian culture, the government eased his naval duties and created a post especially for him: Inspector of Naval Bands. He held this post for a decade, and during this time he also served as conductor of the bands.

The government was not always on Rimsky-Korsakov's side, however. Severe censorship of his last opera, *Le Coq d'Or* ("The Golden Cockerel")—a satire on an inept monarchy, based on a text by the great poet Aleksandr Pushkin—caused a great deal of tension between Rimsky-Korsakov and Russian officials. Whether it was a matter of coincidence or the result of stress, Rimsky-Korsakov died of a fatal heart attack on June 21, 1908. The world premiere of *Le Coq d'Or* took place in Moscow on October 7, 1909.

From 1871 on, in addition to his governmental duties, Rimsky-Korsakov was a member of the faculty at the St. Petersburg Conservatory; he taught composition and orchestration. Among his students were Anton Arensky (1861–1906), Aleksandr Glazunov (1865–1936), and, his prize pupil, Igor Stravinsky (see Chapter 7, page 153), who later studied privately with him from 1903 until Rimsky-Korsakov's death in 1908. In 1905 there was a student uprising at the conservatory and Rimsky-Korsakov was dismissed for siding with the students, who were protesting various administrative and regulatory practices. Along with his dismissal came a two-month ban on public performance of his

works. Rimsky-Korsakov accepted reinstatement after certain reforms were made at the conservatory and stayed on staff until he died.

For popular appeal, *Scheherazade*, the Russian Easter Festival Overture, and the *Spanish Caprice* probably rank highest among Rimsky-Korsakov's compositions.

Considering his prodigious musical output, one might wonder why Rimsky-Korsakov meddled with—or enhanced—the works of his colleagues. In the case of *Boris Godunov*, its composer, Modest Mussorgsky, had had minimal formal musical training, especially in the area of orchestration. Mussorgsky and Rimsky-Korsakov were roommates during the period when they were writing, respectively, *Boris* and *The Maid of Pskov*. There is no evidence of ego on the part of Rimsky-Korsakov in posthumously orchestrating *Boris Godunov*. In fact, John W. Freeman wrote in *Stories of the Great Operas* that Rimsky-Korsakov's so-called meddling "made Mussorgsky available to a much wider public than would otherwise have known about him."

THE TITLE CHARACTER OF RIMSKY-KORSAKOV'S LAST OPERA, *LE COQ D'OR* ("THE GOLDEN COCKERFEL"), WAS PART OF A SATIRE ABOUT AN INEPT MONARCHY BASED ON A WORK BY THE GREAT RUSSIAN STORYTELLER ALEKSANDR PUSHKIN.

CHAPTER 6

THE IMPRESSIONISTS

CLAUDE DEBUSSY

FREDERICK DELIUS

MAURICE RAVEL

MANUEL DE FALLA

OTTORINO RESPIGHI

DARIUS MILHAUD

THE IMPRESSIONISTS

More is heard about Impressionist painting—in which images are created using dabs or strokes of paint and stippled effects rather than solid lines and shading—than its musical counterpart, but the the artists and composers who worked in that genre were of the same time period, approximately the late 1880s to the early 1900s, and so the era overlaps both the Romantic period and the twentieth century. Impressionist art was centered in France; leaders in the movement included Claude Monet (1840–1926), Pierre Auguste Renoir (1841–1919), and Camille Pissarro (1830–1903). In their works, Impressionist painters focused mostly on nature and people in the natural world.

Similarly, the Impressionist composers illustrated nature in some of their work, and most of these composers were also French. An exception was Manuel de Falla, a Spaniard who was a disciple of the French composer Claude Debussy and who is perhaps best known for his *Noches en los jardines de España* ("Nights in the Gardens of Spain"). Debussy's well-known entries in the realm of "nature" compositions are *Prélude à l'Après-midi d'une Faune* ("Prelude to the Afternoon of a Faun"), *Clair de Lune* ("Moonlight"), and *La Mer* ("The Sea").

One distinct element of Impressionist painting is its somewhat unusual mix of colors to convey impressions, and this concept of color was carried over into musical compositions in various ways. *Clair de Lune,* for example, suggests blue, whereas the vivid tone and timbre of de Falla's *The Ritual Fire Dance* "sound" like orange and red flames. This parallel of color and music is, of course, not confined to Impressionism, and the assignment of specific colors to certain sounds is partially dependent on personal reaction.

CLAUDE DEBUSSY
(1862–1918)

FOR SOME PEOPLE, THE IDEAL VACATION SPOT IS THE BEACH, WITH THE sea either gently lapping or surging against the shoreline; for others it is the woods. Both of these locales are evoked in the music of Achille-Claude Debussy, specifically *La Mer* ("The Sea") and *Prélude à l'Après-midi d'une Faune* ("Prelude to the Afternoon of a Faun"). In a sense, his music is a vacation, if you consider a vacation as a departure from the daily routine.

Debussy's music is considered Impressionistic, although it was not his idea to identify his work in this way. As far as we know, this adjective was first applied to Debussy's work in an evaluation of his orchestral suite *Printemps*. There was a desire among critics of the late 1800s to find a musical counterpart to the Impressionist school of painters—Claude Monet and Pierre Auguste Renoir among them—and the Symbolist movement in poetry, which was led by Paul Verlaine (1844–1896) and Stéphane Mallarmé (1842–1898). Impressionist or not, Debussy serves as the bridge between the Romantic and Modern periods in music.

Debussy, born in 1862, was not from a musical family. At the time of his birth, the family was living in Saint-Germain-en-Laye,

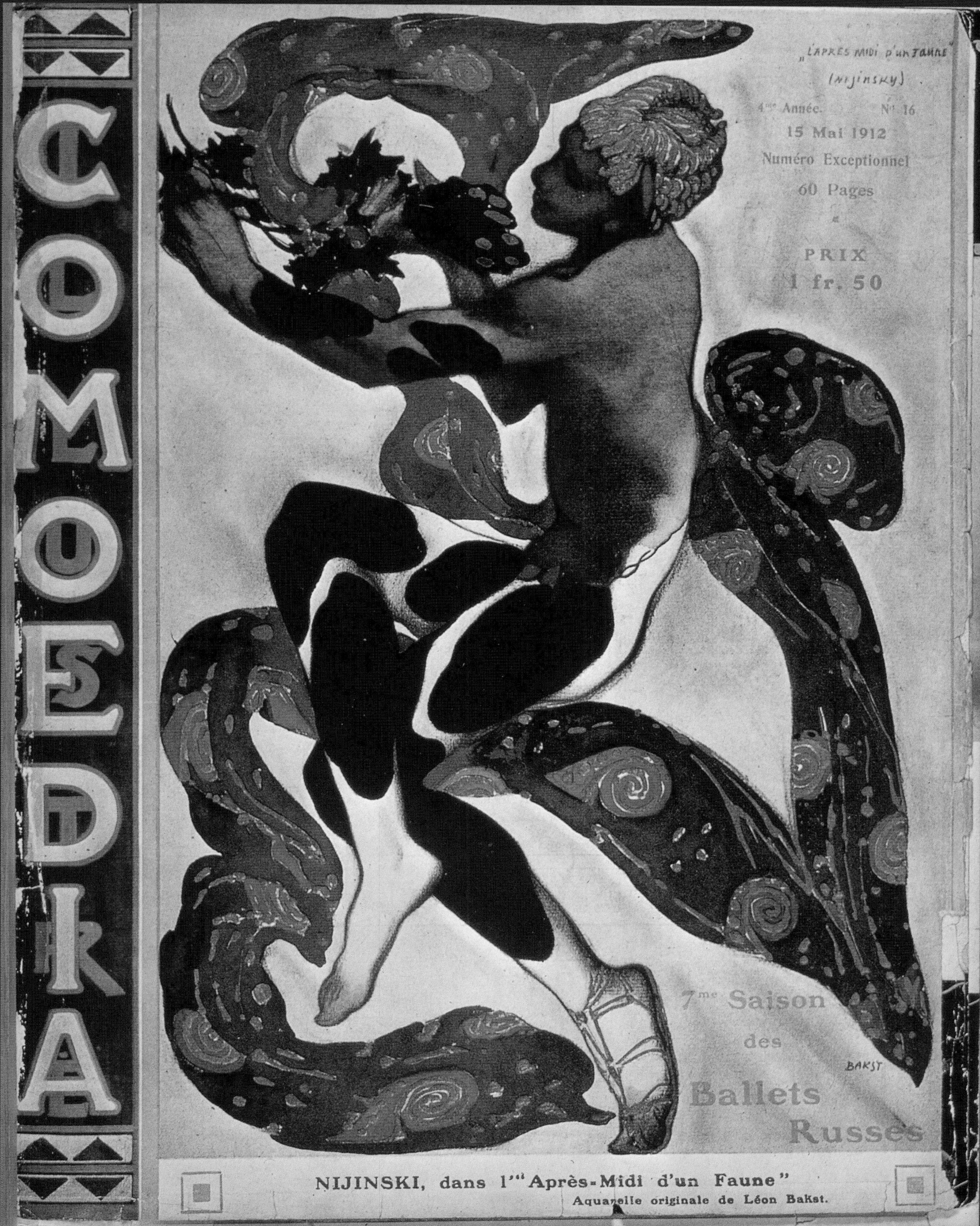
COMOEDIA
ILLUSTRÉ
„L'APRES MIDI D'UN FAUNE"
(NIJINSKY)
4me Année. No 16
15 Mai 1912
Numéro Exceptionnel
60 Pages
PRIX
1 fr. 50
7me Saison
des
Ballets
Russes
BAKST
NIJINSKI, dans l'"Après-Midi d'un Faune"
Aquarelle originale de Léon Bakst.

France, where his father had a china store. When they later moved to Paris, he took on a variety of jobs. When Claude was eleven years old, his aptitude at the piano led him to the Paris Conservatory. Toward the end of his eleven years there he won the Prix de Rome, a scholarship to study in Rome, for his cantata *L'Enfant Prodigue* ("The Prodigal Child"); this enabled him to continue his studies in Italy, not because he wanted to but because he knew it would be good for him.

The first time the concertgoing public took notice of Debussy was in 1893 and 1894, with the premieres of *La Damoiselle Elue* ("The Blessed Damsel"), the Quartet in G Minor, and the *Prelude to the Afternoon of a Faun,* based on a Mallarmé poem. (While many people assume that this work is about a baby deer [a fawn], it is actually about the wanderings of a mythical part man–part animal creature known as a faun.) *Faun* later became a popular ballet choreographed and performed by Vaslav Nijinsky (1890–1950) and produced by Sergei Diaghilev (1872–1929).

Around this time, Debussy attended a performance of the play *Pelléas et Mélisande*, by the Belgian poet and playwright Maurice Maeterlinck (1862–1949); this play became the inspiration for Debussy's operatic masterpiece (and the only opera he completed), which the composer spent a decade writing. Debussy followed the Belgian writer's script almost word for word, but he did not follow Maeterlinck's desire to have his common-law wife, Georgette Leblanc, play Mélisande. Albert Carre, director of the Opéra-Comique, one of Paris's two leading opera companies, decided to feature one of the company's stars, Mary Garden. Apparently Debussy agreed, and Maeterlinck placed the blame on the composer. (Garden became the quintessential Mélisande. The part of Pelléas in the world premiere was played by tenor Jean Perier.) Maeterlinck even went so far as to take the row to the press, clouding the premiere with controversy. Even without this public argument, the opera would have been controversial. Debussy brought his so-called Impressionistic style to the Symbolist play, creating a composition unlike anything previously heard in opera. The opera has no arias nor choruses, and no distinctive melodies; instead, *Pelleas et Melisande* is a flowing musical narrative. Public and press reactions were mixed. One particularly negative response came from the director of the Paris Conservatory, Théodore Dubois (1837–1924), who prohibited the students from attending *Pelléas et Mélisande*. Despite the

controversy—or perhaps because of it—the opera was a success, earning Debussy enough money to address his precarious financial situation (during the rehearsal period, he had been about to be prosecuted for unpaid bills).

Debussy, who had been involved in several romantic entanglements, and a woman named Emma Bardac left their respective spouses in 1904 to live together. A number of Debussy's friends who were sympathetic to his wife distanced themselves from the composer. The following year, Debussy and Bardac's daughter, Claude-Emma, was born. For Claude-Emma, the composer wrote one of his non-Impressionistic works, a piano suite which he titled *The Children's Corner*; probably the most familiar of the six parts of the piece is "Golliwog's Cake Walk." (A golliwog is an African-American doll, and the cakewalk, which has African-American roots. was a popular dance when Debussy wrote the piece.) Debussy composed the suite in 1908, the same year that he and Emma Bardac decided to marry. It was also around this time that money again was a problem for Debussy; to address this situation, the composer traveled throughout Europe playing piano recitals and conducting his own compositions.

Later Debussy works include *Images, Jeux* ("Games"), and, written just prior to World War I, twenty-four outstanding piano preludes divided into two sets. Especially noteworthy for its popular appeal is the ethereal *Clair de Lune*, from the Suite Bergamasque, which has become one of the most popular concert pieces in the classical repertoire.

In 1918, after an extended stay at home, Debussy died of cancer.

FREDERICK DELIUS (1862–1934)

IT IS A LONG WAY, BOTH GEOGRAPHICALLY AND PHILOSOPHICALLY, FROM a Florida orange grove to a Norwegian fjord. Both places, however, share the beauties of nature, albeit dramatically diversified. Frederick Delius related to both and translated these surroundings into his music.

To the influences of Florida and Scandinavia, add those of the English countryside, for Delius's birthplace was Bradford,

Yorkshire, England. A domineering father kept Frederick, born in 1862, from pursuing a career in music, although the senior Delius did allow his son piano and violin lessons and a visit, when Frederick was thirteen years old, to London to hear Wagner's *Lohengrin* at Covent Garden. It was understood that after his schooling, young Delius would become involved in the family wool business. The business, however, permitted Frederick to travel to faraway places and provided his first encounter with the natural glories of Norway.

Lured by the tropical paradise of Florida, young Delius convinced his father to loan him money to obtain an orange grove outside Jacksonville. At twenty-two, Delius was not a very successful orange grower, but he did meet up with Thomas Ward, a musician living in Jacksonville who became his friend and music tutor. Even though Delius returned to Europe and enrolled in the Leipzig Conservatory, he credited Ward as his strongest musical guide. During his eighteen months at the conservatory, he met Norwegian composer Edvard Grieg (see Chapter 4, page 105). Impressed with the young man's talent, Grieg convinced Delius's father to provide the necessary funding for his son to devote himself to composing. This accomplished, Delius went off to Paris where he became involved in important artistic circles.

Perhaps hearing *Lohengrin* as a teenager had an influence on Delius's several operas, for they have the flowing orchestral style of Wagner. Some of Delius's stage works are identified as lyric dramas; Wagner referred to his operas as music dramas. *Irmelin* and *The Magic Fountain,* although composed in the 1890s, were not performed during Delius's lifetime, nor was *Margot la Rouge,* which was written in 1902. *Koanga,* which dealt with voodoo and slavery, was strengthened by

what Delius absorbed of African-American culture during his Florida sojourn; librettist Charles Keary collaborated on the text and *Koanga* premiered in 1904 in Germany. It is said that Delius approached his complete musical maturity with *A Village Romeo and Juliet,* composed in 1900. Delius's last opera, *Fennimore and Gerda*, written in 1910, showed the composer's love for Scandinavia.

While living in the United States, Delius settled for a time in Danville, Virginia, and this provided background for his composition *Appalachia. Sea Drift,* based on a poem by the American poet Walt Whitman (1819–1892), was another ode to nature. These compositions, along with *A Mass of Life,* were written for orchestra, chorus, and vocal soloists. Nature shows up again in Delius's tone poems, *On Hearing the First Cuckoo in Spring* and *Summer Night on the River.*

Many of Delius's compositions were premiered in Germany; in fact, his music was hardly known in his native England until 1907, when *Appalachia* and the Piano Concerto were performed there. While he was not always successful with formally structured music, Delius did compose orchestral pieces with piano, violin, and cello solo parts.

With his wife, the painter Jelka Rosen, Delius lived most of his life in France at Grez-sur-Loing. Ill health contributed to his becoming a recluse. Overtaken by blindness and paralysis in 1922, Delius depended on his music secretary Eric Fenby in order to keep composing.

THE TALENT OF FREDERICK DELIUS, WHO WAS ENCOURAGED BY EDVARD GRIEG DURING HIS TIME AT THE LEIPZIG CONSERVATORY, IS MOST APPARENT IN HIS MANY EVOCATIVE SYMPHONIC SKETCHES, INCLUDING *A SONG IN THE HIGH HILLS.*

THE IMPRESSIONISTS

Sir Thomas Beecham (1879–1961), conductor extraordinaire, was a champion of Delius's music. He organized the Delius Festival of 1929, which the composer, waning physically, struggled to attend. Beecham conducted Delius's compositions in the concert hall and promoted Delius's operas at Covent Garden. Although the conductor did not live to see it through to culmination, he also helped plan the 1962 festival honoring the centenary of Delius's birth.

Delius, who died in 1934, kept working until 1931. *Fantastic Dance* and *Irmelin Prelude* were his last compositions. "So long as I can enjoy the taste of my food and drink and hear the sound of my music," said Delius, "I want to live...I have seen the best of the earth and done everything that is worth doing."

MAURICE RAVEL
(1875–1937)

MAURICE RAVEL IS PROBABLY MOST FAMOUS FOR HIS ORCHESTRAL WORK *Boléro*, which actually introduced many moviegoers to Ravel's music when it was used as background in the film *10* (1979).

However, a unique evaluation of *Boléro* earlier on was related by composer Arthur Honegger (1892–1955), a contemporary of Ravel's: "Ravel said to me, in that serious, objective manner which was characteristic of him: 'I've written only one masterpiece—*Boléro*. Unfortunately, there is no music in it.'"

But there is sensuality in it, which was why it was chosen for *10,* and pulsating rhythms, which suited the original visual interpretation of the work, a ballet commissioned by dancer Ida Rubinstein. Choreographed by Nijinsky's sister, Bronislawa (1891–1972), *Boléro* the ballet was premiered by Rubinstein at the Paris Opera in 1928. Of course, *Boléro* was not Ravel's first or only ballet. Although ballet was certainly not his focus, the composer was known for ballet music as early as 1912, when his *Daphnis et Chloé,* choreographed by Michel Fokine (1880–1942), was performed by Diaghilev's Ballets Russes with great success.

Ravel also wrote a great many piano compositions, including the Concerto for Left Hand Alone and *Histoires Naturelles*, a piece for voice and piano that was one of his first successes. *The Histoires* and other early compositions unfortunately suffered from being compared to the writings of Claude Debussy, who, like Ravel, composed in the Impressionist style. Ravel's response to such criticism was, "And if I have been influenced by Debussy, I have so deliberately, and have always felt that I could escape him whenever I chose."

Despite this criticism, the works of Ravel and Debussy are generally quite different. Except for a few compositions, including 1899's *Pavane pour une Infante Défunte* ("Pavane for a Dead Princess"), Ravel's music is generally less emotional than Debussy's. This piano piece was first publicly

performed by Ricardo Vines (1876–1943), who had been one of Ravel's fellow students at the Paris Conservatory. Vines became one of the foremost interpreters of Ravel's music for the piano. While the pianist had a good deal to say about Ravel's "intellectual powers," he also evaluated the composer's eating habits, describing him as a "devoted gourmet" with a predilection toward exotic recipes and toward condiments—particularly pickles, peppers, and mustard.

Apparently, Ravel's manner of dress was also somewhat exotic. Jane Bathori, a well-known singer who was the first to present several of Ravel's vocal pieces, said that "He liked to be the first to wear certain clothes, for example the double-breasted waistcoat; and at one time he started the mode for white socks and rather open patent shoes." There are also reports of violet-colored jackets and powder-blue tailcoats. "But all this was done with great simplicity," said Mademoiselle Bathori, "and without consciously seeking to attract attention."

Ravel was also intrigued by mechanical knickknacks, of which he owned many. This hobby perhaps influenced his two operas—both of them involve clocks. *L'Heure Espagnole* ("The Spanish Hour") had its world premiere at the Opéra-Comique in 1911 and *L'Enfant et les Sortilèges* ("The Child and the Enchantments") in 1925 in Monte Carlo. *L'Enfant* was delayed by World War I when Ravel took time off to be a truck and ambulance driver in the vicinity of Verdun.

In 1921 Ravel settled into a house, Le Belvedere, in the village of Montfort l'Amaury. There he reveled in his knick-knacks, his garden, long walks in the forest of Rambouillet, and his Siamese cats. Hélène Jourdan-Morhange, violinist and close friend of the composer, recalled working with Ravel when the cats "used to come prowling among the pages of manuscript, leaving their fivefold muddy footprints as an emblem of friendship. Only [Ravel] could have written the cats' duet in *L'Enfant et les Sortilèges* with such accurate onomatopoeia."

Equally popular as *Boléro* are Ravel's *Rhapsodie Espagnole* ("Spanish Rhapsody"), *Ma Mère L'Oye* (the French equivalent of Mother Goose), and *La Valse* ("The Waltz"). In 1932, Ravel was injured in an auto accident; he never regained his health and died in December 1937 after brain surgery. According to the French writer Léon-Paul Fargue, who was perhaps the composer's closest friend, popularity was not very important to Ravel: "He attached little importance to honors or fame but was sensitive to true, spontaneous demonstations of enthusiasm." ♪

MANUEL DE FALLA (1875–1946)

THE RENOWNED AMERICAN COMPOSER GEORGE GERSHWIN ONCE described Manuel de Falla as "The Spanish Gershwin." Quite a compliment from one composer to another!

Gershwin and de Falla were contemporaries who shared a number of musical sensibilities. Like Gershwin, Falla delved into opera as one of several forms of musical expression; his first opera was *La vida breve* ("The Short Life"). This piece won first prize in a Spanish opera competition sponsored by the Madrid Academy of Fine Arts in 1905. It was quite some

time, however, before *La vida breve* was produced—in 1913 it was introduced with great success in Nice, France, after which it traveled to the Opéra-Comique in Paris; it also played successfully in Madrid in 1914. Falla's versatility (and perhaps his sense of humor) showed when he wrote an opera to be performed by puppets, *El ratablo de maese Pedro* ("Master Peter's Puppet Show"). In 1935 Falla started working on another opera called *L'Atlántida,* a depiction of Columbus's coming to the New World that has sometimes been referred to as a choral trilogy. Unfortunately, the composer died before finishing this work and the task was taken on by Ernesto Halffter, who had studied with Falla.

Opera, of course, was not the only musical form in which Falla created. Lauded as a solo pianist, Falla was also known for keyboard compositions he wrote for others, including a harpsichord concerto dedicated to Polish pianist Wanda Landowska (1879–1959) and his *Fantasia Betica* ("Andalusian Fantasy," from Betica/Baetica, the Roman name for Andalusia), which was dedicated to pianist Arthur Rubinstein (1886–1982), a Polish-born American emigré.

It is probably ballet, however, for which Falla is best known. *El amor brujo* ("Love, the Sorcerer"), is considered by some critics to be Falla's masterpiece. This piece was requested by Pastora Imperio, one of the greatest flamenco dancers of her

---

OPPOSITE: PROBABLY BECAUSE BOTH COMPOSERS WORKED IN THE IMPRESSIONIST STYLE, THE EARLY WORKS OF MAURICE RAVEL WERE OFTEN COMPARED TO DEBUSSY'S, EVEN THOUGH THEY HAVE MANY DIFFERENCES. ABOVE: MANUEL DE FALLA WAS BOTH IMPRESSIONIST AND NATIONALIST—HIS ART WAS ROOTED BOTH IN STRICT HISTORICAL TRADITIONS OF SPANISH MUSIC AND IN THAT COUNTRY'S FOLK SONGS.

time; she danced the premiere in Madrid in 1915. From this work comes the *Ritual Fire Dance,* which stands on its own as a popular concert choice. Another outstanding Falla ballet is *El sombrero de tres picos* ("The Three-Cornered Hat"), which was given its premiere by Sergey Diaghilev's company in London in 1919. Based on the novel *El Corregidor y la Molinera* ("The Governor and the Miller's Wife"), by Pedro de Alarcon, the story was also used by the Austrian composer Hugo Wolf (1860–1903) for his opera *Der Corregidor.*

Also of note is the symphonic nocturne *Noches en los jardines de España* ("Nights in the Gardens of Spain"), a piece that is both nationalistic and Impressionistic. According to Falla, "The music has no pretensions to being descriptive; it is merely expressive."

As a young man, Falla studied at the Madrid Conservatory, where he was particularly influenced by a teacher named Felipe Pedrell and by the concept of basing the nation's contemporary music on Spanish folk tunes. Falla employed this idea, not note for note, but in the spirit of his music. "Falla's music represents by far the finest and most effective use that has yet been made of the Spanish idiom," says Richard Anthony Leonard, author of parts of *The Music Lovers' Encyclopedia.* "It is infinitely more subtle and truer to the spirit of Spain than any of the attempts made by foreign composers, with the exception of Debussy. For Falla, although steeped in the folk music and popular dance tunes of Spain, never makes direct use of them. In his music the conventional mannerisms of melody, the dance rhythms, the characteristic harmonies and ornamental figures are suggested, insinuated, but rarely referred to directly."

The reference to Debussy is a significant one, for during his years of study in Paris (after he composed *La vida breve*) Falla absorbed the Impressionistic style of Debussy. "To 'suggest, insinuate, but rarely refer directly,' the impressionistic technique is, of course, invaluable," according to Leonard, "and Falla's debt to Debussy is undeniably large."

Like many composers, Falla's nationalistic feelings were not limited to his music. During the Spanish Civil War, he associated strongly with the fascist ideals of General Francisco Franco. In time, however, the composer became disillusioned with Franco's precepts; in 1939 he left his native Spain and settled in Argentina, where he lived until his death seven years later.

OTTORINO RESPIGHI (1879-1936)

NEITHER PHOTOGRAPHS NOR PAINTINGS CAN ILLUSTRATE MORE SUCcinctly the fountains, pines, and festivals of Rome than does the music of Ottorino Respighi. His masterpiece is the trilogy made up *of Le fontane di Roma, I pini di Roma,* and *Feste romane* ("The Fountains of Rome," "The Pines of Rome," and "Roman Festivals"), all composed and premiered between 1916 and 1929. His depictions of the natural and artistic treasures of Rome are crystal-clear.

The first suite Respighi created was *The Fountains,* which evokes different fountains in Rome at different times of the day: Valle Giulia at dawn, Triton at morn, Trevi at midday, and Villa Medici at sunset. The four segments of *The Pines* are intended to be less visual and more visionary, evoking memories of what went on in the areas around the pines of the Villa Borghese, near a catacomb, of the Janiculum, and of the Appian Way. Rounding out the trilogy is *The Roman Festivals,* which evokes the Circus Maximus, the Jubilee, the October Excursions, and Epiphany. Each part of the trilogy is like a musical postcard.

Born into a musical family in Bologna, Italy, in 1879, Ottorino learned the fundamentals of music from his father and entered Bologna's Liceo Musicale at the age of twelve. By the time he graduated in 1899, he had already written and seen the successful premiere of his *Symphonic Variations.* To further bolster his musical education, Respighi journeyed to St. Petersburg, Russia, to study orchestration and composition with composer Nikolai Rimsky-Korsakov (see Chapter 5, page 120) and then to Berlin, Germany, to work with composer Max Bruch (1838–1920). Home again in 1903, Respighi played viola with the Mugellini chamber ensemble.

As a professor of composition at Santa Cecilia Academy in Rome, Respighi met academy student Elsa Olivieri-

A MASTER OF MODERN ITALIAN ORCHESTRATION, OTTORINO RESPIGHI IS RENOWNED NOT ONLY FOR HIS OPERAS, BALLETS, AND SYMPHONIC TONE POEMS, BUT ALSO FOR THE INNOVATIVE INSERTION OF A PHONOGRAPH RECORDING INTO THE SCORE OF THE TONE POEM *THE PINES OF ROME.*

Sangiacomo, who later became a singer and composer; in 1919 she also became Respighi's wife. In 1923 Respighi was appointed director of Santa Cecilia, but after two years he relinquished the position, preferring to concentrate on his composing while continuing his professorship.

Although Respighi's success with the Rome Trilogy was tremendous, his other compositions must not be overlooked. In the category of opera, *Belfagor* was undoubtedly his most successful; other notable works include *Maria Egiziaca, Re Enzo,* and *Semirama.* The opera *La Campana Sommersa* ("The Sunken Bell") was based on a play by Gerhart Hauptmann (1862–1946) with a libretto by Claudio Guastella. Its world premiere was in Hamburg in 1927, and the United States premiere, which was designed by the renowned scenic designer Joseph Urban, was held the following year at the Metropolitan Opera. An incredible cast sang in the Metropolitan's *Campana* production: Elisabeth Rethberg, Giovanni Martinelli, Giuseppe deLuca, and Ezio Pinza. Respighi, who traveled to America three times and was present to hear them at the Met premiere, observed, "In heaven itself I could not wish for such a production!"

Along with his operas, Respighi composed ballets, chamber works, choral music, and a quantity of orchestral compositions. Descriptive music, such as 1927's *Gli uccelli* ("The Birds"), was Respighi's forte. For *The Birds*, Respighi made a composite of seventeenth- and eighteenth-century works written for the lute and harpsichord and tagged their respective themes "dove," "hen," "nightingale," and "cuckoo," with those four movements anticipated by a prelude.

Respighi's last opera, *Lucrezia,* was completed by Elsa Respighi, his wife. It premiered at La Scala in Milan in 1937, a year after his death. In 1979, *Lucrezia* and a choreographed version of *The Birds* were performed at the Caramoor Festival in Katonah, New York, for a centenary celebration of Respighi's birth. ⸮

DARIUS MILHAUD
(1892–1974)

DARIUS MILHAUD FOUND INSPIRATION IN RATHER UNUSUAL PLACES: HE musically transcribed descriptions of farm machinery from an agricultural catalog and gave the same treatment to a florists' brochure. *Machines Agricoles* is a song cycle and *Catalogue des Fleurs* ("Catalog of Flowers") is a musical setting of poems by Lucien Daudet (1840–1907) based on a commercial book for those in the floral business.

Of course, Milhaud also had his more serious, more conventional side. He wrote symphonies, concertos, chamber music, film scores, songs, and choral works. Born in 1892 at Aix-en-Provence, France, Milhaud had a privileged youth. In 1909 he entered the Paris Conservatory to concentrate on conducting and composition and to further his violin study. Three years later, at age twenty, Milhaud had his first composition, the Sonata for Violin and Piano, performed publicly.

When Milhaud was in his late twenties, he was able to visit South America when he became secretary to France's ambassador to Brazil, Paul Claudel. Claudel was also a poet and provided texts for some of Milhaud's music. The young composer later interpreted his Latin surroundings in the compositions *Saudades do Brazil,* "Scaramouche," and "Le Boeuf sur le Toit."

Upon returning to France from Rio de Janeiro in 1918, Milhaud helped to organize the French musical mavericks Georges Auric (1899–1983), Louis Durey (1888–1979), Germaine Tailleferre (1892–1983), Arthur Honegger (1892–1955), and Francis Poulenc (1899–1963) (see Chapter 7, page 161), along with himself, into the group who later became recognized as "Les Six." This name was coined by critic Henri Collet when he reviewed these composers' collection of piano selections; "Les Six" was a reference and perhaps an homage to the group of Russian composers of a somewhat earlier period known as "The Five" (Mily Balakirev, Aleksandr Borodin, Modest Mussorgsky, Nikolai Rimsky-Korsakov, and César Cui—see Chapter 5 for more on these composers and their accomplishments, both as individuals and as a group). During this period, he also became a professor of composition at the Paris Conservatory.

Throughout his career, Milhaud looked into all ramifications of polytonality—simultaneous use of two or more keys-and applied his research to his compositions, regardless of form or venue. He wrote chamber operas such as *Les Malheurs d'Orphée* ("The Misfortunes of Orpheus"), *Le Pauvre Matelot* ("The Poor Sailor"), and the trilogy *L'Enlèvement d'Europe* ("The Abduction of Europa"), *L'Abandon d'Ariane* ("The Abandonment of Ariadne"), and *La Délivrance de Thésée* ("The Liberation of Theseus"). On a grander scale, he wrote *Maximilien, Bolivár,* and *Christophe Colomb* (with a text by Claudel), all of which may have been carryovers from the Spanish influence of his two years in South America. Milhaud's interpretation of the Columbus epic was first presented in Berlin in 1930; strangely, although this premiere was successful, the opera was not produced again until three decades later.

Another grandiose opera, *David,* was influenced by his Jewish background. Actually part oratorio, the work was commissioned for the 1952 Festival of Israel on the occasion of the three-thousandth anniversary of King David and the founding of Jerusalem. Always an avid traveler, Milhaud journeyed to Israel to take in the atmosphere as preparation for writing *David.*

WITH *LA CRÉATION DU MONDE*, DARIUS MILHAUD, SHOWN HERE IN CARICATURE, ANTICIPATED GERSHWIN IN USING BLUES AND JAZZ IN A SYMPHONIC SCORE.

Among Milhaud's many travels were frequent trips to the United States—he was a regular faculty member at Mills College in Oakland, California, and often guest-taught at other American institutions.

In the 1920s jazz started to spread its wings across the world; Milhaud was a great enthusiast of not only jazz, but also blues and ragtime. Like so many of his interests and moments of inspiration, his attraction to jazz began on a trip abroad: in London he heard Billy Arnold and his band, and at a nightclub in New York City's Harlem he heard jazz as performed by black musicians; what he heard in Harlem was his inspiration for one of his numerous ballets, *La Création du Monde* ("The Creation of the World"). At the same time, jazz was being brought into the concert hall by George Gershwin. When Gershwin was about to write *An American in Paris* in 1928, he spent time in the French capital to get in the mood—just as Milhaud had done by going to Jerusalem in preparation for *David.* In response to the rousing success of *An American in Paris*, the RCA recording company commissioned Milhaud to compose *A Frenchman in New York*. While this did not enjoy the great success of Gershwin's counterpart *An American in Paris, A Frenchman in New York* was given the distinction of being recorded back to back with *An American in Paris* by Arthur Fiedler and the prestigious Boston Pops.

Later in life, Milhaud suffered crippling arthritis; this could have limited his trips, which involved conducting and lecturing, but Milhaud never let the pain slow him down. Toward the end of his life, however, he did have to rely on a wheelchair. Darius Milhaud died in 1974, two years after his eightieth birthday, which had been widely celebrated both publicly and privately. In the year preceding his death, Milhaud composed his last work (Opus No. 441): *Ani Maamin, Un Chant Perdu et Retrouvé* ("I Believe, A Song Lost and Found"), a cantata for the 1973 Festival of Israel.

C H A P T E R 7

The Twentieth Century

GUSTAV MAHLER

RICHARD STRAUSS

JEAN SIBELIUS

RALPH VAUGHAN WILLIAMS

SERGEI RACHMANINOFF

GUSTAV HOLST

ARNOLD SCHÖNBERG

CHARLES IVES

BÉLA BARTÓK

PERCY GRAINGER

IGOR STRAVINSKY

SERGEI PROKOFIEV

VIRGIL THOMSON

GEORGE GERSHWIN

FRANCIS POULENC

AARON COPLAND

DMITRI SHOSTAKOVICH

SAMUEL BARBER

BENJAMIN BRITTEN

LEONARD BERNSTEIN

PHILIP GLASS

The Twentieth Century

Twentieth-century music employs the tried-and-true elements of the past, intermingles those elements, and adds new touches, which gives the era its definition and distinction. Probably the newest addition to music in the twentieth century was the twelve-tone technique, an experiment of composer Arnold Schönberg concocted because the composer felt that the possibilities of existing combinations had been exhausted.

Webster's Dictionary defines the twelve-tone technique as "a modern system of tone relationships in which the twelve tones of an octave are not centered around any one tone, but are unified by a selected order of tones for a given composition." The twelve-tone row, Webster states, is "a series of tones in which no tone is duplicated, and in which the tones may appear in the same sequence."

The twentieth century has also developed Neoclassicism, a form of music incorporating features of the Classical and previous periods. Neoclassicism was based on a feeling of some composers that those writing in the late Romantic period, immediately preceding the twentieth century, had strayed off course. Ferruccio Busoni (1866-1924) launched Neoclassicism, and Paul Hindemith carried on the movement along with Sergei Prokofiev and Igor Stravinsky.

At the end of the twentieth century, new traditions such as the twelve-tone system and Neoclassicism have become integrated into the musical canon. Just as previous traditions have influenced the twentieth century, new techniques based on innovations of the twentieth century will chart future phases of music, and examinations of contemporary composers can therefore provide some clues as to what will occur in the next century of music.

A CONSUMMATE CONDUCTOR, GUSTAV MAHLER HAD TO CONVERT FROM JUDAISM TO CATHOLICISM, THE PREVAILING RELIGION IN AUSTRIA, TO OBTAIN THE MUSIC DIRECTORSHIP OF THE VIENNESE COURT OPERA. OPPOSITE: AN ILLUSTRATION OF ONE OF MAHLER'S MANY SONGS.

GUSTAV MAHLER
(1860–1911)

GUSTAV MAHLER SUBTITLED HIS SYMPHONY NO. 1 "THE TITAN," A name which could serve as well for the composer himself. Certainly Mahler had a titanic effect on the music world, influencing later twentieth-century composers with his use of new and more traditional elements side by side.

After "The Titan" came several additional symphonies. Mahler had a strange feeling about a ninth symphony. Beethoven had died after his ninth, and Anton Bruckner (see Chapter 4, page 85), a peer of Mahler's, had died before completing his. According to renowned conductor Bruno Walter (1876–1962), who authored a biography on Mahler, the composer was hesitant to continue the numerical sequence after his eighth symphony. Shying away from number nine, he called the next major work in the manner of his other symphonies—*Das Lied von der Erde* ("The Song of the Earth")—

Und nun a-de, mein herzaller-liebster Schatz

G. Mahler

a "song-symphony." Eventually, he did write a symphony that he called the Ninth. Maestro Walter, who revered Mahler and was influential in promoting his music, conducted the premiere of Symphony No. 9 in Vienna in 1912—the year after Mahler died. A Tenth symphony had been in progress, and through the years, several authorities on Mahler's music have rounded out the work using musical sketches left by the composer. The symphonic treatment most performed was pieced, patched, and pasted together by Deryck Cooke.

Unlike many composers, Mahler did not come from a musical family—his father ran a distillery and a string of taverns in Bohemia to support his large family. Born in Kalischt, Bohemia, in 1860, Gustav was nevertheless drawn to the piano; he gave his first recital when he was about ten years old. It is said that the sounds he absorbed in his youth—the blaring of the band at a local military installation, along with the rustles, warbles, and gurgles of nature—can be heard in his work. When Mahler was fifteen, his father was persuaded to let the youngster go to Vienna, where he enrolled in the Imperial Conservatory; he stayed for three years, transferring his interest from the piano to composition, took some courses at the University of Vienna, and then set off to pursue a career. Through a booking agent, Mahler was hired as conductor for several provincial opera houses throughout Germany and Austria. His first engagement was as conductor for a performance of Verdi's *Il Trovatore* ("The Troubadour") in the town of Halle on October 3, 1881. While the two operas he wrote were never published, Mahler built a reputation as an opera conductor.

Composing symphonies and songs was Mahler's real forte. His first major composition was the cantata *Das Klagende Lied* ("Song of Lament"). Mahler's symphonies detour somewhat from the accepted symphonic form, especially in the use of the human voice in several of them. The Eighth, for instance, calls for chorus and vocal soloists. On one occasion for this "Symphony of a Thousand," as it was subtitled, the combined choruses tallied 950 voices and the orchestra totaled 110 instruments, supplemented by celesta, pianoforte, organ, and mandolin, with extra trumpets and trombones situated in the theater boxes for stereo effect. Mahler's symphonies run unusually long; the shortest, the Fourth, lasts almost one hour.

In 1888 Mahler was called on to be artistic director of the Royal Opera in Budapest, a position he held for three years.

Mahler's enhancement of the Royal Opera brought cultural focus to Budapest. To achieve quality, Mahler was extremely demanding. When the administration sought to soften his approach, he resigned. Soon after, Mahler was hired by the Hamburg Opera, where he remained for six years. Before Mahler departed Hamburg, he also led the symphony orchestra, whose conductor, the celebrated Hans von Bülow, had to step down due to ill health.

Johannes Brahms, having heard Mahler conduct Mozart's *Don Giovanni* in the Budapest days, eagerly recommended him to conduct the Vienna Opera in 1897, a crucial event for both the Opera and Mahler. By 1900 Mahler advanced to the position of artistic director, putting all his energies into every detail of production and bringing the Vienna Opera to an incredibly high level. However, his despotic behavior, which had caused him trouble in Budapest and Hamburg, reached the breaking point in Vienna. Beethoven's *Fidelio* was the last opera Mahler conducted in Vienna; his tenure there ended in 1907. Around this time, the older of Mahler's two daughters, who was five, died from scarlet fever. This was certainly tragic, but also seemed rather eerie—two years earlier Mahler had composed *Songs on the Death of Children,* set to poems by Friedrich Ruckert, who had lost two children. A few days after the little girl's death, Mahler was diagnosed with a serious heart condition.

After Vienna, Mahler's next position was in New York's music world. Contracted in 1908 by the Metropolitan Opera, Mahler made his debut conducting Wagner's *Tristan und Isolde.* He conducted the American premieres of Smetana's *The Bartered Bride* and Tchaikovsky's *Queen of Spades*, along with numerous other operas. Doing double-duty, he conducted the New York Philharmonic, receiving the highest salary at that time for a conductor in the United States. By the start of the 1910 season, however, Mahler was affiliated solely with the New York Philharmonic.

Early in 1911, a streptococcus infection combined with his weakened heart to debilitate the fifty-year-old Mahler. The titan went back to Vienna, where he died in May. ♪

OPPOSITE: COMPOSER AND CONDUCTOR RICHARD STRAUSS, ONE OF THE MOST INVENTIVE MUSIC MASTERS OF THE TWENTIETH CENTURY, SUCCEEDED HANS VON BÜLOW AS PRINCIPAL CONDUCTOR AT THE WEIMAR OPERA.

RICHARD STRAUSS (1864-1949)

DON'T LET THE WALTZ FOOL YOU: RICHARD STRAUSS AND JOHANN Strauss were not related. While there is an exquisite waltz theme in Richard's *Der Rosenkavalier* ("The Knight of the Rose"), produced in 1911, it is coincidence that his last name is the same as that of the Waltz King.

Der Rosenkavalier's lighthearted, comic aura represented a change of tempo for Richard Strauss, whose earlier successful operas, namely 1905's *Salome* and 1909's *Elektra*, were laden with doom and gloom. While the moods were quite different, the librettist for *Elektra* and *Der Rosenkavalier*, as well as four other Strauss operas, was the same, the celebrated Austrian poet and dramatist Hugo von Hofmannsthal (1874–1929). The friendship and collaboration between Richard Strauss and Hofmannsthal spanned twenty-five years.

A number of Strauss's fifteen operas focused on women; in addition to *Salome* and *Elektra*, there was *Die Frau ohne Schatten* ("The Woman Without a Shadow," 1917) and *Arabella* (1932). In *Der Rosenkavalier*, the dominant woman is the Marschallin, Princess von Werdenberg.

This considered, it is perhaps not surprising that Strauss's wife, Pauline de Ahna, was a strong woman and also a professional soprano who portrayed Freihilde in Strauss's *Guntram*, his first opera. Strauss said his wife was "impulsive, violent, and brusque," but this was not by way of a negative criticism, for he had great regard and affection for his marital partner. Pauline was undoubtedly an interesting character; as Strauss wrote to a friend, "One could make ten plays out of my wife."

Born in Munich in 1864, Strauss was a wunderkind who had piano lessons at age four and started composing when he was six. His father, a highly regarded musician, was principal horn player in the Munich Opera orchestra, but young Strauss turned to conducting after taking his academics at

the University of Munich. At twenty-one, he became conducting assistant to the renowned Hans von Bülow, with the Meiningen Orchestra, and succeeded him as principal conductor. Strauss's fame as an extraordinary conductor would become international. For twelve years, he was music director of the Berlin (Royal) Opera, followed by five years (1919–1924) at the Vienna State Opera as principal conductor and co-music director.

The story goes that Strauss was an avid card player, very fond of the game "skat." He would play against the musicians and soloists in the

orchestras he conducted, and there were reports of colleagues losing large sums of money to Strauss. By way of introducing himself to a new orchestra, Strauss would say, "I need some players for skat. Who will join me?"

Early in his composing career, Strauss was successful with orchestral tone poems, which had their day in the second half of the nineteenth century. Also known as program music or symphonic poems, Strauss's orchestral poems, notably *Don Juan, Death and Transfiguration,* and *Till Eulenspiegel's Merry Pranks*, are among the best-known works in this form. Concertgoers eagerly awaited each new one, wondering what turn Strauss would take next. The composer combined his respect for the master composers of the past with contemporary dissonance. His music demanded large orchestras to complement his style.

Strauss composed three symphonies, the best known being the Symphony in F Minor, as well as other orchestral music. Vocal recitalists often incorporate Strauss's songs and lieder into their programs.

The Nazi regime in Germany found Strauss with mixed attitudes. To the satisfaction of the Nazis, he did not hesitate to replace conductor Bruno Walter, who was Jewish, or conductor Arturo Toscanini (1867–1957), who refused to come to Nazi Germany. Strauss, however, became suspect when he worked with a Jewish writer, and when he openly opposed the Nazi invasion of Poland he was placed under house arrest for a time. He further fell from Nazi favor when his son married a Jewish woman.

Strauss lived for several years after the war and died in Garmisch-Partenkirchen, Germany, but before he passed on, he composed his final opera: the quasi-autobiographical *Capriccio*, written during World War II. *Capriccio* is primarily a debate between a musician and a poet as to which is more important in opera, the music or the words. Strauss's conclusion, befitting his career, was that they are equal. ♪

OPPOSITE: THE TITLE PAGE OF THE MANUSCRIPT FOR STRAUSS'S OPERA *SALOME*, WRITTEN TO THE GERMAN TRANS-LATION OF OSCAR WILDE'S PLAY. RIGHT: THE GENIUS OF JEAN SIBELIUS, A NATIONALIST COMPOSER WHO WAS GREATLY INFLUENCED BY FINNISH LEGENDS AND MYTHS, WAS MOST ELOQUENTLY EXPRESSED IN HIS SYMPHONIES AND SYMPHONIC POEMS.

JEAN SIBELIUS
(1865–1957)

HAMEENLINNA SUOMALAINEN NORMAALILYSEO IS NOT FINNISH FOR supercalifragilisticexpialidocious; it is the name of the school where eleven-year-old Jean Sibelius was enrolled, an educational institution that instilled early nationalistic pride in the future composer. It was the first Finnish-speaking grammar school in Finland, which was a grand duchy of Russia from 1809 and had most of its home rule taken away during the reign of Czar Nicholas II (1868–1918), which began in 1894 and ended in 1917. Finland's desire for independence, declared December 6, 1917, after the October Revolution, was a strong influence on Sibelius, generally considered Finland's greatest composer.

Sibelius, the son of an army medical doctor who died during the 1867–1868 cholera epidemic, was born in Tavastehus in 1865. Jean and his brother and sister were comfortably brought up by their mother and grandmother in a musical environment. In his teens, Jean was becoming an accomplished violinist and composing chamber music. A law student at the University of Helsinki, he soon switched to composition and then departed for a more intense musical education in Berlin and Vienna. Sibelius's musical aptitude made him acceptable to high society, under the influence of whom he developed lifelong expensive tastes that often had him deep in debt.

Most artistic eras have their organized groups of intellectuals who are talented musicians, painters, and writers. The "Symposium," to which Sibelius belonged when he returned to Finland in the early 1890s, was just such a group. Sibelius's compositions had started to be well received while he was teaching at the Helsinki Conservatory. A few years later, the government granted him a small annual stipend with the idea that Sibelius would be able to devote more time to composing.

The nationalistic Sibelius was also inspired by Finnish mythology and legends. Finland's great folk epic, the *Kalevala*, touched Sibelius early on. It was the source of several of Sibelius's symphonic poems, an orchestral form of descriptive music that was well suited to the composer. *Finlandia* (1899) is his supreme masterpiece. Both a symphonic poem and a hymn titled "This Is My Song," *Finlandia* is most of all a documentation of Sibelius's love of his country. Some of his other successes are also symphonic poems, including *En Saga* (1892), the five-movement *Kullervo* (1892), and *Lemminkainen* (1895), or *The Four Legends,* which includes the famous *Swan of Tonela.*

In 1892, around the time he wrote those compositions, Sibelius married Aino Jarnefelt. He found himself in an authoritative family aligned with his nationalistic ideals. As of 1904, Sibelius and his wife lived in Jarvenpaa near Helsinki in a house called "Ainola," named to compliment her.

Sibelius traveled far and wide to fulfill conducting contracts, and he received honors from all over the world. In 1914 he journeyed to the United States to conduct his symphonic poem *The Oceanides* at the Norfolk Festival in Connecticut. On that visit, he received an honorary doctor of music degree from Yale University. In France he had received the Legion of Honor, and in Vienna he was offered the official chair of composition at the Imperial Academy of Music. Following World War I, Sibelius was asked to be director of the Eastman School of Music in the United States, a position he declined. In fact, he never journeyed to America again. A fervor for Sibelius's music was prevalent in the 1930s and 1940s in England and the United States, with renowned conductors Sir Thomas Beecham (1879–1961) and Serge Koussevitzky (1874–1951) performing complete cycles of Sibelius's symphonies. A poll by the Columbia Broadcasting

System (CBS) in the 1940s revealed Jean Sibelius as the favorite classical composer of U.S. listeners.

Sibelius composed seven symphonies, each quite distinct from the other. An eighth symphony was under way but became fragmented. Robert Kajanus, colleague and friend to Sibelius and composer and conductor of the Helsinki Philharmonic Orchestra, helped promote the First Symphony and Sibelius's other works when the orchestra performed at the Paris World Exhibition of 1900. Sibelius also composed for the violin and the piano, and more than one hundred songs flowed from his musical pen.

Celebrations of Sibelius's birthday in Finland have several times taken on the aura of a national holiday, none more so than his ninetieth. Concerts and other events abounded, and the composer received gifts from Scandinavian royalty, an estimated twelve hundred congratulatory telegrams, and a box of cigars from Winston Churchill.

Strangely, Sibelius stopped composing after 1929; at the same time, he also discontinued conducting. His last composition was the symphonic poem *Tapiola*—referring to Tapio, the Finnish forest god—which is regarded as one of his masterpieces. There are, of course, various theories as to why he ceased writing music when he was only sixty-four, considering he lived to be ninety-one. Perhaps he did not want to contend with the atonality that was popular in twentieth-century music. Perhaps he stopped for personal reasons, such as the cumulative effects of his heavy drinking or the loss of close friends. However, what he did compose was enough to place him in the annals of music history. ♩

RALPH VAUGHAN WILLIAMS (1872–1958)

RALPH VAUGHAN WILLIAMS WAS A TIRELESS COMPOSER WITH A WIDE range of interests, musical and otherwise. He was a bright and creative octogenarian when he wrote his *Romance for Harmonica and Orchestra*, followed by the Concerto for Tuba. Throughout his life, he also wrote for more traditional instruments, including piano, violin, and cello. Furthermore, he composed eleven variations for brass band for the 1957 National Brass Band Championship, which took place just a year before he died.

Born in 1872 in Down Ampney, Gloucestershire, England, Vaughan Williams was the epitome of the sophisticated country British gentleman. His country roots surfaced in the intense interest he took in English folk music. Vaughan Williams had another interesting root: his great-uncle was the renowned and controversial naturalist Charles Darwin (1809–1882), and Ralph was about seven when his great-uncle's treatise on evolution, *The Origin of Species*, was published.

Vaughan Williams was schooled at Charterhouse and Trinity College, Cambridge, after which he studied at the Royal College of Music from 1890 to 1896. He later became professor of composition there for three decades following World War I. After his time as a student at the Royal College, he studied with Max Bruch in Berlin and Maurice Ravel (see Chapter 6, page 128) in Paris.

Joining the English Folk-Song Society in 1904 influenced his early compositions, such as the *Norfolk Rhapsodies*, which included "The Captain's Apprentice" and "A Bold Young Sailor Courted Me," folk songs Vaughan Williams collected in England's Norfolk County, located on the east coast along the North Sea.

Religious texts also attracted Vaughan Williams, probably because of his early environment—his father was an Anglican clergyman, and religion was viewed as an integral part of the English social scene. The younger Vaughan Williams became organist at St. Barnabas Church in South Lambert for several years. He also edited *The English Hymnal*, for which he arranged numerous hymns and composed several new melodies that have been presented in various denominational hymnals. Segments of Vaughan Williams's Mass in G Minor were performed at the 1953 Coronation of Queen Elizabeth II (1926–) in Westminster Abbey in London.

Vaughan Williams adapted poems by well-known authors to music, including "Toward the Unknown Region," based on the writings of the American poet Walt Whitman (1819–1892). The first of the composer's nine symphonies, written in 1910 and known as "A Sea Symphony," was also inspired by Whitman's work.

At age forty-two, Vaughan Williams enlisted in the Royal Army to fight in World War I. He survived, but his colleague George S.K. Butterworth was killed in action. Vaughan Williams dedicated his second symphony to Butterworth

upon its publication. This piece premiered in 1914, but the composer revised it twice and it was presented in its final form when the New York Symphony Society played the United States' premiere in December 1920. Symphony No. 2, "A London Symphony," which Vaughan Williams preferred to have called "Symphony by a Londoner," travels musically from the Houses of Parliament to the slums of London. After the war, he continued composing symphonies. The Third, written in 1913, is a prime example of how the composer utilized the human voice as an orchestral instrument. Vaughan Williams's first visit to the United States, in 1922, was to the

RALPH VAUGHAN WILLIAMS, THE QUINTESSENTIAL ENGLISH COUNTRY GENTLEMAN, HAD WIDE MUSICAL INTERESTS—HE WROTE RELIGIOUS MUSIC, RE-CREATED BRITISH FOLK SONGS FOR HIS ORIGINAL WORK, AND EVEN COMPOSED TWO FILM SCORES.

Norfolk Music Festival in Connecticut to conduct this symphony, which was called the "Pastoral." (His third and last trip to America was when he was eighty-two.)

Vaughan Williams began writing for the theater in the 1920s, and his first opera was *Hugh the Drover*, first produced in 1924. While opera was not his main forte, probably his best one was *Sir John in Love*, based on the Shakespearean character John Falstaff, produced in 1930. Incorporated into this work was "Fantasia on Greensleeves," his adaptation of an old English folk tune.

Vaughan William's interests spanned centuries. Research into forgotten English music unearthed a theme written in 1567 by Renaissance composer Thomas Tallis, which Vaughan Williams converted into his *Fantasia on a Theme by Tallis* (1910), employing two string orchestras for an antiphonal effect of the original music. Later in his career, Vaughan Williams wrote film scores for *The 49th Parallel* (a.k.a. *The Invaders*), a World War II saga, and *Scott of the Antarctic*, a dramatization of the first British expedition to the South Pole.

Although defined as a nationalist composer, Vaughan Williams's utilization of folk music was not always direct—he was talented enough to create original music in the folk style. Interestingly, his nationalism was not limited to music: during the 1930s, he helped shelter European refugees from Hitler's scourge, housing them in his home in Surrey and in a refugee shelter in Dorkey.

Indefatigable, Vaughan Williams was approaching his eighty-sixth birthday in 1958 when his Symphony No. 9 was premiered, a few months before he died. ♪

SERGEI (1873-1943) RACHMANINOFF

AFTER BEING HYPNOTIZED FOLLOWING THREE YEARS OF DEPRESSION, Sergei Rachmaninoff returned to composing with enthusiasm. Despondency had set in with the failure of his First Symphony, even though some of the negative reviews were attributed to a slovenly performance of the work. Family and friends prevailed upon Rachmaninoff, then in his early twenties, to seek counseling, which led him to Dr. Nikolay Dahl.

After a few sessions of auto-suggestion, Rachmaninoff got back into the musical mainstream. Apparently, the composer was quite grateful to Dr. Dahl, to whom he dedicated his second piano concerto.

Rachmaninoff's career as a composer was equaled by his success as a conductor and especially as a concert pianist. As a boy, Rachmaninoff's musical training was at the keyboard. Born in 1873, he had a comfortable childhood on his father's vast estate in Oneg/Novgorod, Russia, until the property had to be sold. When the serf system ended, more money had to be poured into wages for those who managed and worked the land; the financial drain on the family was made worse by the senior Rachmaninoff's intense gambling habits. Around Sergei's tenth year, his parents separated, and he lived with his mother in St. Petersburg, where he studied at the College of Music. Rachmaninoff found little challenge there, however, and was transferred to the Moscow Conservatory at age twelve. In the company of two other pupils, he boarded with one of the instructors, Nikolai Zvereff, who imposed strict academic discipline. As Rachmaninoff became more dedicated to his studies, he asked Zvereff for a private room and his own piano. This caused a rift between the two, and, after four years guided by Zvereff, Rachmaninoff was told to leave.

One of the perks of being in Zvereff's household had been meeting gifted personalities of the late 1800s, and one of these, Pyotr Ilyich Tchaikovsky (see Chapter 4, page 98) became Rachmaninoff's mentor. To maintain this artistic relationship, sixteen-year-old Rachmaninoff remained in Moscow after the fracas with Zvereff, residing with relatives. Tchaikovsky died about four years later, in 1893, after which Rachmaninoff wrote the *Trio Elegiaque* and dedicated it to his fellow Russian.

The influence of Tchaikovsky can be heard in Rachmaninoff's one-act opera, *Aleko*, which he wrote for his final exams at the Moscow Conservatory (he graduated with honors). *Aleko* was premiered at the Moscow Opera in 1893. Although Rachmaninoff wrote two other operas that were produced, *The Miserly Knight* (for which Tchaikovsky's brother Modest wrote the libretto), and *Francesca da Rimini*, composing opera was not his forte.

His conducting of opera was better received. Rachmaninoff was conductor at the Moscow Private Russian Opera and then at the Bolshoi Opera until 1906, when political upheaval prompted him to leave the country. He and his wife and daughter settled in Dresden, Germany, where a second daughter was born in 1907. In 1909 Rachmaninoff went on his first American concert tour. Though he did return to his homeland eventually, Rachmaninoff made the final break with Russia in 1917, at the time of the February Revolution. Having been offered a Scandinavian concert tour, Rachmaninoff and his family lived in Stockholm, Sweden, and then in Copenhagen, Denmark. At this time, suffering from lack of money, Rachmaninoff also went on an extensive tour as a pianist, filling an opening temporarily left by renowned pianist Ignace Paderewski (1860–1941). When the Rachmaninoffs came to the United States in 1918, he played almost forty concerts in four months.

In the meantime, Rachmaninoff did not let up in his criticism of the new government of his native land. With two compatriots, he wrote a letter to *The New York Times* in January 1931, criticizing the policies of what had become the Union of Soviet Socialist Republics (U.S.S.R.). This drew a hostile response from *Vechernyaya Moskva*, a leading Soviet newpaper. More than that, the Soviet government forbade its citizens from performing or even studying Rachmaninoff's compositions (this ban was lifted in 1933).

By the early 1930s, Rachmaninoff had written his Second Symphony (the Third would come in 1936) and four piano concertos. The melodic Second Piano Concerto contains a theme that was transposed into the pop song "Full Moon and Empty Arms" in 1946. Most of Rachmaninoff's songs came earlier in his career, as did various piano preludes, sonatas, and études. The symphonic poem *Die Toteninsel* ("The Isle of the Dead") was written in 1907 as Rachmaninoff's reaction to a painting by Swiss artist Arnold Bocklin. *Kolokola*, a choral symphony inspired by Edgar Allan Poe's "The Bells," had its first performance conducted by Rachmaninoff in 1913. However, one of Rachmaninoff's most resounding compositions, *Rhapsody on a Theme by Paganini*, was not written or performed until 1934, and his last work, the *Symphonic Dances*, was written in 1940 in the United States, where he took refuge during World War II.

Cutting short a U.S. concert tour in February 1943 due to ill health accentuated by a diagnosis of pleurisy, Rachmaninoff returned to his Beverly Hills, California, home, where he died of cancer on March 28. ♪

SERGEI RACHMANINOFF, A PROTÉGÉ OF TCHAIKOVSKY, BECAME DISENCHANTED WITH THE RUSSIAN REVOLUTIONARY GOVERNMENT AROUND 1917 AND EMIGRATED TO AMERICA, WHERE HE CONTINUED HIS MUSICAL CAREER AND REMAINED A CRITIC OF HIS NATIVE LAND'S NEW REGIME.

GUSTAV HOLST
(1874–1934)

NO ONE WAS MORE SURPRISED THAN GUSTAV HOLST WHEN *THE PLANETS* became his most applauded composition, for when he had composed this piece he had not regarded it as exceptional. *The Planets* consists of seven tone poems, each named after a planet: Mars, Venus, Mercury, Jupiter, Saturn, Uranus, and Neptune. (Pluto had yet to be discovered at the time of *The Planets'* composition, or there might have been eight tone poems.) *The Planets* was first performed in public in 1919 by the Royal Philharmonic Society; the reception of this work made previously indifferent publishers take notice that Gustav Holst occupied a stellar place in the musical universe.

Though his very German name may be misleading, Holst was an Englishman. His ancestry has been traced to Matthias von Holst, who migrated from Scandinavia to Great Britain in 1807. Gustav was born in Cheltenham, England, in 1874. He dropped the "von" during the conflict with Germany in World War I.

Holst's childhood aptitude on the piano seemed to destine him for a career as a pianist, but that hope diminished when he developed severe neuritis in one of his hands. This affliction, however, did not deter him from pursuing a career in music. He took up the trombone and performed with the Carl Rosa Opera Company and the Scottish Orchestra, and in the lean years played on the piers at Blackpool and at Brighton.

In 1893, in his eighth attempt, Holst was finally admitted to the Royal College of Music in London. One of his joys at the Royal College was fellow student Ralph Vaughan Williams, who became one of England's most highly regard-ed composers. The two became lifelong friends and listened to one another's compositions as they were creating them. Vaughan Williams turned Holst on to English folk songs. But in the composition he dedicated to Vaughan Williams, "Two Songs Without Words," the music was pure Holst. During his days at the Royal College, Holst conducted the Hammersmith Socialist Choir, where he met the young soprano Isobel Harrison, who became his wife in 1901.

Teaching was a major part of Holst's professional life and something he perfected. His students adored him. His credo was "learn by doing," and he was patient with amateurs but merciless with professionals. His first assignments were as music master at James Allen's Girls' School in Dulwich from 1903 to 1919, and at St. Paul's Girls' School in Hammersmith, a post he held from 1905 to the end of his life. Later, he taught composition at the Royal College of Music and served on the faculties of Morley and Reading colleges. Not satisfied with the published music available at the school level, Holst composed works that he thought were suitable and challenging. For the James Allen School, Holst wrote a group of songs called *The Princess* and for St. Paul's School he composed the Brook Green Suite and the St. Paul's Suite.

His neuritis and his very poor eyesight kept him from military service, but under the auspices of the YMCA, he went to Salonika in Greece, Constantinople in Turkey, and all over Asia Minor with a music program for the British troops.

Some of Holst's earlier music, written between 1903 and 1910, reflects the appeal that Hinduism had for him. He learned Sanskrit so that he could better comprehend Hindu philosophy and literature. Under this exotic influence, Holst wrote several pieces, including "Choral Hymns from the Rig-Veda;" "Sita," based on an episode from "Ramayana"; and an opera called *Savitri*, based on the *Mahabharata*, one of the great classical Sanskrit epics of ancient India.

There were three operas in addition to *Savitri*, but *Savitri* was the most dramatic of the four. *At the Boar's Head* was the setting of tavern scenes from Shakespeare's *Henry IV*. Holst's other two operas were *The Perfect Fool* and *The Wandering Scholar*. Wagner's music deeply impressed Holst, and some of Holst's early writings, besides opera, show a glimmer of his influence.

Among Holst's most notable compositions are the Concerto for Two Violins and Orchestra; *The Hymn to Jesus*, which defied the standard oratorio form; the tone poem *Egdon Heath*, from a passage out of *The Return of the Native*, by Thomas Hardy (1840–1928); and the orchestral suite *Beni Mora*, another exotic piece, inspired by a vacation in Algeria, where, it is said, Holst rode a bicycle in the desert. No wonder he had a reputation of being unconventional.

Because of his multiple teaching jobs, finding time to write music was a monumental problem for Holst. He had a soundproof booth at St. Paul's School where he would closet himself to compose on weekends and during summer recess. Only when his stressful routine was complicated from the effects of a fall off an orchestra podium in 1923 did Holst accept his doctor's advice and slow down.

After 1925 he did minimal teaching and learned to relax and enjoy the pleasures of extensive reading, rambling walks through the countryside, and traveling. His traveling included several trips to the United States, where he lectured at the University of Michigan and at Harvard University and received the Howland Memorial Prize from Yale University for distinction in the arts. By 1934 Holst's health had deteriorated; he died in London on May 25, two days after abdominal surgery. His ashes were buried in Chichester Cathedral.

OPPOSITE: FOR MOST OF HIS PROFESSIONAL LIFE, GUSTAV HOLST, A DEDICATED, INNOVATIVE TEACHER, WAS HARD PRESSED TO FIND TIME TO WRITE MUSIC BECAUSE OF HIS MANY TEACHING ENGAGEMENTS. RIGHT: BECAUSE OF HIS RELIGIOUS BACKGROUND—THOUGH HE CONVERTED TO CHRISTIANITY, HE WAS BORN JEWISH—ARNOLD SCHÖNBERG, WHO PERFECTED THE SO-CALLED TWELVE-TONE TECHNIQUE, WAS FORCED TO LEAVE HIS NATIVE GERMANY AS HITLER ROSE TO POWER.

ARNOLD (1874–1951) SCHÖNBERG

ONE-THIRD OF THE AUDIENCE HISSED, ANOTHER THIRD LAUGHED, AND the remaining third sat there puzzled. This is the essence of a review by the esteemed critic Ernest Newman of the 1912 premiere of Arnold Schönberg's *Five Pieces for Orchestra*.

The reason for this harsh rejection was the piece's use of the twelve-tone technique, a radical musical method of the era. Composer Josef Matthias Hauer (1883–1959) had previously dabbled with twelve-tone mechanics, but Arnold Schönberg was the real developer of the twelve-tone technique. Critics, enthusiasts, and historians often refer to this kind of music as "atonal," but Schönberg always objected strenuously to this characterization. In fact, in the twelve-tone technique, the composer uses all twelve notes of the

ALBAN BERG (1885-1935)

Alban Berg was nineteen years old when he met Arnold Schönberg, the master of the twelve-tone system. For the next six years, Schönberg was the younger man's teacher and in many ways a surrogate father to him. The conservative tastes and constraints of the Viennese in the early 1900s were not conducive to use of the twelve-tone technique Berg and Schönberg were working with. The 1913 Vienna premiere of Berg's *Five Orchestral Songs*, for instance, created a furor.

Berg's experience working for the Austrian War Ministry during World War I inspired him to write an opera based on *Woyzeck*, a play by Georg Buchner about the plight of a soldier by that name, which in turn had been based on a court case of the 1820s. Three excerpts of the opera *Wozzeck* were performed at the Frankfurt Music Festival in 1924, and, like Schönberg's works, they sparked violent response. Sufficient positive interest was stirred, however, to lead the Berlin State Opera to stage *Wozzeck* the following year. Public and critics who were advocates of the twelve-tone technique hailed Berg's opera; those who were not in favor of this music, of course, did not. But enough of the music world had been intrigued, and frequent performances were scheduled in Europe, with American premieres scheduled for 1931.

Berg's approach to the twelve-tone system was not expansive. Certainly influenced by Schönberg's technique, Berg softened the system with tonal, or traditional, forms for both vocal and instrumental music. Still, Berg, Anton von Webern (another Schönberg student), and Schönberg himself are considered the ultimate composers of atonal music. Berg incorporated letters from their three names in "Epigraphe," the opening section of his *Chamber Concerto for Violin,* *Piano, and Thirteen Wind Instruments*, first performed in Frankfurt, Germany.

With the reasonable success of *Wozzeck* in Europe, Berg was inspired to write another opera, *Lulu*, which is a composite of the dramas *Earth Spirit* and *Pandora's Box*, by Frank Wedekind. Berg compiled his *Lulu* music into an orchestral suite that met with the usual polarized response when it was first performed in Berlin in 1934. A year later in Vienna, the suite fared better. This was to be the last concert attended by Berg, who had never been a healthy man; he died two weeks after the concert, the final physical blow being blood poisoning precipitated, oddly enough, by a bee sting.

When he died, Berg had completed only two acts and part of the third—and final—act of *Lulu*. This unfinished piece was presented as *Lulu*'s world premiere in Zurich in 1937, although subsequent performances have employed the "Lulu" Suite to fill out Act III. Hélène Berg, whom Berg married in 1911, refused to release the material she held as Act III, claiming she was fulfilling her dead husband's wishes communicated to her from "the beyond." There is also a theory that she withheld the existing music because she not only detested the sordid story of *Lulu* but also saw her refusal as retaliation for her husband's infidelity. When Hélène died in 1976, her stand was reiterated in her will. However, this was circumvented when the publisher Universal Edition designated composer Friedrich Cerha to write Act III based on existing Berg manuscripts. With Cerha's additions, the completed *Lulu* had its world premiere at the Paris Opéra in 1979 and its United States premiere the same year at the Santa Fe Opera, which had presented the earlier version in 1963. New York's Metropolitan Opera premiered the fragmented version in 1977 and was finally able to perform the completed *Lulu* in 1980.

chromatic scale, eliminating the dominance of one tone with the modulation of others, which is characteristic of traditional classical music. It is not that there is no tone, but that all the notes being treated equally makes it impossible for one tone to be heard above the others. The twelve-tone technique is difficult for laymen to accept and understand because it sounds extremely unmelodic and is exceedingly complex.

Born in Vienna in 1874, Schönberg started composing for the violin when he was around twelve years old. He soon came to the attention of composer and teacher Alexander von Zemlinsky, who nurtured Schönberg's career. The young composer married Zemlinsky's sister, Mathilde, in 1901, and they had two children. After Mathilde died, Schönberg married Gertrude Kolisch in 1924, with whom he had three more children.

Schönberg's earlier compositions were in a more conventional style. One of the most performed Schönberg compositions, *Transfigured Night*, first heard as an instrumental sextet in 1902, was rewritten for chamber orchestra in 1917, and was choreographed in 1942 by Antony Tudor for the Ballet Theatre as *The Pillar of Fire*.

Pierrot Lunaire, based on symbolist poems by Albert Guiraud, further established Schönberg's uniqueness after *Five Pieces for Orchestra*, with the overriding use of *sprechstimme*, or *sprechgesang,* a form of song-speech or recitative. The difficulty of performing such a piece is indicated by the fact that forty rehearsals were necessary before *Pierrot Lunaire* premiered in 1912 in Berlin, again eliciting negative outcries. Schönberg enthusiasts were also in the audience, however, and the confrontation between both factions produced great verbal and even physical antagonism.

In response to the intense opposition to his work, Schönberg founded the Society for Private Performances in 1918. Critics were refused admission and applause was not allowed, even from his followers.

Although Schönberg, born Jewish, had converted to Christianity, his religious background was objected to by the

OPPOSITE: FOLLOWING IN THE MUSICAL FOOTSTEPS OF HIS MENTOR, SCHÖNBERG, ALBAN BERG CREATED MANY WORKS IN THE TWELVE-TONE SYSTEM, THOUGH HE MADE IT EASIER FOR THE LISTENER TO UNDERSTAND BY INCORPORATING MORE TRADITIONAL FORMS.

Nazis, who also rejected his experimental music. Schönberg left Germany, where he had done much of his composing, reinstated himself as a Jew, and arrived in the United States in 1933, becoming a citizen eight years later.

Political events in Europe are reflected in Schönberg's *Ode to Napoleon*, an orchestral composition protesting the tyranny of dictatorship; *A Survivor From Warsaw,* a choral work depicting the atrocities of the Nazi concentration camps; and an opera, *Moses and Aaron*, based on the Old Testament book of Exodus. *Moses and Aaron* was incomplete when Schönberg died; Acts I and II have been performed since 1954 and the text he wrote for Act III is sometimes performed with other Schönberg music.

In 1903 Schönberg had organized a school for composition in Berlin. Among his admiring students were Alban Berg (see sidebar) and Anton von Webern (1883–1945), who went on to establish themselves as highly regarded composers, often writing in the Schönberg style. In the United States, Schönberg taught at the Malkin School of Music in Boston and was a professor of music at the University of Southern California and then at the University of California, Los Angeles. He was also named Professor for Life at the Academy of Arts in Berlin.

Numerous commemorative concerts for Schönberg's seventieth and seventy-fifth birthdays were not welcomed by the composer, who was still bitter over critical and public response to his twelve-tone technique. He expressed his retroactive anger when receiving a Special Award of Distinguished Achievement from the National Institute of Arts and Letters. The hurt showed even when a composition was well received, as with the cantata *Gurrelieder* (1903), after which Schönberg refused to acknowledge the ovation.

His surliness apparently did not carry over to his personal life. In Los Angeles, his home for many years until his death in 1951, Schönberg reportedly enjoyed large gatherings; grandchildren abounded, and there were lots of pets. Schönberg enjoyed his hobby of furniture-building and often played tennis, with George Gershwin a frequent partner on the court.

No matter which side one comes down on in the twelve-tone controversy, everyone agrees that Schönberg certainly made his mark on music.

CHARLES IVES
(1874–1954)

WHEN IS AN INSURANCE SALESMAN A COMPOSER? THE ANSWER IS: when he is Charles Ives.

Around 1909 Ives's insurance office was achieving the highest sales of any such business in the United States. Ives and his partner, Julian Myrick, comprised an agency of the Mutual Insurance Company. In addition to normal business, they operated a training school for agents, and Ives wrote orientation pamphlets, some of which continued to be used long after his demise.

Soon after Ives's graduation from Yale University in 1898, a relative who was medical examiner for the Mutual Insurance Company arranged for "Charlie" to work in the actuarial department of Mutual's New York City office. Subsequently qualifying as an insurance agent, Ives went to Washington Life, but when that company sold out Ives returned to Mutual. Along the way he met Myrick, and the two men, realizing that they complemented each other well in business, began their partnership.

Ives was a nighttime and weekend composer. Part of his weekends were spent as an organist for Sunday services at various churches in and around New York City. On relinquishing one post, Ives generously left some of the anthems and organ music he had composed in the choir library. When that church changed locations in 1915, an unsavvy person or committee threw out the sheet music for Ives's compositions. Not much of Ives's written organ music survives; as for anthems, only the outlines remain for some of them.

Born in 1874, Ives grew up in Danbury, Connecticut, and later settled in West Redding. "Charlie" was very young when he began to receive his music instruction from his father, who had been a bandmaster in the Union Army during the Civil War. At the age of twelve, Charlie was playing drums in his father's civilian band, and at fourteen he became the youngest paid church organist in Connecticut. Ives was also an avid athlete, especially when it came to baseball, football, and tennis, and was often selected team captain.

Between music and sports, his schoolwork suffered, but not enough to keep him out of Yale. While Ives did not engage in college sports (his father wisely prohibited athletics to allow Charlie more time for his prescribed studies), he was elected to various student societies—he was quite obviously well liked. During this time, Ives wrote the waltz-like "The Bells of Yale," which became part of the glee club's repertoire, and composed a graphic orchestral composition called *The Yale-Princeton Football Game*, depicting an actual confrontation in 1897 ending with a 6–0 Yale victory.

Ives's first known composition is called "Slow March," a rather generic title considering the colorful ones that were to come. *Concord, Mass., 1840–1860* is the name of Ives's second piano sonata, written between 1909 and 1915; its four movements are called "Ralph Waldo Emerson," "Nathaniel Hawthorne," "Bronson and Louisa May Alcott," and "Henry David Thoreau," named after famous residents from Concord.

Ives's music was polytonal, polyrhythmic, and polytextured. Although he experimented with new styles of music, he also employed many themes originating from standard marches, pop tunes, and hymns, of which there was a great store in his brain from his years as a church organist. Ives overlapped, interspersed, and generally blended familiar melodies so much that often only a keen ear could identify the original well-known tunes. Much of his music comes out sounding dissonant.

Considering the nature of Ives's music, it is ironic that his wife's name was Harmony. Harmony Twichell, the sister of one of Ives's Yale classmates, and Charles Ives were married in 1908 in Hartford, Connecticut, by her clergyman father. The couple designed their own house in West Redding and moved in around 1913. Through the Fresh Air Fund, which brought those less fortunate to the country, they invited families to spend time at a cottage on the property. They even adopted one child, and Edith Osborne Ives brought them great joy.

Ives was awarded a Pultizer Prize in 1947 for the third of his four symphonies, *The Camp Meeting,* written in 1911. In the 1940s, his music started to be performed more frequently and became more popular. Despite the prestigious prize, however, much of his music was not performed until well after his death in 1954. In 1956 Harmony Ives gave her husband's manuscripts to the Yale School of Music Library. Ives composed very little music following a heart attack in 1918, but he did not retire from the insurance business until 1930. Around 1926 he wrote his last composition, an instrumental piece, "Sunrise."

"American as apple pie" might be a good phrase to describe Ives's music, with composition titles such as *Three Places in New England*; "General William Booth Enters Into Heaven," Ives's most acclaimed song; "Central Park in the Dark;" and *Holidays*, which includes the sections "Washington's Birthday," "Decoration Day," "The Fourth of July," and "Thanksgiving." Blissfully oblivious of what contemporary European composers were up to, Ives created his own style and was in his own way a nationalistic composer. ♪

OPPOSITE: ONE OF THE GREAT AMERICAN MUSICAL EXPERI- MENTERS, CHARLES IVES WAS IN FACT ONLY A NIGHTTIME AND WEEKEND COMPOSER, AS HE HAD TO SPEND WEEKDAYS RUN- NING HIS INSURANCE BUSINESS. BELOW: CHARLES IVES AND HIS WIFE, HARMONY, WERE VERY GENEROUS FOLK; VIA THE FRESH AIR FUND, WHICH BRINGS LOW-INCOME CITY DWELLERS TO EXPERIENCE THE PLEASURES OF THE COUNTRY, THEY OFTEN INVITED FAMILIES TO SPEND TIME ON THEIR CONNECTICUT PROPERTY.

BÉLA BARTÓK
(1881–1945)

AN OUTSTANDING ETHNOMUSICOLOGIST, BARTÓK STUDIED PRIMITIVE and folk music. His research into ethnic folk songs, especially in his native Hungary, was far-reaching and has become long-lived.

Bartók was born in 1881 in Nagyszentmiklos, Hungary (ceded to Rumania after World War I and now known as Sinnicolau Mare). His father headed an agriculture college and, although the older Bartók died in 1888, he and Bartók's mother, a piano teacher, left a strong musical influence on their son. When Béla was in his late teens, his mother intended for him to study in Vienna, then capital of the Austro-Hungarian Empire. Instead, young Bartók chose the Royal Academy of Music in Budapest, apparently attracted by the Hungarian nationalistic movement that was brewing in that city.

In that environment, it is not surprising that one of Bartók's earliest musical successes was a symphonic poem about Lajos Kossuth (1802–1894), a revered Hungarian national hero. A member of parliament who was a leader for liberal government reform, Kossuth led the unsuccessful 1848–1849 rebellion in Hungary and was exiled for his involvement. Kossuth represented independence and is sometimes called the "Hungarian George Washington." The 1903 composition *Kossuth* premiered at the Halle Orchestra and was conducted by the eminent Hans Richter.

Bartók s own nationalistic feelings found their niche in his folk-music research. His interest in this field was shared by composer Zoltán Kodály (1882–1967), who joined Bartók on numerous expeditions into the outermost areas of Hungary and its neighboring countries. Bartók authored five books and numerous articles on his findings. A fantastic number of more than fourteen thousand examples of folk music were collected, catalogued, and transcribed, as well as used, at least in essence, in Bartók's own creations. In his use of folk music, he sought out elements that were well off the beaten path of melody, creating dissonant compositions.

In composing his only opera, *Duke Bluebeard's Castle*, which premiered in Budapest in 1918, Bartók followed the path of Modest Mussorgsky (see Chapter 5, page 119) in adapting the vocal line to fit the idiosyncrasies of the national language of the piece. *Duke Bluebeard's Castle*, a one-act work, is sometimes coupled in performance with Bartók's ballets, 1916's *The Wooden Prince* and 1919's *The Miraculous Mandarin*.

Whereas *Kossuth* was in the style of Richard Strauss and *The Wooden Prince* reflected Debussy, Bartók showed his own style with *The Miraculous Mandarin*. While fame in the international music world came to Bartók because of *Mandarin*, it was not all positive because Bartók's dissonant music and the violence and sexuality of the story were shocking to many. His first success in a popular sense

was the orchestral *Dance Suite*, composed in 1923 for the celebration of the fiftieth anniversary of the joining of the cities of Buda and Pesth to create Budapest.

Somewhat like Kossuth, Bartók's nationalism was not always well received in Europe, which was experiencing waves of communism. From time to time Bartók thought of emigrating, but his strong personal allegiance to Hungary kept him in Budapest for most of his life. Eventually the composer did leave; in 1940 he went to the United States with his second wife, Ditta Pasztory, whom he had married after his divorce in 1923 from Marta Ziegler. He had taught at the Royal Academy of Music for many years and had a research position with the Hungarian Academy of Sciences. In the United States he did research at Columbia University for a while, but his failing health, his straitened financial circumstances, and the lack of public enthusiasm for his music had whittled Bartók down to a depressed state.

Regarded as an excellent pianist, Bartók went on numerous concert tours, often performing his own music, which included sonatas, three concertos for piano, and the monumental *Mikrokosmos* ("Microcosmos"), the six-volume set of 153 piano pieces written between 1926 and 1939. He also wrote for solo violin and viola and composed six string quartets. Well-known musicians commissioned works by Bartók. The composer wrote *Sonata for Solo Violin* for violinist Yehudi Menuhin (1916–), *Concerto for Orchestra* for conductor Serge Koussevitzky, and *Contrasts* for a trio made up of jazz clarinetist Benny Goodman (1909–1986), classical violinist Joseph Szigeti, and Bartók himself at the keyboard.

The popularity of Bartók's music rose greatly after his death in 1945, but his compositions were not then, nor are they now, pleasing to all audiences. It is Bartók's great contribution to folk-music research that was and is universally accepted and hailed. ♩

OPPOSITE: BÉLA BARTÓK IS PERHAPS AS IMPORTANT TO MUSIC HISTORY FOR HIS EXTENSIVE RESEARCH INTO ETHNIC FOLK SONGS AS FOR HIS OWN COMPOSITIONS. <u>RIGHT:</u> AN AUSTRALIAN EMIGRÉ TO THE UNITED STATES, PERCY GRAINGER WAS A SORT OF PIONEER OF ELECTRONIC MUSIC—AROUND 1937 HE WROTE A QUARTET FOR ELECTRONIC INSTRUMENTS.

PERCY GRAINGER
(1882–1961)

BEST KNOWN FOR WHAT HE HIMSELF CALLED HIS "FRIPPERIES," GEORGE Percy Aldridge Grainger has not been taken as seriously as a composer as, according to some authorities, he should be.

The Twentieth Century

But by writing such delightful "fripperies" as "Country Gardens" and "Shepherd's Hey," Grainger earned a solid place in music history.

Grainger holds multiple places in music history: as a composer, an outstanding concert pianist, and an interpreter of the music of the Norwegian composer Edvard Grieg (see Chapter 4, page 105). Grainger showed a predilection for Nordic composers, and when he met Grieg through a mutual friend in 1906, the two men formed an instant rapport. On this occasion, Grainger, in his twenties, played Grieg's *Slatter* for the older composer, who entered his reaction in his diary: "I had to reach the age of 64 to hear Norwegian piano music interpreted with so much understanding and genius." At Grieg's instigation, Grainger was engaged as soloist for the older composer's Piano Concerto in A Minor at England's Leeds Festival the following year. Grieg himself was scheduled to conduct, but he died suddenly in September 1907. Nevertheless, the October performance, conducted by Sir Charles Stanford, went on as scheduled, and was a great success for Grainger.

Grainger had first learned the Grieg concerto when he was a student at the Hoch Conservatory in Frankfurt, Germany, from 1895 through 1899. He shone as a soloist in the work for nearly half a century, playing the composition with the top orchestras and conductors. Grainger received his earliest piano lessons from his mother, a professional teacher, and from Louis Pabst in Grainger's native Melbourne, Australia. At age ten, Grainger was earning money as a recitalist; these monies were in part what enabled him to study in Germany. In the early 1900s, Grainger toured Great Britain, Australia, New Zealand, and South Africa, receiving acclaim as a pianist; he made his United States debut with a New York recital in 1915. Just a month later, Grainger was the soloist, as he had been at Leeds in 1907, for Grieg's Piano Concerto in A Minor with the New York Philharmonic. Around that time, he moved to the United States; he became a naturalized citizen in 1919.

One of the links between Grainger and Grieg was a shared active and exuberant interest in folk music. On his worldwide concert tours, Grainger would search out and record local singers and their songs. In 1922 he joined a Danish folk song-collecting expedition to Jutland and returned there twice, expanding his collection to two hundred Danish songs.

In 1928 Grainger married Swedish painter and poet Ella Strom during a Hollywood Bowl concert attended by twenty-two thousand people; on that occasion, Grainger conducted his "To a Nordic Princess," which was inspired by and dedicated to his bride.

Grainger's compositions, other than his "fripperies," are sometimes referred to as "free music." As a boy, he was supposedly inspired by the sounds of water flowing and rushing; this seems quite possible, for later on he wrote "Sea Song" and other songs emulating nature. In the choral work *Love Verses from The Song of Solomon*, he attempted to use music to re-create the rhythms of human speech.

Some of his compositions are founded on British and Irish folk songs, such as "Irish Tune from County Derry," which was inspired by "Londonderry Air" (which dates back to 1855). "Shepherd's Hey" represents four variations of a Morris dance tune typical of certain agricultural districts in England. "Mock Morris," however, is a Grainger original with only the rhythm in the Morris dance style.

"Country Gardens" has its roots in what is known as a "handkerchief dance" bearing the same title. Grainger started publicly improvising on the "Country Gardens" melody when he was a member of the Army Band during World War I, playing saxophone, oboe, and piano. The popularity of this ditty with audiences prompted the composer to send his adaptation to his publisher, G. Schirmer, and "Country Gardens" became a bestseller in sheet music.

Grainger's research papers, manuscripts, and other memorabilia are preserved in the University of Melbourne's Grainger Museum, which he helped establish; at the Library of Congress in Washington, D.C.; and in the Grainger Library in White Plains, New York, where he lived from 1940 until his death in 1961. ♩

OPPOSITE: IGOR STRAVINSKY, PROBABLY BEST KNOWN FOR HIS INSPIRED AND RADICAL *RITE OF SPRING* BALLET, IS CELEBRATED ALSO FOR THE *FIREBIRD* BALLET, AND *NOAH AND THE FLOOD*.

IGOR (1882–1971) STRAVINSKY

WHILE MANY BIOGRAPHIES OF IGOR STRAVINSKY BEGIN BY DESCRIBING his work as "shocking," "wild," "bizarre," "grinding," "harsh," "revolutionary," "violent," or "hideous," the composer substantially contributed to a wide range of more conventional musical styles in addition to adding to the more radical work of the twentieth century. As for Stravinsky himself, a man who wrote music to "The Owl and the Pussycat" by Lewis Carroll and composed a ballet for elephants could hardly be considered "harsh" or "hideous"—humorous perhaps.

Actually, the radical adjectives apply almost exclusively to *Le Sacre du Printemps* ("The Rite of Spring"), Stravinsky's third major ballet. Before and after the presentation of this work, his compositions were not reviewed with words of extreme rejection. *The Rite of Spring*'s premiere in Paris on May 29, 1913, whipped its listeners into a frenzy during and long after the performance because of its harshness and dissonance. But that is how the public often responds to something unfamiliar. *The Rite of Spring* broke all the accepted rules of rhythm and music. In the 1990s the public is willing to listen to—though not always approve of—music that is sometimes dissonant and discordant, but we must remember that it was Stravinsky who pioneered this type of music.

The thirty-year-old composer who created such a stir was the son of Fyodor Stravinsky, an operatic bass who was the predecessor of the great Fyodor Chaliapin (1873–1938) at the Imperial Opera House in St. Petersburg. Igor, born in 1882, studied criminal law at the University of St. Petersburg near his childhood home of Oranienbaum (since renamed Lomonosov). This academic pursuit was the result of practical guidance from his parents, but when Igor was twenty, his father died and the youth was free to pursue music. A university friend named Andrei introduced Igor to his father, the esteemed composer Nikolai Rimsky-Korsakov (see Chapter 5, page 120), who was so impressed with the young man's talent that he took Stravinsky on as a student. Stravinsky was instructed by Rimsky-Korsakov for three years and had his compositions performed at weekly musical gatherings hosted by the older composer. Stravinsky became part of the family, and when Andrei's sister was to be married, Stravinsky wrote the orchestral fantasy *Fireworks* for the occasion.

Another providential meeting took place when Stravinsky's *Fireworks* and *Scherzo Fantastique* premiered and impresario Sergei Diaghilev (1872–1929), mastermind of the Ballets Russes, was in attendance. After having Stravinsky prepare scores for compositions by others, Diaghilev engaged him for an original ballet, resulting in *The Firebird*. This Russian fairy tale set to music brought Stravinsky international notice, which was furthered by the success of *Petrouchka* in 1911. These works were traditional but had a modern flavor.

Stravinsky's international fame soured a bit when, in 1913, he presented *The Rite of Spring.* In spite of the furor over this ballet, which was regarded as visually as well as audibly offensive, Stravinsky's progress as a composer was not harmed.

However, the Russian Revolution in 1917 did create a detour. Property in his homeland was confiscated and financial stress precipitated the formation of a low-budget touring company, whose initial ballet offering was Stravinsky's *L'Histoire du Soldat* ("The Soldier's Tale"). An extensive flu epidemic cut the tour short, and Stravinsky turned to Diaghilev for support. Diaghilev was uninterested in *Soldat,* but he did produce other Stravinsky works, including *Pulcinella,* which was enhanced with sets designed by Pablo Picasso (1881–1973), in 1920, and in 1923 *Les Noces* ("The Wedding"), the last Stravinsky ballet for the Ballets Russes. Stravinsky was expecting to hear from Diaghilev in August 1929 when a telegram arrived advising him of the death of the impresario. Diaghilev, promoter of concerts, opera, and art, as well as ballet, was buried in St. Michel, the island cemetery in Venice.

Diaghilev had introduced Stravinsky to Vera de Bosset Sudeikin in 1921, and she had quickly become his devoted companion. Stravinsky married her in 1940, a year after the death of his first wife, with whom he had had four children. Vera and Stravinsky settled in Los Angeles, California; though he had become a French citizen in 1934, he subsequently became a naturalized citizen of the United States.

Stravinsky was heavily involved in the American music world. For bandleader-clarinetist Woody Herman 1913–1987),

Stravinsky wrote the *Ebony Concerto.* In *The Seven Lively Arts,* produced for Broadway by Billy Rose, there was "Scène du Ballet" with original music by Stravinsky. The "Circus Polka," choreographed by George Balanchine (1904–1983), was composed by Stravinsky for a herd of elephants along with Vera Zorina as premier danseuse.

Stravinsky continued to compose chamber music and symphonies for concert halls as well as ballet compositions. He was commissioned by the Boston Symphony Orchestra and the Chicago Symphony Orchestra to compose works for their respective fiftieth seasons. On Stravinsky's frequent worldwide concert tours, he would often conduct his own works. Stravinsky also composed operas, most notably *The Rake's Progress.* Inspired by a series of William Hogarth (1697–1794) lithographs with the same title, Stravinsky solicited poet W.H. Auden (1907–1973) and his colleague Chester Kallman to prepare the libretto. *The Rake's Progress* had a successful premiere in 1951 at the Venice Festival.

Of Stravinsky's numerous awards and honors, the one he considered the greatest was being invited back, after more than forty years, to his native land. In September 1962, the year of his eightieth birthday, Stravinsky went to the U.S.S.R. for a round of banqueting, sightseeing, and conducting performances of his *Petrouchka, Orpheus, Firebird* and *Sacre du Printemps.* Premier Nikita Khrushchev invited Stravinsky to again take up residence in the Soviet Union, but the composer declined.

Stravinsky, who died in 1971, is interred at St. Michel, just like his mentor Diaghilev. ♪

SERGEI (1891–1953) PROKOFIEV

DURING COMMUNIST RULE IN RUSSIA, COMPOSERS—INCLUDING Prokofiev and Dmitri Shostakovich—and leaders in all the arts were forced to operate under the strictures of the government. Political pressure and intrigue may have changed the course of composition by Sergei Prokofiev, but he nonetheless completed a number of influential works.

Prokofiev's early music, written in the second decade of the twentieth century, was startling to conservatives but refreshing to modernists. Prokofiev used dissonance and discord in his composition, unlike the melody and refinement present in the music of the preceding Romantic period. In time his writing mellowed, either from natural progression in his development or from the Communist Central Committee's demands.

While his adult life occurred under the communists, Prokofiev's childhood was in a different era: the time of Czarist Russia. He was born in Sontsovka, Ukraine, in 1891 to parents who had lost two daughters before his arrival. A prodigy, Prokofiev wrote an opera at the age of twelve and then spent a decade at St. Petersburg Conservatory, graduating with honors at age twenty-three. After the 1917 Revolution, Prokofiev left his native land and wended his way through London, Paris, and Tokyo before arriving in New York in September 1918. He resided in the United States until 1922, when he moved to Paris; in 1932 he returned to the U.S.S.R. Through those years and into 1938, Prokofiev performed worldwide as a piano virtuoso, in recital and as

OPPOSITE: PICASSO, ANOTHER AVANT-GARDE TWENTIETH-CENTURY ARTIST, SKETCHED THE COVER FOR THE PROGRAM OF STRAVINSKY'S WORK *RAGTIME*; THE ARTISTS ALSO COLLABO-RATED ON STRAVINSKY'S *PULCINELLA*, FOR WHICH PICASSO DESIGNED THE SETS. RIGHT: ONE OF THE FOUR TWENTIETH-CENTURY RUSSIAN MUSIC MASTERS, SERGEI PROKOFIEV, IS PROBABLY BEST KNOWN FOR HIS CHILDREN'S PIECE *PETER AND THE WOLF*, WHICH SERVES AS AN INTRODUCTION TO THE INSTRUMENTS OF THE ORCHESTRA BY USING SPECIFIC INSTRU-MENTS TO REPRESENT SPECIFIC CHARACTERS.

soloist with top symphony orchestras, often playing his own sonatas and concertos.

By the time of the 1917 Revolution, Prokofiev had made his musical mark. Meeting ballet impresario Sergei Diaghilev in 1914 had resulted in a commission for a ballet, *Ala and Lolli,* and the music was arranged into the Scythian Suite, which premiered in 1916 and is generally regarded as Prokofiev's first public success. The Scythians were an ancient nomadic tribe and Prokofiev's wild music was descriptive of their lifestyle.

After the success of these pieces, Prokofiev stepped out of character and, as a challenge to himself, wrote a symphony in the manner of Haydn and Mozart. He named it the Classical Symphony. This work, the first of his seven symphonies, had its premiere in Russia shortly before Prokofiev departed for the West.

Although the Classical Symphony is one of Prokofiev's most frequently performed concert compositions, *The Love for Three Oranges* ranks as his most popular opera. Commissioned by the Chicago Opera Company, Prokofiev prepared the libretto based on the work of the eighteenth-century Italian playwright Carlo Gozzi. This piece premiered in 1921, with the composer conducting. *Oranges* did not immediately prosper, but it did acheive tremendous success in 1949 when it was performed by the New York City Opera. The stately march from *The Love for Three Oranges* served as theme music for the long-running CBS radio program *Your FBI in Peace and War.*

The Twentieth Century

In the United States, Prokofiev studied film music techniques in Hollywood and brought what he learned to Russian filmmaking. Prokofiev's scores for the movies *Alexander Nevsky, Ivan the Terrible*, and *Lieutenant Kije* were transcribed into orchestral suites; *Kije* has become especially familiar.

Under Communist rule, the safest territory for composers was works for children. Before the revolution, he had composed a piece for voice and piano on "The Ugly Duckling," by Hans Christian Andersen (1805–1875); in 1936 he wrote twelve piano pieces grouped together as *Music for Children;* seven of these pieces were later transcribed into the orchestral suite *A Summer's Day*. His *Cinderella* ballet was first performed in 1945.

Prokofiev's most outstanding piece in the children's music genre—and perhaps his best-known work—is *Peter and the Wolf*, which premiered in Moscow in 1936 for an audience of youngsters at a concert by the Moscow Philharmonic Orchestra. *Peter and the Wolf* was first performed outside Russia as part of an all-Prokofiev program by the Boston

Symphony Orchestra in March 1938. In *Peter and the Wolf*, each character is represented by a different instrument— Peter, for example, is represented by the orchestral strings and the wolf by three horns. Many well-known personalities have been chosen to play the important part of the narrator, a cherished role. The narrators include: political writer William F. Buckley (1925–), actor Peter Ustinov (1921–), and First Lady Eleanor Roosevelt (1884–1962). One special narrator was former opera singer Lina Llubera, who made a recording of *Peter and the Wolf* in 1986 at the age of eighty-eight. Lina was special because she had been the wife of Prokofiev; the couple wed in 1923 and had two sons.

Around 1938 Prokofiev had met Mira Mendelson, who prepared text for some of Prokofiev's works, including the operas *The Duenna* and *The Tale of a Real Man*. In the political upheaval of the 1940s, Lina, who was Spanish and had maintained some of her Western contacts, became politically suspect. In 1947 the Supreme Soviet decreed that Soviet citizens could not marry foreign nationals and that this law was to be retroactive. Prokofiev's marriage to Lina, therefore, became illegal and their sons "illegitimate." Lina was arrested on trumped-up espionage charges and sent to a Siberian labor camp for eight years. In 1948 Prokofiev married Mira Mendelson.

Prokofiev died on the same day—March 5, 1953—as Josef Stalin (1879–1953), and news of the composer's passing was almost entirely subdued by the response to the death of the Soviet premier.

One of Prokofiev's most highly regarded works is his Symphony No. 5, which seems to be a summation of its composer's ideologies, which were battered by the age in which he lived. "It is," Prokofiev said, "a symphony about the spirit of man." ♪

LEFT: IN ADDITION TO *ALA AND LOLLI*, PROKOFIEV WROTE ANOTHER BALLET FOR IMPRESARIO SERGEI DIAGHILEV, *LE FILS PRODIGUE* ("THE PRODIGAL SON"), PERFORMED HERE BY IRINA BARONOVA AND ANTON DOLIN. OPPOSITE: VIRGIL THOMSON COLLABORATED WITH THE AVANT-GARDE AUTHOR GERTRUDE STEIN ON TWO OF HIS THREE OPERAS, THE MOST RADICAL OF WHICH WAS *FOUR SAINTS IN THREE ACTS*, FOR WHICH THOMSON ASSEMBLED A CAST MADE UP COMPLETELY OF AFRICAN AMERICANS.

VIRGIL THOMSON
(1896–1989)

WHEN SOMEONE SITS FOR A PORTRAIT, IT IS USUALLY FOR A PHOTO-graph or an oil painting, but when the person was a friend of Virgil Thomson, his or her likeness was captured in music. Other composers have similarly immortalized people, but with Thomson's portraits, the subject actually sat in front of the composer, just as one would for an artist painting a portrait on canvas. Thomson did numerous musical portraits in this manner. Usually the work would be accomplished in one sitting and, if the composition was to be orchestrated, that would be done at a later time.

Some of these musical pictures were grouped into *Five Portraits*, which was first performed in 1944 by the Philadelphia Orchestra, with Thomson as guest conductor. (He was often invited to conduct major symphony orchestras.) The five portraits are "Bugles and Birds," of painter Pablo Picasso;

"Percussion Piece," of Mrs. Chester Whitin Lasell, a Californian turned New Englander; "Cantabile for Strings," of Russian painter Nicolas de Chatelain; "Tango Lullaby," of Mademoiselle Flavie Alvarez de Toledo; and "Fugue," of American conductor Alexander Smallens.

Born in Kansas City, Missouri, in 1896, Thomson learned to play the piano at the age of five and, in his teens, was sufficiently gifted at the keyboard to be hired as a church organist. Thomson's American nationality is reflected in his compositions through hints of various hymns, marches, dance rhythms, and folk tunes. His talent as a composer did not emerge until he matriculated at Harvard University. As a member of the Harvard Glee Club, Thomson toured Europe in the summer of 1921 and was given several opportunities to conduct the vocal ensemble.

After the Glee Club tour, Thomson elected to remain in Paris for a year of study, courtesy of a John Knowles Paine Traveling Fellowship. Not only did he study with the esteemed Nadia Boulanger (1887–1979), but he relished the fringe benefits of meeting with poet Jean Cocteau (1889–1963), associating with the composers known as Les Six (see Chapter 6, page 131) and being introduced to their contemporary, Erik Satie (see sidebar, page 158), whose style influenced Thomson's writing.

Back in Massachusetts, Thomson served as organist and choirmaster at King's Chapel in Boston, and graduated from Harvard University in 1923, after which he received a Juilliard Grant to study in New York. Paris beckoned, however, and he made his residence there from 1925 until World War II, when the Germans took over and Thomson returned to the United States.

Soon after his return to Paris, Thomson met the enigmatic author Gertrude Stein (1874–1946). Without knowing her, he had turned her "Susie Asado" into a vocal solo; now he gave musical treatments to other Stein texts to create "Preciosilla," a song, and *Capital Capitals*, a cantatalike work. Thomson and

ERIK SATIE (1866–1925)

With a bowler hat atop his head and an umbrella tucked under one arm—whether or not it was raining—Erik Satie was a familiar and rather comical sight on the streets of Paris. His musical style, however, was not familiar; it did not bear resemblance to anything in the concert halls in the early 1900s. As for comical, it can be wondered if it was Satie's intention to look amusing, just as he intended his music to tease and to taunt. Satie was called "The Velvet Gentleman" because he wore velvet suits, in spite of the extremely meager lifestyle he lived.

Satie was born in Honfleur, France, in 1866, and he received his early music education from the local organist, Vinot, who introduced the boy to the Gregorian chants that would influence his early composing. A year at the Paris Conservatory was all the teenage Satie could take of the formal curriculum, and perhaps a year was all his instructors could take of Satie's unusual approach to music.

Satie's first compositions, *Valse-Ballet* and *Fantaisie-Valse*, were for the piano. He numbered them Opus 62 upon publication in 1887. Satie's wry sense of fun is also revealed by composition titles such as "Three Pieces in the Shape of a Pear" (1903), a piano duet; "The Dreamy Fish" (1905); and "Flabby Preludes for a Dog" (1912). His musical manuscripts bore odd instructions, such as one to perform a particular piece as a "nightingale with a toothache."

Satie played piano in the cafés of Paris; at one of these, Auberge du Clou, he met composer Claude Debussy (see Chapter 6, page 124), who was intrigued by Satie's avant-garde attitude toward music. Debussy, in self-evaluating his *Pelleas et Melisande*, allowed that Satie had influenced the ethereal mood of his opera.

When Satie was almost forty years old, he became a student again, undoubtedly with a more mature approach than when he had attended the Paris Conservatory. Three years at the Schola Cantorum broadened his compositional ability. Classes with composers Vincent d'Indy and Albert Roussel gave Satie the impetus to attain greater heights as a composer. Among his later compositions are two operettas, *Pousse d'Amour* and *Le Piège de Meduse*; "Socrate" for four sopranos and orchestra; and two ballets, *Mercure* and *Relache*.

His ultimate composition, the ballet *Parade*, premiered on May 18, 1917, at the Ballet Russe de Monte Carlo in Paris. It was a collaboration of genius, with a scenario by Jean Cocteau, sets and costumes by Pablo Picasso, and choreography by Léonide Massine (1896–1979). In spite of this plethora of talent, *Parade* drew negative response from the critics and the public. The frivolous surface theme of *Parade* was considered an insult, considering that World War I was creating death and destruction less than 100 miles (160km) from Paris. Furthermore, in addition to the unfortunate timing, Satie radically introduced into the score not only ragtime but also background sounds of sirens, typewriters, and airplane engines. *Parade* was also noteworthy because its program notes were the first place the word "surrealist," coined by French poet Guillaume Apollinaire (1880-1918), was used in print. In the intervening years, with the freeing up of musical perceptions, *Parade* has become accepted. The Metropolitan Opera, for instance, brought it into its repertoire in 1981 on a triple bill with *Les Mamelles de Tiresias* ("The Breasts of Tiresias"), by Francis Poulenc (see page 161), and *L'Enfant et les Sortilèges* ("The Child and the Enchantments"), by Maurice Ravel (see Chapter 6, page 128).

Stein collaborated on two of the composer's three operas. *Four Saints in Three Acts* was a "succès de scandale," at least at its first performance, in Hartford, Connecticut, in 1934. While Thomson's score had melody and traditional musical logic, Stein's libretto was true to her avant-garde form (so the cellophane costumes did not seem unusual). Artist Maurice Grosser was called upon to create staging that would give the work some coherence. Stressing good diction as his purpose, Thomson chose an all-African-American cast, a custom that carried through subsequent performances. Not quite as radical, Thomson's second opera, *The Mother of Us All*, about suffragette Susan B. Anthony, was commissioned by the Alice M. Ditson Fund of Columbia University, where it had its world premiere in 1947. Stein completed the libretto just four months before she died in 1946. Thomson's nationalism is apparent in this opera in his use of vernacular music.

With Stein gone, Thomson chose writer Jack Larson to be the librettist for his third opera, *Lord Byron*. Although this piece was commissioned by the Metropolitan Opera's general manager, Rudolf Bing, it was not performed at the Met, but at the Juilliard Theater at Lincoln Center.

In addition to his operas and portraits, Thomson created musical landscapes. "Wheat Field at Noon," "Sea Piece with Birds," and "The Seine at Night" are among his orchestral works. His ballets include *Filling Station* and *The Harvest According*. He also wrote scores for several films, including *The River, Tuesday in November*, and *The Plow that Broke the Plains.*

Perhaps it was his journalistic skill that prompted such picturesque titles. Thomson was one of the most highly regarded critics and authors of music. He held the top music post at the *New York Herald Tribune* from 1940 to 1954 and wrote an autobiography and several other books. Almost ninety-three years old when he died in 1989, Thomson had spent his later years lecturing, conducting, and writing. Published in 1971, the last book Thomson wrote was *American Music Since 1910*, about a musically prolific era of which he was an integral part. ⸙

GEORGE GERSHWIN, WHO WROTE MANY WONDERFUL POP SONGS WITH HIS BROTHER, IRA, ALSO PAINTED AS A HOBBY. HE IS SHOWN HERE WITH HIS PORTRAIT OF ARNOLD SCHÖNBERG.

GEORGE GERSHWIN (1898–1937)

THE AUDIENCE IN NEW YORK'S AEOLIAN HALL ON FEBRUARY 12, 1924, was becoming restless during orchestra leader Paul Whiteman's program *An Experiment in Modern Music* when the mood was changed by the next-to-last selection on the program, the premiere of George Gershwin's exciting, jazzy *Rhapsody in Blue*. The successful *Rhapsody in Blue* brought jazz into the concert hall, and it gave Gershwin, who was already a popular theater composer, his passport to the world of classical music.

Gershwin had a keen interest in the classics, prompted by his grade-school classmate Maxie Rosenzweig, who became

The Twentieth Century

an acclaimed violinist under the name Max Rosen. Born in Brooklyn in 1898, Gershwin was the second of four children; the eldest was Ira (1896–1983), who became an esteemed lyricist who worked with his brother as well as other song-writers. Aiming for a career as a concert pianist, Gershwin quit high school and headed for the songwriting center of Manhattan known as Tin Pan Alley. There he became a song plugger, pounding out the hits of the day, trying to sell them for the publisher.

Gershwin became a familiar face along Tin Pan Alley and started getting invited to parties; inevitably, there would be a piano on the scene and he would head straight to it, playing for hours. It was in just such a scenario that entertainer Al Jolson (1886–1950) heard Gershwin play his tune "Swanee." The eager Jolson had the song interpolated into the Broadway hit *Sinbad*, in which he was then appearing. From that point on, Gershwin's place in theater was assured. Musical after musical followed, including *La La Lucille* (1919), *Lady, Be Good!* (1924), *Oh, Kay!* (1926), *Funny Face* (1927), *Girl Crazy* (1930), and *Of Thee I Sing* (1931), which was the first musical ever to win a Pulitzer Prize.

The year after *Rhapsody in Blue* premiered, Gershwin wrote his Piano Concerto in F, which premiered in Carnegie Hall with himself as soloist. Then followed the *Piano Preludes* (1926), *An American in Paris* (1928), *Second Rhapsody* (1932), and *Cuban Overture* (1932).

Although Gershwin's opera, *Porgy and Bess,* did not fare well during his lifetime, its acceptance has since been definitely secured. While the Metropolitan Opera was interested in *Porgy and Bess*, it was the Theatre Guild that first produced it. Gershwin and several colleagues, including DuBose Heyward (1855–1940), author of the the novel *Porgy*, spent the summer of 1934 in Charleston, South Carolina, the story's locale. Frequenting nightclubs, churches, and social events, collaborators Heyward, Gershwin, and Ira Gershwin absorbed Southern African-American culture to better equip themselves for writing their work. The Broadway premiere in October 1935 was not greeted with enthusiasm; public and critics alike could not find a place for it. Was it opera? Was it a Broadway musical? Gradually, *Porgy and Bess* found its rightful place and, fifty years after its debut, Gershwin's opera was brought into the Metropolitan's standard repertoire.

Hollywood also benefited from Gershwin's talent, starting with the movie *Delicious* in 1931. He wrote scores for two Fred Astaire films in 1937: *A Damsel in Distress*, costarring Joan Fontaine, and *Shall We Dance*, with Ginger Rogers. The score to 1947's *The Shocking Miss Pilgrim* was assembled posthumously from previously unused songs. Gershwin was at work on music for *The Goldwyn Follies* when he was stricken with a brain tumor and died in 1937, shortly before his thirty-ninth birthday.

FRANCIS POULENC
(1899–1963)

WITH THE AIR OF MUSICAL COMEDY STAR MAURICE CHEVALIER, FRANCIS Poulenc brought an element of the bon vivant to his personal life and to his profession, while possessing the aura of another Chevalier, brother of the distressed Blanche in Poulenc's opera *Les Dialogues des Carmélites*, who seeks solace for his distress in religion. For all his gaiety, Poulenc was prone to nervous breakdowns during his creation of *Dialogues*, and he sometimes made pilgrimages to the shrine of Vierge Noire at Rocamadour before writing.

The Dialogues of the Carmélites, written in 1957, is unquestionably Poulenc's masterpiece. It is based on a text by playwright Georges Bernanos, which was suggested to the composer as a choice opera libretto by Guido Valcarenghi, president of Ricordi, one of the foremost music publishing companies in the world. Bernanos' play was based on the 1931 novel *The Last on the Scaffold*, by Gertrud von le Fort, which was based in history: sixteen nuns of the Carmelite Order went to the guillotine in July 1794 during the Reign of Terror that followed the French Revolution. A seventeenth nun, Blanche, was the creation of author le Fort, who made Blanche the last on the scaffold. Poulenc's deep religious

devotion, coupled with his keen theatrical awareness, made *The Dialogues of the Carmelites* extraordinary. Perhaps writing *The Dialogues* was a natural progression from Poulenc's composing religious choral works.

Dialogues was a tremendous success at its 1957 premiere at La Scala in Milan, in January. Among the numerous early productions was a December 1957 version produced by the NBC Opera Company and aired on NBC-TV; this televised performance received the New York Music Critics' Circle Award.

Most of Poulenc's choral works are sacred rather than secular. Between 1937 and 1961, he wrote a Stabat Mater, a Gloria, a Mass in G, and *Sept Repons des Tenebres*, among other choruses. The composer had drifted from his Roman Catholic heritage in his youth, but he returned to religion in the mid-1930s upon the death of his friend and fellow composer Pierre-Octave Ferroud.

Poulenc started his musical training with piano lessons at the age of five. Subsequently a student of the highly regarded piano teacher Ricardo Vines, Poulenc's classical education was balanced by an uncle who exposed his nephew to the theater world of Paris. Poulenc was born in the French capital in 1899; the family was well-to-do and Francis had a privileged upbringing. Military service between 1918 and 1921 did not stop him from composing. A simpler, Neoclassical French style of music was emerging, and before long Poulenc was identified with an ensemble of composers known as "Les Six" (see Chapter 6, page 131). Poulenc scored in his mid-twenties with the ballet *Les Biches* (1920), produced by impresario Sergei Diaghilev. He achieved still further success with other ballets, including *Les Animaux Modeles* (1941).

Poulenc's piano studies served him well both as composer and as accompanist. The fifteen improvisations he wrote for piano were his favorite compositions. As piano accompanist, Poulenc worked with the best performers, including baritone

---

OPPOSITE: FIFTY YEARS AFTER GEORGE GERSHWIN'S *PORGY AND BESS* PREMIERE, THE SHOW BECAME PART OF THE NEW YORK METROPOLITAN OPERA'S REGULAR REPERTOIRE. ABOVE: FRANCIS POULENC, WHO DISPLAYED HIS THEOLOGICAL CONCERNS IN HIS OPERA *THE DIALOGUE OF THE CARMÉLITES*, WAS IMPORTANT AS A MEMBER OF THE GROUP OF FRENCH COMPOSERS KNOWN AS "LES SIX."

ALBERTO GINASTERA (1916–1983)

"He's a very smart cookie, in the best sense," said Aaron Copland of Alberto Ginastera, one of South America's most celebrated composers. The American composer and the Argentinian met when Ginastera came to the Berkshire Music Center (Tanglewood) to study composition with Copland, and the association developed into friendship for life.

Ginastera was thirty years old at the Tanglewood meeting and already had several compositions to his credit. *Panambi*, for example, is performed both as an orchestral suite and as a ballet; in the latter form, it received the National Prize in Argentina in 1940. It was composed around the time Ginastera graduated with honors from the National Conservatory of Music in Buenos Aires, the city where he was born in 1916.

Many commissions were awarded Ginastera throughout his life, signifying the esteem in which he was held. One of the early ones came jointly from the Carnegie Institute of Technology and the Pennsylvania College for Women. This led to the composition of a piano sonata that was so well received that it was selected for the festival of the International Society for Contemporary Music in Oslo in 1953. Ginastera was invited by the Festival Casals of Puerto Rico and the Puerto Rican Bicentennial Commission to compose a memorial for cello virtuoso Pablo Casals (1876–1973), which became *Glosses for String Orchestra.* This piece premiered in 1978 in Washington, D.C., at the National Symphony Orchestra with the well-known Mstislav Rostropovich conducting.

For the gala opening season of the New York Philharmonic at Lincoln Center, Ginastera was commissioned to compose a violin concerto; the piece was not finished in time, and the premiere was postponed to the autumn of 1963, when Leonard Bernstein conducted and Ruggiero Ricci was the violin soloist. For the opening of the Kennedy Center for the Performing Arts, the Opera Society of Washington, D.C., commissioned Ginastera to write an opera, *Beatrix Cenci*, which was conducted at the 1971 premiere by Julius Rudel.

Ginastera, a mild-mannered man who dressed ultraconservatively and was extremely fastidious in his habits, wrote operas on profoundly degenerate and perverse subjects, allowing all the gross details to be witnessed. *Don Rodrigo*, written in 1964, was the inaugural offering at the New York City Opera in its Lincoln Center quarters. The music is descriptive and utilizes considerable *sprechstimme*, or song-speech, a technique often used by Arnold Schönberg (Ginastera once named Schönberg, Stravinsky, and Bartók his composers of choice).

Ginastera's second opera was *Bomarzo*. The world premiere was in Washington, D.C., in May 1967, and when the staging was reviewed, the President of Argentina banned *Bomarzo*'s August premiere in the composer's native Buenos Aires.

Heralding the four-hundredth anniversary of the founding of Buenos Aires, Ginastera wrote *Iubilum*; this piece, which Ginastera called a "symphonic celebration," premiered in the city it was meant to celebrate in 1980, three years before Ginastera died.

Pierre Bernac and soprano Denise Duval on their numerous respective recital tours. Bernac's firsthand biography of the composer, *Francis Poulenc: The Man and His Songs,* was published in 1977.

Duval was in the premiere performances of Poulenc's other two operas, one preceding *Dialogues* and the other succeeding it. *Les Mamelles de Tiersias* ("The Breasts of Tiersias") is a surrealistic and convoluted antiwar tale. The libretto is by poet Guillaume Apollinaire, who also provided text for numerous nonoperatic songs by Poulenc. *Les Mamelles* premiered in Paris during June 1947, first at the Maubel Conservatory and soon after at the Opéra Comique. *La Voix Humaine* ("The Human Voice") was written especially for Duval, who had a flair for both musical theater and opera. This forty-minute opus had its first performance at the Opéra Comique in 1959. Duval was the sole performer in a staged one-sided musical telephone conversation between parting lovers.

Apollinaire was not the only noted poet to work with the composer. Poulenc's more serious songs employed the talents of Paul Eluard and Louis Aragon. One of the most unusual Poulenc-Aragon songs was "C"; written during the German occupation of France in World War II, this tune is a dirge that alludes to a bridge crossed by enemy armies through the centuries. The lighthearted verses were supplied by Apollinaire and Max Jacob. The piece "Trois Poèmes de Louise Lalanne" was devised as a lark written by a fictitious poet conjured up by Apollinaire and Marie Laurencin.

There was to be a fourth Poulenc opera, *La Machine Infernale*, with text by Jean Cocteau, who also collaborated with other members of "Les Six." But that effort ended when Poulenc died from a sudden heart attack in 1963. ♪

AARON COPLAND
(1900–1990)

NOT UNLIKE THE EXHILARATING SPIRIT OF THE BALLET *APPALACHIAN Spring*, one of Aaron Copland's most popular compositions, the composer brought a refreshing spirit to his classical compositions.

An amiable man who was always extending a helping hand to aspiring composers, Copland was himself helped by Serge Koussevitzky, the legendary conductor of the Boston Symphony, and Nadia Boulanger, who was considered the finest teacher of composition in the twentieth century. Copland was studying at the School of Music for Americans at Fountainebleau outside Paris when he met Koussevitzky. They were introduced by Boulanger, who was Copland's teacher at the school. By his own account, Copland was unaware of Boulanger before he enrolled at the school, but he then studied with her for three years. Koussevitsky then helped Copland's Symphony for Organ and Orchestra receive its 1925 premiere in New York, which was conducted by

OPPOSITE: ALBERTO GINASTERA, AN IMPORTANT SOUTH AMERICAN CLASSICAL COMPOSER, CITED SCHÖNBERG, BARTÓK, AND STRAVINSKY AS HIS FAVORITE COMPOSERS, AND THEIR INFLUENCES SHOWED IN HIS MUSIC. RIGHT: PERHAPS ONE OF THE GREATEST CLASSICAL COMPOSERS TO COME OUT OF THE UNITED STATES, THE INNOVATIVE AARON COPLAND CREATED IN A WIDE ARRAY OF STYLES, INCLUDING TWELVE-TONE, AND WITH A BROAD RANGE OF TECHNIQUES.

Walter Damrosch (1862–1950). Boulanger was on her first United States concert tour when the Organ Symphony made its debut, and she was the organ soloist. Soon thereafter the Organ Symphony had its Boston performance, with Koussevitzky conducting.

Paris in the 1920s was synonymous with the avant-garde. While there, Copland was privileged to attend Wednesday afternoon teas at Boulanger's apartment. It was a gathering place for the musical greats of the era—Stravinsky and Poulenc, for instance—and the yet-to-be-great, such as Copland.

Copland was born in Brooklyn in 1900, and for his first twenty years, he lived in the house next to H. M. Copland's department store, his father's business. Aaron was the youngest of the five children of Harris and Sarah Copland, who had emigrated from eastern Europe. As a teenager, Copland attended New York Symphony concerts conducted by Damrosch at the Brooklyn Academy of Music. After graduating from Boys High School, Copland studied music with Rubin Goldmark, a composer and teacher who was head of the composition department at the Juilliard School, before going on to Paris.

Copland's early compositions were radical. His jazz-motivated *Piano Concerto of 1926*, in fact, drew severe criticism from the reserved Boston audience. Gradually, Copland eased into a more melodic, almost folksy, phase. The 1936 piece *El Salon Mexico*, which premiered in Mexico City, with Carlos Chávez (1899–1978) conducting, bridges Copland's two styles.

Ballet danced into Copland's repertoire in 1938 with *Billy the Kid,* followed four years later by *Rodeo*, commissioned by the Ballet Russ de Monte Carlo in collaboration with choreographer Agnes de Mille (1909–1993). The same year, Copland wrote *A Lincoln Portrait,* an orchestral piece with narration culled from the words of Abraham Lincoln, followed by *Fanfare for the Common Man*, an orchestral work with emphasis on brass and percussion.

A long association with Leonard Bernstein started in the 1930s, when Copland was well on this way as a composer and Bernstein was a student at Harvard University. Bernstein has been called Copland's protégé. It is curious that the date in 1943—November 14—when Bernstein unexpectedly substituted as conductor at a New York Philharmonic concert happened to be Copland's birthday; conducting that concert sky-rocketed Bernstein's career. Coincidentally, the composers died in the same year, 1990.

In 1940 Copland helped found the Summer Music School at the Berkshire Music Center (Tanglewood); he remained chairman of its faculty for twenty-five years.

Undoubtedly the best-known Copland composition, *Appalachian Spring*, written in 1944, was commissioned by modern dance choreographer Martha Graham (1894–1991). Copland makes eloquent use of the Shaker hymn "'Tis a Gift to Be Simple" in his work. A Pulitzer Prize for composition was awarded to Copland in 1944 for the suite from *Appalachian Spring*.

Copland received many other honors, including the Presidential Medal of Freedom and a 1979 Kennedy Center Award. Another distinction bestowed on Copland was having his orchestral work *Connotations* performed at the inaugural concert in Lincoln Center's Philharmonic (renamed Avery Fisher) Hall in September 1962, which was televised live. Performed by the New York Philharmonic with Bernstein conducting, *Connotations* precipitated tremendous controversy. Copland had returned to his avant-garde mode of composing, now employing the twelve-tone technique. *Inscape*, an orchestral piece written for the 125th anniversary of the New York Philharmonic in 1967, set off a similar stir.

As sometimes happens with composers of classics, their other credits get swept aside. While not known primarily for his work in Hollywood, Copland wrote the background music for *Our Town, The Red Pony*, and *The Heiress*, for which he received an Academy Award in 1949 for best score.

Although Copland ceased composing around 1970, he continued to travel around the world to conduct and lecture on the topic of American music. When he died twenty years later, his obituary in *The New York Times* called him "America's best-known composer of classical music and a gentle yet impassioned champion of American music in every style. " ♪

DMITRI (1906–1975) SHOSTAKOVICH

ONE OF THE TWENTIETH CENTURY'S MOST FAMOUS COMPOSERS, DMITRI Shostakovich was an incredibly versatile artist. He achieved success with his first symphony at the age of nineteen and went on to compose fourteen more symphonies, fifteen string quartets, and several operas, ballets, and oratorios.

Shostakovich's first symphony served as his thesis for graduation from the Conservatory at St. Petersburg. He was only nineteen at the time, having been born in 1906 in St. Petersburg. The 1926 premiere had the distinction of being performed by the Leningrad Philharmonic. Surging forward from the success of his initial composition, Shostakovich wrote two more symphonies within the next three years. "Ode to October" is the subtitle of his second symphony, commemorating the tenth anniversary of the 1917 Revolution, which took place in the month of October. The "May First Symphony" is the subtitle for Shostakovich's Third, which has a May Day anthem for the Soviet holiday incorporated into the choral finale.

The political and national enthusiasm that these pieces met with did not always accompany Shostakovich's compositions. As a composer, his acceptance by the government and by the populace rose and fell like waves and the reaction depended to a large extent on the dictates of the Kremlin.

Shostakovich's first wife, Nina, endured his changing fortunes with him. They were married in 1932; their daughter Galya was born in 1936 and their son Maxim in 1938.

In addition to his composing talents, Shostakovich excelled as a pianist. In 1927 he was a prizewinner in the Warsaw Chopin Competition. During hard times following the revolution, he helped support his widowed mother and two sisters by playing piano in theaters as background music to silent movies. Later, he wrote the scores for several films. One of his most prominent works—the Quintet in G Minor, first performed in Moscow in 1940—is primarily for piano.

The Nose, based on a comic tale by the Russian author Nikolay Gogol (1809–1852), was Shostakovich's first opera; it premiered in January 1930. Highly satirical, the opera was given "thumbs down" by the Russian Association of Proletarian Composers, and after several performances it was removed from the repertoire. *Lady Macbeth of Mtsensk*, which followed in 1934, met with even greater disaster than *The Nose*—it was ordered withdrawn by Premier Josef Stalin. Both the story, by Nikolai Leskov, and the music were regarded as distasteful. *Pravda*, the leading Soviet newspaper, topped off the criticism with its "Chaos Instead of Music" editorial, followed by another vindictive article. *Lady Macbeth* reappeared as *Katerina Ismailova* in 1956. The opera was then acceptable not only for its content but also because of somewhat alleviated cultural demands after the death of Stalin in 1953.

Restoration of Shostakovich's reputation came with his Symphony No. 5 in 1937. Generally valued as his finest, this symphony commemorated the twentieth anniversary of the revolution.

World War II did not deter Shostakovich from composing; his Seventh, Eighth, and Ninth symphonies echo the U.S.S.R.'s position during that devastating conflict, musically documenting that phase of Russian history. Symphony No. 7 (late 1941) reflects the Siege of Leningrad by the Nazis, the Eighth (1943) documents the Red Army driving back the invaders (but not without great suffering), and the Ninth (1945) conveys the triumph of the Soviets (and the Allies) over the Third Reich.

After World War II, Shostakovich's fortunes changed again when his music was branded bourgeois and degenerate by the Central Committee of the Russian Communist Party. His colleagues Sergei Prokofiev and Aram Khachaturian (1903–1978) were similarly maligned. Symphony No. 8, which had been exalted during World War II and known as the "Monumental," fell from favor during this period.

In addition to his symphonies, Shostakovich worked in numerous other forms. The Second Violin Concerto, written for virtuoso David Oistrakh, was introduced in the United States by Leonard Bernstein and the New York Philharmonic. His ballet scores include *The Limpid Stream, The Bolt*, and *The Age of Gold* (a.k.a. *The*

Golden Age), which lambasted capitalism. An oratorio, *Song of the Forests*, praised Stalin's reforestation plan and was later adapted as the Tenth of Shostakovich's fifteen symphonies.

Nina Shostakovich, the composer's first wife, died in 1954, and the composer remarried twice, first Margarita and then Irina, who accompanied him on his last visit to the United States in 1973. Shostakovich died two years later and was interred in Moscow.

During his lifetime, Shostakovich was awarded various honors, both abroad and in his own country. On one of his trips to the United States, he was an "honored member" of the Soviet delegation at the 1949 Cultural and Scientific Conference for World Peace, which took place in New York. In spite of the badgering he received from the Soviet government throughout his life, he was honored by his home country many times. He received several Stalin Prizes and Russia's highest honor, the Hero of the Soviet Union award (1996), as the first musician to be so designated. ♪

SAMUEL BARBER
(1910–1981)

WHAT AN HONOR IT WAS FOR SAMUEL BARBER TO BE COMMISSIONED TO write the inaugural opera for the new Metropolitan Opera House situated in New York's Lincoln Center for the Performing Arts. Although the 1966 world premiere of his *Antony and Cleopatra* was not a great success (due in part to the music being overwhelmed by the elephantine production), it certainly was an incomparable distinction for the fifty-six-year-old composer.

More artistically agreeable was Barber's opera *Vanessa,* which had premiered eight years earlier in 1958, also at the Met, and won him a Pulitzer Prize in music. When *Vanessa* had its European premiere later the same year, it was the first opera by an American composer ever produced in Salzburg, Austria, one of the world's musical meccas. In 1937 Barber's First Symphony had been the first American symphony ever to be performed at the Salzburg Festival.

Vanessa's libretto was written by Gian Carlo Menotti (1911–), Barber's longtime companion from their days at the Curtis Institute. Barber did much of his composing at

"Capricorn," the Mount Kisco, New York, house they shared for thirty years. From 1973 until his death in 1981, Barber lived in New York City and had a villa in the Italian Dolomites.

"Capricorn" was also the title Barber gave to his concerto for flute, oboe, trumpet, and strings. One might suspect he came under the sign of Capricorn, but in fact he was a Pisces, born on March 9, 1910, in West Chester, Pennsylvania, near Philadelphia. His father was a doctor and his mother was an accomplished amateur pianist. Samuel showed an affinity for the piano and for composing early on, but his parents tried to steer him away from music. He persevered, however, and by the time he was twelve years old, Barber was organist in a West Chester church, was playing piano at social functions, and had organized an orchestra at the high school. With these accomplishments, Barber soon

ABOVE: DESPITE HIS DISTANCE FROM THE SOPHISTICATED, DISSONANT STYLE THEN IN VOGUE, SAMUEL BARBER ATTEMPTED TO CREATE A "MODERN" GRAND OPERA, *ANTONY AND CLEOPATRA*, WHICH WAS THE FIRST TO BE PERFORMED AT THE NEW METROPOLITAN OPERA HOUSE IN NEW YORK CITY ON SEPTEMBER 16, 1966. OPPOSITE: BENJAMIN BRITTEN, SHOWN HERE WITH FREDERICK ASHTON, REHEARSING HIS OPERA *ALBERT HERRING*, WAS EQUALLY ADEPT AT DEPICTING COMEDY, TRAGEDY, AND SURREAL OR SUPERNATURAL SUBJECTS.

came to the attention of the director of the Peabody Conservatory, who encouraged his musical studies. In 1924 Barber became a charter student at the newly opened Curtis Institute in Philadelphia; he studied there until 1932, in the interim earning his high school diploma. Later, Barber would teach at Curtis, specializing in orchestration and conducting.

Louise Homer, the famous contralto who had a long, albeit intermittent, career at the Metropolitan (which lasted from 1900 to 1929), was Barber's aunt. It is perhaps not odd, therefore, to learn that he had a penchant for singing and was exceptionally talented at it. During a sojourn in Vienna in the mid-1930s, while in Europe on a Pulitzer Traveling Scholarship and an American Prix de Rome, Barber sang recitals of lieder.

Legendary conductor Arturo Toscanini selected Barber as the first American composer to be represented on a program of the NBC Symphony Orchestra, over which Toscanini reigned. In 1938 Barber's Adagio for Strings and his Essay No. 1 for Orchestra were performed.

World War II found Barber inducted into the U.S. Army with a subsequent transfer to the U.S. Air Force and assignment to musical duties. He was commissioned to compose a symphony in honor of the Air Force; this work was premiered by the Boston Symphony in 1944 and a week later was heard worldwide via shortwave radio.

In 1962 Barber won a second Pulitzer Prize, this one for his Piano Concerto. Commissioned by the G. Schirmer music publishing company, the concerto was part of the centenary celebration of the company's founding, and the composition premiered during opening week of Philharmonic (now known as Avery Fisher) Hall in Lincoln Center.

Barber's music—aristocratic in an old-world sense but not without a modern flair—ranges beyond concertos for violin, cello, or piano, operas, and symphonies. His catalog also includes piano compositions, choral works, and ballets, one of which, *Medea*, was commissioned for the Martha Graham Company by the Ditson Fund of Columbia University.

High regard for Barber was obvious by the numerous observances of his seventieth birthday in 1980, the year before he died. He was celebrated in New York by the Chamber Music Society of Lincoln Center, in Philadelphia by the Curtis Institute, in London and in Naples, and at The White House, where First Lady Rosalynn Carter presented Barber with the prestigious Wolf Trap Award. ♩

BENJAMIN BRITTEN
(1913-1976)

RECOGNIZING A SENSE OF THEATER IN TWENTY-EIGHT-YEAR-OLD Benjamin Britten, the renowned conductor Serge Koussevitzky asked the young composer why he had not written opera. Britten replied that he did not have the funds to support himself during the time he felt was required to compose an opera. Eight days later, the conductor's beloved wife died, and shortly thereafter, the Koussevitzky Foundation was founded in her honor and the foundation's first financial grant went to Britten to write an opera. The eventual result was the tremendously successful *Peter Grimes*, a tale of a seafaring man based on "The Borough," a poem by the English writer George Crabbe (1754–1832).

The success of *Peter Grimes* at its London premiere in 1945 firmly established Britten as an opera composer; the American premiere was held the following year at the Berkshire Music Center (Tanglewood), which was appropriate considering the opera's sponsorship by the Koussevitzky Foundation and the fact that Tanglewood was founded by Koussevitzky. *Peter Grimes* breathed new life into English opera, which had been limping along for years.

Britten's roots were along the British coast, where he was born at Lowestoft, Suffolk, in 1913. Musically precocious, Britten was ten years old when he heard the Frank Bridge song "The Sea," which had a tremendous impact on the youngster. Three years later he met Bridge and the older songwriter became Britten's teacher. Britten honored his mentor in 1938 by composing *Variations on a Theme of Frank Bridge,* which premiered at the Salzburg Festival.

At age seventeen, Britten earned a scholarship to The Royal Academy of Music, but once he got there he felt insufficiently challenged and left after about four years. He composed for the British film industry, creating background music for numerous documentaries and, perhaps most memorably, the score for the 1937 mystery *Love From a Stranger*.

After *Peter Grimes*, Britten experienced numerous other notable operatic successes—some were on the grand scale of his first opera, including *Billy Budd* (1951), *The Turn of the Screw* (1954), and *Death in Venice* (1973), and others were chamber-style operas, like *The Rape of Lucretia* (1946) and *Albert Herring* (1947). *Gloriana*, a retrospective of Queen Elizabeth I written in 1953, was commissioned by the British government for the Coronation of Elizabeth II. *Owen Wingrave*, written for BBC-TV in 1971, was enhanced by television filming techniques.

While he vividly turned the brooding story of *Peter Grimes* into an opera, Britten was able to apply a lighter touch to some of his other works, and to appeal to children with his *Let's Make an Opera* in 1949 and *Noye's Fludde* in 1957.

Forever an ardent pacifist, Britten first came to the United States in 1939, disturbed by what he considered to be social injustices in England and the government's soft attitude toward fascism. He settled in New York State's Suffolk County on Long Island, but he yearned for his homeland. Travel during World War II was restricted and there was considerable delay before Britten could book passage to Liverpool via a Swedish cargo ship. During the lengthy 1942 voyage home, he wrote his well-known *Ceremony of Carols*.

Upon his return to England, Britten, an accomplished conductor and pianist, participated in the war effort by playing concerts for the wounded and for the public distressed by the bombings. Following World War II, Britten composed a monumental War Requiem; this piece premiered in Coventry Cathedral concurrent with the reopening of that historic building, which had been severely damaged during the war.

Britten resided in Aldeburgh, a village not unlike the setting for *Peter Grimes*, with his lifelong companion, tenor Peter Pears. In 1948 they jointly founded the Aldeburgh Festival, which continues to be an outstanding annual musical event. When Britten died in 1976, he was buried in Aldeburgh beside his beloved English sea. ♪

LEONARD BERNSTEIN (1918–1990)

On Sunday, November 14, 1943, Leonard Bernstein (pronounced "BURN-stine," not "BURN-steen"), then twenty-five years old, was summoned on short notice to conduct the New York Philharmonic in its weekly nationwide CBS broadcast from Carnegie Hall. Bernstein, assistant conductor for the Philharmonic, had been alerted the day before that conductor Bruno Walter was ailing. On Sunday morning, Bernstein was informed that he would have to conduct. Bernstein deftly led the mighty Philharmonic through a program of Schumann, Richard Strauss, Rosza, and Wagner and, by doing so at the last minute and at such a young age, became the subject of a front-page story the next day in *The New York Times*. He was called "Wunderkind of the Western World" and "Pinup Boy of the Podium," but later earned a more meaningful title as "Maestro," which indicated the profound respect people had for his musical ability.

Bernstein was born in 1918 in Lawrence, Massachusetts. He was about ten years old when his Aunt Clara stored her piano at the Bernstein home, and the youngster was drawn to it like a magnet. When piano lessons escalated from $1 to $3 per lesson, he paid for them himself from his band-job earnings. One of his piano teachers was Helen Coates, who became his longtime secretary.

Bernstein went to Harvard as a member of the Class of 1939. There he met composer Aaron Copland and conductor Dmitri Mitropoulos (1896–1960), both of whom urged him to take up conducting. Following their advice, he studied at the Curtis Institute with conductor Fritz Reiner (1888–1963) and at the Berkshire Music Center (Tanglewood) with Serge Koussevitsky, conductor of the Boston Symphony. Artur Rodzinski, music director of the New York Philharmonic, observed Bernstein conducting a rehearsal at Tanglewood and hired him for the Philharmonic's 1943–1944 season. In 1958 Bernstein was named music director of the Philharmonic, a post he held until 1969, when he gave it up to devote more time to composing. The New York Philharmonic is America's oldest orchestra; Bernstein was its youngest conductor and the first to have been born in the United States.

Through the years, Bernstein was busy composing. *Fancy Free*, which he wrote for the Ballet Theatre (now known as the American Ballet Theatre), was developed into the hit musical *On the Town*. Bernstein's other Broadway triumphs included *Wonderful Town, West Side Story,* and *Candide*, although the commercial success of the latter was much delayed. *Candide* lasted for merely 73 performances on Broadway in 1956, though it won the New York Theatre Critics award, but the revised production in 1974 ran 740 times

Bernstein's first symphony, *Jeremiah*, was premiered in 1944 by the Pittsburgh Symphony Orchestra with Bernstein conducting. His Symphony No. 2, *The Age of Anxiety,* had its first performance in 1949 with Koussevitzky leading the Boston Symphony Orchestra and Bernstein as piano soloist. There followed a third symphony, *Kaddish*, in 1977 with Bernstein conducting the Israel Philharmonic Orchestra,

which he served as music director. Bernstein also composed the choral piece *Chichester Psalms* and *Songfest,* a cycle of American poems. *Mass* was commissioned by the family of President John F. Kennedy and was first heard in 1971 at the opening of the Kennedy Center for the Performing Arts in Washington, D.C.

Humanitarian politics were an active concern of Bernstein's. He conducted Beethoven's triumphant Ninth Symphony on Christmas Eve in 1989 immediately after the Berlin Wall had been torn down. On the fortieth anniversary of the atomic bombing of Japan, Bernstein went to Hiroshima and conducted the West European Youth Orchestra in a commemorative concert.

His concern for youth was equally strong. Bernstein and his wife, Chilean actress Felicia Montealegre, were the parents of three children. Bernstein created the celebrated

Young People's Concerts, many of which appeared on television; these performances were a distinct means of building the audience of the future.

On Bernstein's seventieth birthday in 1988, two years before he died, there was a grand summertime celebration at the Berkshire Music Center (Tanglewood). On November 14 of that year—on the forty-fifth anniversary of his first time at the podium with the New York Philharmonic—the Philharmonic played a gala all-Bernstein concert with the composer conducting. ♪

LEONARD BERNSTEIN, A RENOWNED CONDUCTOR AND COMPOSER WHO DREW TREMENDOUS AUDIENCES AROUND THE WORLD, WAS JUST AS GOOD AT WRITING PROFOUND SYMPHONIC PIECES AS HE WAS AT CONSTRUCTING EXTREMELY EFFECTIVE BROADWAY SHOWS.

The Twentieth Century

PHILIP GLASS
(1937-   )

PHILIP GLASS IS ONE OF A VERY FEW CONTEMPORARY COMPOSERS WHO has been heard consistently in the concert halls and opera houses during the past half-century.

To celebrate the five-hundredth anniversary of Christopher Columbus's arrival in the New World, the Metropolitan Opera gave Glass a $325,000 commission to write an opera. Glass had presented the concept of *The Voyage* to the Met in 1986. The fifteen pages of text by playwright David Henry Hwang, the librettist, seem brief compared to the two and a half hours of music by the composer, but it is typical of Glass's work to let the music speak for itself. The world premiere took place on October 12 (Columbus Day), 1992, and while it received mixed reviews from critics and the public, *The Voyage* enjoyed a half-dozen performances that season and was presented again during the 1995–1996 Metropolitan Opera season.

This was not the first time the Met housed an opera by Glass. In 1976 his first full-length opera, *Einstein on the Beach*, was given two performances at the opera house at Lincoln Center. This was *Einstein*'s United States premiere, and was held under the auspices of the Byrd-Hoffmann Foundation; the world premiere had taken place earlier that year at Paris's Opéra-Comique, commissioned by Michel Guy, France's Secretary of State for Culture. *Einstein* is five hours long—with no intermission—and its score calls for a stan-

dard early-Glass orchestra consisting primarily of electronic keyboards and amplified wind instruments; to this was added a solo violin played by the Einstein character. In this piece, the vocalists sing syllables and numbers as they maneuver through ethereal sequences, the "stage pictures" of director Robert Wilson. *Einstein* toured Europe before its two appearances in New York, and although both of those performances were sold out, a huge deficit loomed, so Philip Glass went back to driving a taxicab in New York City.

In his earlier days as a composer, driving was one of several vocations Glass took up to earn a living. From the age of seventeen, he had various stints as an airport baggage handler, hotel night clerk, film extra, furniture mover, crane operator for a steel company, and plumber.

Glass's educational credentials qualified him for something more academic, but he needed time and space to concentrate on his particular kind of music. At fifteen, Glass went from his Baltimore home to matriculate at the University of Chicago, finishing with a degree in mathematics and philosophy, and proceeded to New York's Juilliard School of Music to study composition, graduating in 1962. Two years later, at age twenty-seven, Glass was in Paris, sponsored by the Ford Foundation and Fulbright grants, studying counterpoint with Nadia Boulanger, pedagogue par excellence.

In Paris, Glass had the privilege of working as assistant to Ravi Shankar, the virtuoso of the sitar, an Indian lute with a long neck and a varying number of strings. Glass quickly took to Indian music and went to India to absorb the techniques of Hindu music with another authority on the subject, Alla Rakha. Probably influenced by his experiences there, Glass's second opera was about the early life of Mohandas Gandhi when he was in South Africa advocating peaceful resolve to racial prejudice. *Satyagraha* was commissioned by the city of Rotterdam, Holland, for the opening of its 1980 opera season. This opera, sung in Sanskrit, was subsequently produced by the New York City Opera.

Akhenaten, Glass's third opera, about the Egyptian pharoah who was Nefertiti's husband, first appeared in 1985 and has since been produced in Stuttgart, Houston, New York, and London. In each of these operas, as in most of Glass' work, the emphasis is on characterization rather than a story with a beginning, middle, and end. From *Einstein* to *Gandhi* to *Akhenaten*, there is a very slight move toward what is considered musically more traditional. His next opera, *The White Raven*, is scheduled to premiere in 1998 in Portugal.

In addition to his operas, Glass has composed film scores, such as that for *Mishima*, recognized by the Cannes Film Festival; dance music, for instance, "Glassworks," used in part for the hit show *Glass Pieces*, created by Jerome Robbins; and many compositions for his Philip Glass Ensemble, which consists basically of seven keyboards and woodwinds.

As Glass has said himself, his work is more about discovering music than redoing what has already been presented. ∫

SELECTED BIBLIOGRAPHY

Arnold, Denis, general ed. *The New Oxford Companion to Music.* New York: Oxford University Press, 1983.

Blom, Eric. *Everyman's Dictionary of Music.* Philadelphia, Pa.: David McKay Company

Bordman, Gerald. *American Musical Theatre: A Chronicle.* New York: Oxford University Press, 1986.

Condon, Denis. Album notes for *The Historic Percy Grainger Piano Roll/Stokowski Conducts Grainger Favorites.* RCA Records, 1919.

Crofton, Ian, and Donald Fraser. *A Dictionary of Musical Quotations.* New York: Schirmer Books, 1985.

Dearling, Robert and Celia. *The Guinness Book of Music.* Lincolnshire, England: Guinness Books, 1986.

Ewen, David. *Composers Since 1900.* New York: H.W. Wilson, 1969.

————————.*The New Encyclopedia of the Opera.* New York: Hill and Wang: 1971.

Faris, Alexander. *Jacques Offenbach.* New York: Scribner, 1980.

Freeman, John W. *Stories of the Great Operas.* New York: Norton, 1984.

Goulding, Phil G. *Classical Music.* New York: Fawcett Columbine, 1992.

Gutman, David. *Prokofiev.* New York: Omnibus Press,1990.

Hamilton, David. *The Metropolitan Opera Encyclopedia.* New York: Simon & Schuster, 1987.

Harding, James. *Gounod.* New York: DaCapo Press, 1990.

Kennedy, Michael, ed. *The Oxford Dictionary of Music.* New York: Oxford University Press, 1994.

Landon, H.C. Robbins. "George Frideric Handel." *Ovation Magazine,* January 1985, 14-18.

Lebrecht, Norman, ed. *The Book of Musical Anecdotes.* New York: The Free Press/Macmillan, 1985.

Lingg, Ann M. "Pied Piper." *Opera News,* 25 December 1971, 11-14.

Music Lovers' Encyclopedia. Revised and newly edited by Deems Taylor and Russell Kerr from materials compiled by Rupert Hughes. Chicago: Music Times Company, 1939.

Nichols, Roger. *Ravel Remembered.* New York: Norton, 1987.

Orel, Harold. *Gilbert and Sullivan: Interviews and Recollections.* Iowa City, Iowa: University of Iowa Press, 1994.

Raeburn, Michael, and Alan Kendall, eds. *Heritage of Music.* New York: Oxford University Press, 1989.

Reich, Nancy B. *Clara Schumann: The Artist and the Woman.* Ithaca, New York: Cornell University Press, 1985.

Sadie, Stanley. "Johann Sebastian Bach." *Ovation Magazine,* February 1985, 11-15.

————————. *New Grove Dictionary of Music and Musicians.* London: Macmillan, 1980.

————————. *The Norton/Grove Concise Encyclopedia of Music.* New York: Norton, 1988.

Siegmeister, Elie, ed. *The New Music Lover's Handbook.* Irvington-on-Hudson, New York: Harvey House, 1973.

Slonimsky, Nicola. *Baker's Biographical Dictionary of Musicians.* New York: Schirmer Books, 1992.

Stanley, John. *Reader's Digest Classical Music.* Pleasantville, New York: The Reader's Digest Association, 1994.

Stedman, Jane W. "Orpheus In the New World." *Opera News,* 28 November 1955, 12-13.

Thompson, Oscar. *The International Cyclopedia of Music and Musicians.* New York: Dodd, Mead & Co., 1985.

Wechsberg, Joseph. *The Waltz Emperors.* New York: Putnam, 1973.

INDEX